Praise for *The Making of Champions*

"Olver deserves high praise for *The Making of Champions*. It's a story of triumph, and one of the indomitable spirit of youth."

The London Free Press

"Skilfully done, and essential reading for parents who coach their own children or someone else's."

Books in Canada

"A fascinating, and surprisingly honest, look at hockey from the inside as the players deal with parental pressure, injuries and schoolwork in pursuit of their dream — a career in the National Hockey League....Must reading for all hockey parents and aspiring NHLers as well as the most casual fan."

The Gazette (Montreal)

"A genuine slice of Canadiana....In tracing each player's background, Olver tells the story of a country not a game."

Province (Vancouver)

"Mesmerizing....[Olver] manages to get us inside the psyche of six teenagers, all of them away from home, family and friends, as they chase their dream, a career in the NHL."

The Leader Post (Regina)

PENGUIN BOOKS

The Making of Champions

Robert Olver is a feature writer for the *Toronto Sun*, spe-cializing in the people and personalities of the sports world. He has written one novel, *The Bicycle Tree*, and is the recipient of the MacMillan Bloedel Award for a series of articles he wrote on drug addiction.

THE MAKING OF
CHAMPIONS

LIFE IN CANADA'S JUNIOR A LEAGUES

ROBERT OLVER

Penguin Books

PENGUIN BOOKS
Published by the Penguin Group
Penguin Books Canada Ltd, 10 Alcorn Avenue, Toronto, Ontario,
Canada M4V 3B2
Penguin Books Ltd, 27 Wrights Lane, London W8 5TZ, England
Penguin Books USA Inc., 375 Hudson Street, New York,
New York 10014, U.S.A.
Penguin Books Australia Ltd, Ringwood, Victoria, Australia
Penguin Books (NZ) Ltd, 182-190 Wairau Road,
Auckland 10, New Zealand

Penguin Books Ltd, Registered Offices: Harmondsworth,
Middlesex, England

First published in Viking by Penguin Books Canada Limited, 1990

Published in Penguin Books, 1991

10 9 8 7 6 5 4 3 2 1

Manufactured in Canada

Canadian Cataloguing in Publication Data

Olver, Bob
  The making of champions

ISBN 0-14-012080-7

I. Hockey players - Canada - Biography.   I. Title.

GV848.5.A1058   1991   796.962'092'271   C90-094836-1

O *To my wife, Kathy, who helped with the translation, and so much more besides.*

THE MAKING OF
CHAMPIONS

◯ Contents

○ In the Beginning . . .

This is a story about dreams.

It's also a story about dreamers, six of them. They are young men named Mike Ricci, Rob Lelacheur, Patrice Brisebois, Tracey Katelnikoff, Donald Audette and John Tanner.

All of them are Junior A hockey players and their dream is to take their places among the best in the world, as players in the National Hockey League. Each pursues his dream of excellence in his own way, with his own talents, his own handicaps, his own strengths and weaknesses.

They play for teams representing the three Junior A leagues in Canada. Brisebois and Audette are from the Laval Titans of the Quebec Major-Junior Hockey League; Tanner and Ricci are from the Peterborough Petes of the Ontario Hockey League, while Katelnikoff and Lelacheur are from the Saskatoon Blades of the Western Hockey League.

This is also the story of the 1988-89 season, from training camp in the fall to the Memorial Cup the following spring, a full season of dreams. Each of the players fills a special niche in the world of hockey, and a special role on their teams. Just as in everyday life all sorts of people achieve excellence in various ways, so in hockey.

John Tanner is the goalie. The game's goaltenders are among some of the world's grand eccentrics—flakes if you like—and John will tell you himself that he's no exception. But he's also a sensitive and sometimes tortured soul, driven by the demons of his mental genius, his talent as a player, and his love for the game. On the one hand he wants to soar to the top of the hockey world, savour the fame and glory. On the other hand, he dreams of a cottage in the north woods, of peace and quiet and safety.

Mike Ricci is the superstar. He didn't give himself that role; it was thrust upon him by others: coaches and scouts, fans, the media. In short, by anyone who's ever seen him play. And you can't blame them, because even by the age of sixteen his talent was so pure and glorious that to watch him was to feel your pulse beat faster, to feel an excitement. Great gifts can be misused, twisting the lives of those who own them, and that's a danger. Some never learn to use their gifts, but not Mike Ricci. He seems to have been born with that special knowledge.

Donald Audette is the fighter. He's not an enforcer or a goon, not that kind of fighter at all. He is a player of indomitable will whose fights take place within. He's had to fight for a spot on every team, then fight even harder for acceptance. That's because he must bear the handicap of being small in size. Instead of letting his handicap defeat him, he has turned it into a strength that he uses so effectively that he's not just a good player, he dominates. His spirit flames so fiercely that the handicap is simply burned away.

Patrice Brisebois is the worker. His mother says that as a very small boy, he was, in her words, "fast as a fish." She'd give him an errand and he'd zip off and zip back and be done faster than you'd think possible. He's still like that, bright and flashing, on the ice or off. Although he's highly talented, he knows talent is not enough, that hard work is needed, too. He's the sort who works hard at everything in life, not just hockey, but that's okay. Talk to him for a few moments and you sense his enthusiasm, for life and for his dream.

Rob Lelacheur is the kid. Although none of our dreamers is exactly old, Rob Lelacheur is the youngest. He's in his first year of Junior A, a rookie, with everything still to learn and everything possible. He's not flashy, a player in the mould of, say, Brad Marsh at this stage rather than Al Iafrate. But he's learning acceptance, learning what he's about, in terms of hockey and in terms of life. There's an air of excitement about Rob Lelacheur as he discovers himself, learns to be a man.

Tracey Katelnikoff is the veteran. Captain of his team, all-time leading scorer, this is his last year of Junior A. Whatever happens at season's end, he will never play another Junior game. If he is ever to make it to the NHL, ever to see the fulfillment of a dream to which he has devoted his life, it must be this year or not at all. So Tracey Katelnikoff has much to lose this year, and all the world to gain. He, more than any of the others, learns what being a champion means. A champion lives inside each of us if we only look, and Tracey forces himself to look deeper than most.

Without the co-operation of the dreamers, none of these stories could be known as fully as we will come to know them. But how to convince six young macho males to share their inner, most private thoughts, that was the question. Although I travelled back and forth across the country many times, spent as much time with them as I could, I couldn't be with them every minute. And even if that were possible, how to know what they're thinking, what they love, what they fear?

They kept diaries and although all agreed to do so, success was limited at first. John and Patrice wrote copiously; the others sometimes did, sometimes did not. Tape-recorders eventually proved to be a useful alternative. Even the most reluctant, those who wouldn't normally discuss their deeper feelings face-to-face, would reveal themselves to a tape-recorder. And even more significantly, they'd reveal themselves at the very time, sometimes in their bedrooms at 3 a.m., when they were experiencing the emotions most strongly.

All except Tracey Katelnikoff. Tracey is so modest that he has been known to fracture an ankle and not mention it to anyone. When he set the all-time scoring record for the Blades, the team management and players planned to give a dinner in his honour. He let it be known that he didn't need a dinner, thank you, he was just doing his job. He had several injuries over the season, but even his own teammates didn't know the extent of them. When it comes to his own life, his exploits as a player and as a man, he'll tell you, but you have to ask. So that's what I did. Sitting in the shade of Kiwanis Park in Saskatoon. Drinking coffee in his apartment. Talking on phones and in hotel rooms and on buses and in cold arenas before games.

It wasn't just Tracey, of course. All the boys tended to be shy at first and, tape-recorders and diaries or not, I spent a lot of time with them in a lot of arenas and hotels and homes, slowly, sometimes almost painfully, getting to know them, sharing with them their six journeys towards self-knowledge. In the process of sharing their dreams, we can all learn to live our own.

Robert Olver
Toronto
May 5, 1990

○ Part 1

DREAM THE DREAM

o 1

There is silence.

It is ten o'clock at night in the Centre Sportif de Laval as Donald Audette pauses at the boards before stepping through the gate and onto the ice. He glances up at the empty seats, receding into gloom in the higher reaches, and his imagination fills them with fans. There is no sound now, not a whisper or a breath or a sigh; but he pauses anyway, smiles up into the silence and dreams them full.

"Audette!" they cry as they recognize the number, 28, that graces his jersey. "Audette! Ti' Wayne! *La Vedette! Le Roi!*"

Actually, he is wearing a black warm-up jersey, but in his mind, for that moment, he is wearing the white, black and red of his team, the Laval Titans. They call him Little Wayne and The Star and The King and sometimes even, affectionately, *Ti' Cul*, Little Asshole. They cheer and whistle, these phantoms, and he smiles at the fantasy before stepping out onto the ice. He skates, slowly at first, a leisurely circuit, alone in the arena, and although he does not actually think of it each stride he takes is a stride closer to a dream he has held as long as he can remember. He is eighteen now and for fifteen years he has followed a dream. He summons it to him briefly, lets it flood into his mind. Instead of the number 28, the Titans' white, black and red and the confines of the Centre Sportif, he wears the number 28, the *rouge, blanc et bleu* of the Montreal Canadiens. The cheering crowds disappear up and up, too far to see, into the high reaches of The Forum. Or the team is the Quebec Nordiques, the blue fleur de lys, and the crowds welcome the darting, dauntless player

3

who came as a long shot and stayed to turn the franchise into a winner. Or sometimes, *merveilleux à dire*, the colours are blue and white, with a maple leaf in the middle of his chest. It is Maple Leaf Gardens and oh, can't he hear them, *les anglais*, roaring their accolades, incomprehensible to civilized ears except for what he takes to be two words, in what sounds like fractured French, and those two words are sweetest music.

"Fren-chay, fren-chay, fren-chay," they holler, *ces fous*, screaming their delight and pride in the saviour from Laval, and he loves them, every one, *formidable, ces anglais*, they sound so sweet that he stops skating, alone here at the Centre Sportif. He stops and the cheering fades, the seats of The Forum and Le Colisée and the Gardens empty in a heartbeat, and he is alone again; he, Donald Audette, right-winger for the Quebec Major-Junior Hockey League Laval Titans.

He skates across the empty rink to centre ice, dumps a pailful of pucks onto the ice, and wrists a shot, low and hard, at the empty net. The first one misses, rocketing off the boards, the sound exploding up ice and into the gloom. He lines up his next shot, flicks it low and hard, settling down now, picking the corners. Low and to the left, low and to the right. High and to the left, high and to the right. Picking the corners, where goalies have the most difficulty, striving to shave the posts. One shot, then another. Finish the pail, then retrieve the pucks and start again. One pail and then another. One hour and then two. Alone in the Centre Sportif as midnight comes and the dream, *le rêve merveilleux*, is that much closer, so close that he can feel its nearness, so brilliant that his eyes fill with tears.

As he leaves the arena shortly after midnight, the air is still warm, the sky clear. Tomorrow will be another scorching day. It is August 17, 1988, and training camp begins today.

More than 2,200 miles west and 400 miles north, Rob Lelacheur encounters another kind of silence as he enters the dressing-room of the Saskatoon Blades. Well, one of the dressing-rooms, because Rob is a rookie and rookies have their own dressing-room, separated so as not to lower the tone of the veterans, who use the team's regular room along the corridor.

The silence is self-imposed because this is not only a room full of strangers, it's a room full of strangers in competition. Unless some rookie is so good that he can take a veteran's spot on the team, there are eight openings available and eighteen rookies to fill them. The only player with whom he has even a nodding acquaintance is Pat Mullins, who comes from someplace in Manitoba—he can't remember where—and with whom he rooms temporarily until one or the other of them is cut.

But Mullins is nowhere in sight, so Lelacheur sits and begins to put on his equipment, adding his isolation to that of the others. A few of the rookies are from Saskatoon and they band together, making halfhearted attempts at communication, but really only emphasizing the silence. Rob, from St Albert, Alberta, looks around, and in spite of himself begins thinking of all the things he would prefer to be doing at this instant instead of sitting in this dressing-room, savouring the smell of sweat and loneliness. Part of him, make no mistake, wants to be here, is excited at the prospect that this is his chance to break into Junior A hockey, last step before the National Hockey League. He has to be here, he wants to be here, because that is the one thing he shares with all others in the room—this dream of someday playing in the NHL.

Still . . . Rob is sixteen years old, and much as he wants to make this team he cannot stop imagining what his family is doing now; his mother, Faye; his dad, Rick; his eight-year-old sister, Christine. He misses them all, but just now he misses Christine more than any. This is his first time away from home and although he hasn't yet suffered a really virulent attack of homesickness, the first symptom is still there, an ache at the back of his throat.

Dressing for this particular practice, he follows the sequence he would normally observe only before a game: left skate on first, then the right. Tape the right ankle, then the left; the right shin, then the left, proceeding carefully so as not, on this day, to alter the whim of any of the Fates who might chance the smells and the loneliness. Into his mind flashes a picture of Christine; her blonde hair, blue eyes, mouth changing shape from smile to pout to glee to anger—she is *such* a pain sometimes—and a small grin lights his own face. He thinks of his two best friends, Chris Larkin and Kevin Lovig, two of the Three Amigos. He wishes he could see them now, just to talk, kid around a bit, have a few laughs. Lord knows there's not much laughter here. But Chris is a right-winger for the Swift Current Broncos and Kevin is trying out for the Lethbridge Hurricanes, so that's that.

Right now, he thinks, they are probably sitting in a smelly dressing-room thinking the same things I'm thinking, and I guess that's just the way it is. There's lots of guys who'd give anything to make the Broncos or the Blades and they never get asked, never get a chance. Well, I've got the chance and you can't keep thinking of all those other things as if you were a baby and break down at the thought of leaving your mother, for God's sake. I am here because that's what I wanted. And I am going to stay here and I am going to make the team. Or if I don't make the team it will not be because I was thinking of something else, crying about things that couldn't be. You've got to focus, that's all. You've got to focus and give it your best shot. That's what my dad says and my dad knows. He got where he is because he gave it his best shot. He started out with not much education and now he's successful, his own business, hundreds of jobs. And all that comes from hard work and being the best you can be, giving it your best shot. So that's what I'm here to do. And if it doesn't work, I don't make the team, then I won't be ashamed. What is there to be ashamed about, you give it your best shot and it's not enough? But I am going to make it, that's one thing for sure. I am going to give it my best shot and I am going to make it.

Rob Lelacheur finishes dressing, picks up his stick and follows the rubber mat along the passage to the ice. He is early but already most of the veterans are there skating, stretching, warming up. He recognizes only two faces, another defenceman, Collin Bauer, who comes from Fort Saskatchewan, near St Albert, and left-winger Drew Sawtell, from Prince George, B.C., who once billeted briefly at Rob's home during a tournament in St Albert.

But really, it's as though they are aliens from another planet for all the response he gets now as he skates past them. Rob realizes from their points of view, it's the rookies who are the aliens, awkward and out-of-place, but still dangerously unknown, threatening and ready to eclipse any veteran who comes in a step slow, a heartbeat away from the play. For now, that menace can be kept contained, at least until the rookies regain their confidence and their faith in The Dream.

Rob Lelacheur smiles at that thought and holds it as the coach, Marcel Comeau, skates to centre ice, pauses for a moment, then blows his whistle.

"Applehead," thinks Rob. The nickname pops unbidden, and not entirely welcome, into his mind as he silently sounds the players' ultra-secret name for their coach. Then he feels a guilty flush at the very thought. Guilty or not, he has to admit that Comeau's red hair, ruddy complexion, roundish face and dark-rimmed glasses, make the name appropriate. In any case, the irreverent moniker makes Rob feel better, makes the coach less intimidating. Comeau blows the whistle again and the team flocks around, veterans crowding confidently in, rookies shifting for position in the rear.

"Listen up, guys," he says, the first of what will be a thousand or, God, maybe 10,000 "Listen up, guys" during the year. And for the first of what will be a thousand, or maybe 10,000 times, Rob Lelacheur listens up.

It has been said, almost accusingly, that John Tanner has a stratospheric IQ, something in the 140 range. But just now, at about the time that Rob Lelacheur is giving rapt attention to Marcel Comeau, the goalie of the Peterborough Petes is aware of a certain irony. The mind that can so ably control affairs in the elegant cerebral universe seems just now to be remarkably inept at controlling them in the vulgar physical one.

He is seventeen and beginning his second year as one of the Ontario Hockey League's top goalies. In fact, last year he and the other half of the Petes' goaltending team, Todd Bojcun (pronounced Boy-soon), were tops in the league in goals-against, winning the Dave Pinkney Trophy with a team average of 3.15. John has a theory about mind over matter. As far as he has been able to work it out, a person whose brain has all its synapses working, all the neurons firing reliably, has got an edge over somebody whose synaptic gaps are too wide for optimal effect, the neurons firing irregularly when they fire at all.

Some people would think, Right. You got a big brain and, sure, you can appreciate the relationship between Percy Bysshe Shelley and Frankenstein. You can look at a tree and see a poem, see a rainbow and go off chasing after a pot of gold, all that shit. But what good's a brain when it comes to something useful? Knowing not to put two shoes on one foot: you can do that without a brain. And when it comes to some dork from Belleville or Sault Ste Marie shooting a puck at you, at maybe 100 miles an hour, a purely physical act, what good's a brain to you then? Well, that's what some people think, but that's where some people are wrong. Because when the dork from Belleville is firing the puck at you, you are way ahead of him, mind over matter. At least, that's how it should work.

At this very moment, however, there appears to be a flaw in the theory. This practice scrimmage of mixed rookies and veterans starts off well enough, but as it progresses, the eager rookies of the Blue Team buzz the net, bombarding Tanner with shots. Taner feels a shaft of resentment at the freewheeling tone of the scrimmage and the way the veteran defencemen seem to be letting the rookie forwards have their way.

This is supposed to be a practice, but the defence just stand around and let me do the work, thinks Tanner. Dip flukes a goal, then dances around like he's won the frigging

Stanley Cup. Even as he thinks this, another shot is past him and he digs it out of the net with disgust.

The Red Team, his team, finally come alive and carry the play up the ice. As he calms down, he realizes that what has been happening actually reinforces his mind-over-matter theory. Tanner has allowed anger to take over, something he prides himself on not doing. Let's be cool, he tells himself. Let yourself get angry and the neurons start firing out of sequence. Keep those neurons coming. Be cool; watch the puck; who's got it? What are they doing with it? Watch the shooter. Think like the shooter. Think ahead of the shooter.

The Blues are moving up again. Here they come.

"Corey, on the boards!" he yells, but it's too late—the rookie's in the corner.

"Here's the pass, man in front! Hit the goddam centre, take your man! Here's the shot! Got it! Rebound, rebound! Shit! Wake up, watch the rebound!"

But the rebound comes trickling in, trickling damned fast, low and on his glove side, a bastard to get. But he gets it and although this is only a scrimmage, the first of the year, and the shooter is only a clueless rookie, Tanner feels a warmth, a glow, as if this scrimmage were, well, the Stanley Cup.

Assistant coach Terry Bovair blows his whistle to end the play and Tanner skates towards the bench. He is overtaken by a feeling of lightness and well-being. His skates raise him above mundane Newtonian theories of gravity, and the weight of the pads on his legs, the feel of the blocker and the catcher, make him feel invulnerable. His mask before he raises it gives him an aura of mystery and he feels that, as he peers from behind it, the events he witnesses are his to control, even while they are somehow happening somewhere else, to other people, in a sort of parallel universe.

"Looking good, John," says Corey Foster, skating past. Another defenceman, Jamie Pegg, taps him on the ass with his stick, and any lingering dark thoughts about defencemen flee.

John Tanner floats to the boards, rests there and lets the warm feeling take him. He smiles, because whether he thinks it or not, he has fallen in love anew, on this first day of training camp. He has once again fallen in love with The Dream, with its siren call to excellence and its lonely splendour.

o 2

On a certain day in the early part of every September, scenes like these take place in each of the 39 training camps of the three Junior leagues strung across Canada and into the Northwest United States. The leagues are the Western Hockey League with 14 teams, the Ontario Hockey League with 15, and the Quebec Major-Junior Hockey League, with 10.

Donald Audette, Rob Lelacheur and John Tanner and three others—Patrice Brisebois, Mike Ricci and Tracey Katelnikoff—have all risen to the Junior A level of hockey through the ranks. All six are dreamers, dreamers who seek to create the reality they want out of something that, at this point, exists only in their imaginations: their chance to play in the National Hockey League, to be the very best doing the thing they love. They are young men for whom the pursuit of excellence is much more than an abstraction. They are among those rare people who realize early in life that the road to a goal is the road to self-knowledge. Although they may not say it in so many words, self-knowledge and happiness, they know, are really the same things.

All six hockey players are dreamers, yes. But not dreamers who ignore present reality. They know the rewards and they know the costs. The costs are paid in devotion, working towards a goal to the exclusion of all else: of family, of girlfriends, of nights on the town, of freedom as others know freedom.

Each has an astonishing capacity to delay gratification, to accept that what they give up now may come back to them,

11

perhaps many times multiplied. Whatever happens, whether they graduate to the NHL or end up living less exotic lives, they will escape one consequence that haunts so many of us, the cry of "what if?". What if I had followed my dream, whatever that dream was? Could I have realized it? What would my life be today if at one sweet moment I had said, "Yes, I can, I will try," instead of "No, I can't, I can't, I can't."

The Ile Jésus seems to be rejoicing in its name as Patrice Brisebois takes Route 25 northeast from Laval. It is one of those early fall days when the world hangs suspended, as if waiting for all eyes to focus on it, ready to witness some display of joie de vivre never before revealed to human eyes. A few days previously he returned from Kitchener and the evaluation camp for the Canadian world Junior team, which will spend Christmas in Anchorage, Alaska, competing with the best Junior teams in the world. He won't be seventeen until January 27. He is the first player in twenty years, the first since Wayne Gretzky, to be invited to the Junior camp at age sixteen. Then he thinks of people dear to him. Two, *exactement*. They are his mother, Pierrette, and his girl-friend, Michèle Gaul. And he thinks that the world is his. The trees with their early blush of fire, the first fall haze that hangs around them like smoke. The breeze on his face from the Rivière des Mille Iles, *un baiser d'une jeune fille*. That's his, too, he thinks. The kiss of a young girl. And Michèle's image fills his heart.

Sixteen years old, thinks Patrice, and the gaunt features lighten with a smile. Not bad for Pat Crackwood, as certain English-speaking players, *les niaiseuses*, would have it, their literal translation of his name. Not bad for a kid from Montreal, from a province where every player aspires to be a star, a Guy Lafleur, a Marcel Dionne. They do not revere the Bobby Orrs and the Doug Harveys here. Oh, they admire them, *certainement*, honour them greatly, but they do not wish to be like them. Here, in La Ligue de Hockey Junior-Majeur du Québec, they score goals, and that is the dream of every young player. That is the tradition, that is the star they follow.

But Patrice Brisebois, is different. He is a defenceman, a defender, in a milieu that values the attacker, the shooter. But where is it written, where is *l'écriture sainte*, that says this has to be? He will show, yes, he will, that it does not have to be so. He will show that it is not written in stone that a defenceman cannot be a star, cannot score goals like Bobby Orr or Paul Coffey or Al MacInnis. This world that is his—if not now, then soon—is ready for the new defenceman, the defenceman who can make the changeover *instantanément*, who can score when his team attacks and defend while his team regroups.

These thoughts crowd his mind as Patrice slows for the Terrebonne exit, then stops near the house on rue Belanger where the Titans' new coach, Paulin Bordeleau, is hosting a pre-season party for the team. Mme Bordeleau, Lynne, *très belle, très chic*, greets him at the door, shows him through to the deck at the back where the coach is telling a story to the assistant coach, Jacques Cossette, and several players. Donald Audette is there, Ti' Wayne, and the two clasp hands. Paulin pauses, raises his eyebrows in welcome, and continues. He is speaking in English because Marty Woodford, a defenceman from Saint John, N.B., is among those listening. Although Woodford gives French his best shot as the occasion demands, he is still most comfortable in his native language. Bordeleau, a former NHLer of awesome talent, has been playing in France the past eight years, for the Megeve Rams. He also played for the French Nationals during the 1986 Calgary Olympics, but now he's left that behind to begin his climb through the Canadian coaching ranks.

Bordeleau is drinking beer but he's talking about wine. Patrice is soon holding his sides along with the rest of the audience as Bordeleau, a connoisseur, mourns the fate of a prize bottle of Côtes du Rhône, 1959. He describes the importance of decanting such an exquisite vintage, warming the bottle over a candle as it is poured into the decanter.

"There I am, my friend and I, the two big wine experts, decanting this absolutely magnificent wine, and we get it too close to the candle," says Bordeleau, the terrible memory haunting the laughter. "All of a sudden, the bottle breaks and there's our lovely wine, all over the table. A catastrophe. So we go mad, we grab paper towels and we're trying to mop up the wine and squeezing it into the decanter, trying to salvage *anything*, so we can at least say we had a taste of 1959 Côtes du Rhône. But it was no use, because as soon as it was exposed to so much air, it turned to sugar, and that was the end of the Côtes du Rhône."

Patrice falls about like everyone else for a moment, but then he and some of the other players remember they are French, after all, and fall silent out of decent respect for the memory of a fine wine. Not all the players display this *délicatesse*. Some guys, Woodford and Gino Odjick, the big left-winger from Maniwaki, for instance, they laugh their heads off, choking on their beer. It serves them right. Barbarians. But still they are *his* barbarians, *his* soulmates, *his* team-mates, so he grabs them in a friendly sort of double hammer-lock and they laugh together.

"We will save our fines up all year," Patrice assures Bordeleau. "We'll break curfew every week, just to get the money. We'll put all our fines for the whole year into a fund and at the end we'll have enough for a new bottle of Côtes du Rhône. Then we'll all help you drink it! Only this time, no candles. We'll take no chances. This time, we'll drink it right out of the bottle."

Afterwards, Patrice finds himself alone with Paulin, the coach showing off his prized rosebushes. Patrice is touched by the moment of intimacy shared. I believe I like this coach very much, he thinks. He is one of us. He is a man who knows how to dream, one who understands. Patrice smiles at the rosebushes, smiles at Paulin Bordeleau, smiles at the world, *tout le monde*.

Air Canada Flight 102 leaves the gate at Saskatoon Municipal Airport at 7:10 a.m., precisely on time. However, because of the vagaries of aircraft protocol—flight attendants rhyming off the safety drill, trundling out to the take-off runway, waiting briefly in line—it is twenty minutes later before take-off for the flight to Toronto, connecting to

Rochester, N.Y., and Washington, D.C.

What else is new? thinks Tracey Katelnikoff, picking out the hockey-puck shape of Saskatchewan Place below as the plane gains altitude. He wonders idly, along with most passengers, why, if the airlines are so concerned about passenger safety, they don't seat them with their backs to the pilot instead of facing front. But the thought passes quickly into limbo until the next time and he glances down to the left again, to see if he can catch a final glimpse of SaskPlace. Sure enough, it's still in view and he thinks he can even see the big blue security door glinting in the sun of a clear day.

He wonders if he will ever again see that blue door, the players' entrance, through which he has passed so often during the past three years with the Saskatoon Blades. He daydreams a bit about that, the notion that this could be the day to which all those other days have been leading, his chance finally to play in the NHL. He is twenty years old, twenty-one on July 17, so this is his last year of Junior eligibility. This season is his last chance to make it from the training ground of Junior A to the big leagues.

Tracey has never been drafted by a big-league club, but weeks earlier he was invited to attend the Washington Capitals' fall training camp, and that's where he's headed. He is elated and nervous at the same time, knowing how much will be at stake in the next days and weeks. He relishes the promise of what is to come and ignores the threat of failure, of not at least getting a contract with the Caps. Then that thought, too, he pushes from his mind. Katelnikoff, known to his Blade teammates as The Russian, or sometimes simply T.K., has long ago given up worrying about things he cannot control.

The Russian is a young man of few words, who has become one of the Blades' most valued players through example, not through words. Some think he's a loner, but in fact he's simply quiet, fiercely loyal to his team and strongly attached to them emotionally. He's glad on this day of all days that three of his friends are sharing the flight with him. Defenceman Devon Oleniuk played for the Blades from 1984 to 1987, then was traded to the Kamloops Blazers and later drafted by Washington. Defenceman Duncan MacPherson, a teammate during Katelnikoff's first year, 1985–86, was the New York Islanders' first pick in the NHL Entry Draft of 1984, and has been playing for the Islanders' American Hockey League affiliate, the Springfield Indians. Pat Beauchesne, a defenceman for the Medicine Hat Tigers and the Moose Jaw Warriors, a fifth-round draft by Washington in the 1986–87 season, is also on the flight.

The four athletes pass the time comparing notes on big-league training camps and Tracey feels like a gooseberry on a date because he has no notes to compare. He suspects that some of the discussion is intended to make him feel less nervous rather than to let him know what it's really like.

"Sure, it's faster up here than in Junior," says Beauchesne. "But long as you keep showing them your basic hockey, then the rest will come. They don't look for razzle-dazzle, not in the first few days, anyway. They look for a guy who knows his game."

It's the part that comes after the "but" that Katelnikoff is skeptical about. He doesn't believe the coaches are going to close their eyes if some player really turns it on, shows what he can do. They want basic hockey, yes, but they want something more than that, too. I never saw a Junior coach who was against a guy putting on a bit of a show and I don't think I'm going to see a big-league coach who is, either. He expresses some of these reservations to his friends, but they will have none of it.

"Who's the guy Marse would send in when things are really serious?" asks Oleniuk, looking, in his anxiety to allay the fears he senses Tracey has, the fears he himself had a year ago, as if he has touched on the heart and soul, the very secret, of major-league excellence.

"Yeah," adds MacPherson. "When the score is 4–4 and there's two minutes left and they've got the puck deep in your end zone and everybody's ass is grass, who does he send in?"

Katelnikoff listens to his friends, appreciating what they are doing. But the doubts, self-knowledge really, are inescapable. Even if he could escape them he wouldn't, for they are really signposts by which he will realize his dream. Without those signs he might have become sidetracked long ago.

"Sure, you have Gretzky and you have Mario Lemieux," he hears Oleniuk say as he tunes back in. "They can do the razzle-dazzle, that's what they do. But those two are in a class by themselves. Those two guys are, well, I don't mean this in any bad way, but those two guys are freaks."

Tracey continues to listen with part of his mind, but he knows, and the others know, too, that there's a lot more than just flash to guys like Gretzky and Lemieux. They do what they can do, all they can do. Their excellence may be on a different planet from other people's but it's based on the same thing. It's based on what they know and then working at it. You have to build on what you can do, not on what you kid yourself about doing, not what you dream you can do. That is just a dream. That is not The Dream.

So although Katelnikoff is comforted by what his friends say, because he knows there is truth in it, he does not allow himself the refuge of illusion. The truth is that he is a sound player, a reliable player who knows his game, a talented player. But he is not a dazzling player.

When they land in Toronto, MacPherson catches a flight to New York, while Katelnikoff, Oleniuk and Beauchesne continue on to Washington via Rochester. A Capitals' van meets them at the airport and ferries them to the Holiday Inn in Alexandria, near the Caps' training camp. They arrive tired and hungry, with time only for a quick meal before they must attend a meeting of the rookies and free agents. Jack Button, Washington's director of player personnel and recruitment, and Richard Rothermel, director of western scouting, give a pep talk about what the team expects of its new faces, how glad and proud they are, blah, blah. It is 9:30 before Tracey is finally alone in his room. Practice is set for 9:30 in the morning and he experiences a brief rush of nervousness as he settles into bed. But it is not enough to hold off sleep.

He is awakened by the phone ringing and at first he is disoriented, wondering where he is. Then he gropes around for

the phone in the dark. He notices the digital readout on the
clock-radio, 4:30 a.m., and then he finds the light switch as
the phone shrills again. He picks up the receiver, hears a
woman's voice, and it takes him a moment, through the
remaining fuzz of sleep, to realize it's his mother.

"Your father passed away last night," she says, speaking
with eerie calm over the miles from Calgary. He has trouble
grasping what she is saying at first, and when he does they
discuss it quietly, each hiding their shock and dismay out of
deference to the other. His mother, Marcia, talks about how
sudden it was, how she can't believe it, a heart attack at
forty-five. They talk quietly for three minutes and then he
sits alone on the bed in the Alexandria hotel room, thinking
of his father, Fred. He was closer to him than anyone in the
world.

"I didn't cry or weep, not then," Tracey recalled later. "It
didn't hit me until I got home."

He sits on the bed and stares at the phone, holding his
anguish at bay. His father's death might also be the death of
The Dream, certainly an enormous setback, but no such
thought enters his mind, then or later.

"I don't remember thinking much of anything," says
Tracey. "It was just a kind of numbness. I still hadn't taken in
that I had really lost him."

By 8:00 a.m. he has relayed the news to the team, and by
9:30, when the other Capital hopefuls are skating onto the
ice for their first practice, Tracey is on a United Airlines
flight home for a funeral. His chance at the big time, for now
at least, is gone. His training camp is effectively over and later he will recall an errant thought: Dad has died on me, he
thinks, in disbelief, amazement even. Why did he die on me
and leave me alone?

It is so hot and humid on the track at Kenner Collegiate that
even the dust does not rise as the feet of the various
Peterborough Petes pummel it this September afternoon.
The sun beats down, the track circles endlessly and Mike
Ricci follows his path to glory. Although the sixteen-year-old
centreman from Scarborough does not think in such grand

terms, this is precisely what he's doing. He is a player of an exotic kind, a potential superstar. Indeed, so awesome is his talent that even veteran hockey people tend to drop the word "potential" in reference to him, as if he were already an established star.

Ricci is already six foot one, and 185 pounds, as if his body is trying to compensate in preparation for the heavy burden his expectations will place on it. For now, he carries them lightly, like a cloak so familiar, so well worn, that he forgets it's there. Perhaps it is part of his gift, this ability to detach himself from his body. He has the sort of talent that sets coaches and scouts to scheming about how they will be the ones to draft him when he becomes eligible in 1990 when he's eighteen. They see in Mike Ricci the potential to single-handedly change the fortunes of a team, to become a franchise player, to be better than Steve Yzerman, maybe even in the same league as The Great One, Wayne Gretzky, or Mario the Magnificent. The scout who can sign Ricci will see his reputation enhanced certainly, or even see it made. His coach, Dick Todd, finds it unnecessary to be his usual wily self when it comes to appraising his budding star.

"Mike Ricci will be the greatest hockey player in the world in four years' time," says Todd. His expression acknowledges the doubts such apparent hyperbole is bound to raise. He never offers praise lightly and in fact can't recall ever having said such a thing before. But he knows hockey and he knows Mike Ricci, so he says it now.

At this moment, in the last heat of summer, Ricci is oblivious to the details, if not to the substance, of these extrapolated dreams. Ricci is known as Ratdawg to his closest teammates; goalie Todd Bojcun is known as Guido or T.B.; and fellow centre Geoff Ingram is G.I., for G.I. Joe. But at this particular moment Ricci is feeling precious little of the enthusiasm and tenacity of a Ratdawg or any other kind of dawg as he circles the track. He has worked out during the summer, adding strength and weight to his frame, but he feels nervous and a little stiff on this first day.

As he comes down the stretch for the first half of his two-mile run, he eyes a patch of shade in a corner off to the side.

If I were any kind of dog today, it would be the kind that just lies in the shade and bites flies, he thinks, as sweat streams into his eyes. Bites flies, bites flies, he repeats to himself, in time with his stride as he pounds the ground. He quickly abandons the bites-flies mantra because the image displeases him, substituting instead the syllables, Cool-er, Cool-er—yeeah, that sounds better, a dawg in the shade thinking cool thoughts. Looking at these fools running around in the heat, thinking cool, superior thoughts. Or maybe a cat, a cool cat, lying in the shade dreaming of nice cold milk, watching the butterflies go by. These stray thoughts fade as he circles into the back stretch for his final lap, however, because he is deep into himself by now, the heat and the dust forgotten. The nervous tightness is gone, too, submerged in the pleasure of his physical being. He has left Bojcun behind, and Ingram, too. John Tanner, whose stride covers about two to his one, is still keeping more or less up with him. But Tanner is tired, Ricci can tell, and he knows from experience that he will leave him behind, too, just about—now. He summons up a little extra kick so that in the backstretch it is as if he has the track to himself. He feels he is here alone, as if his body is running separately from his mind and he is able to lie back and enjoy the sight of the muscles working, the sweat and blood flowing, the oxygen bubbling and fizzing through the arteries. He crosses the line second of the entire team and watches as Jeff Twohey, the trainer, clicks the stopwatch.

"Twelve-oh-three," says Twohey as Ricci swigs water, pours some over his head, then rubs himself with a towel. The team has finished the run by now, and the athletes move on to the standing long jump, which Ricci completes at eight feet three inches. As they finish, the players head back to the Memorial Centre, where they'll complete the fitness tests in the weight-room. Ricci does 85 pushups, 52 situps in 60 seconds, benchpresses 130 pounds 33 times and earns a nod of approval from Todd.

Later Ricci realizes that his nervousness has totally disappeared. He feels completely in command as he skates onto the ice. He celebrates by scoring seven goals in the first of the intra-squad games.

○ **3**

Mike's father, Mario Ricci, was born in the town of Aquino, Italy, in 1929, seven years after Benito Mussolini's Fascist Party became powerful enough to force King Vittorio Emmanuel III to invite the new dictator to form a government. An upstart named Adolf Hitler had finished his *Mein Kampf*, had organized his private army of elite guards, the *Schutzstaffel*, also known as the ss, and had become an important minority political party in Germany.

Anna Peschisolido, Mike's mother, was born nine years later in the town of Ceprano, a year before the Austrian housepainter's obsession with living space and the Italian journalist's visions of empire combined to escalate the troubled times into an orgy of destruction. Both towns are within a one-hundred-kilometer radius of Rome, and both experienced the war in their separate ways.

Anna's parents' home was destroyed during a bombing raid by the Allies, so the family moved in with her grandmother Cecilia, in a large house they were forced to share with German soldiers.

"Because of that, we always had food and the Germans treated us well," recalls Anna. "They told us that as long as we didn't do anything foolish, they would leave us alone, and that's how it was."

All of the menfolk were serving in the Italian army, so the women—great-grandmother Caterina, then seventy; Cecilia, forty-two; fifteen-year-old Aunt Anna; and little Anna herself, then three—faced the terrible experience by themselves. Despite her tender age at the time Anna still has two

vivid memories of those years. One is of Aunt Anna holding
her in her arms as bombs fell nearby. One blast left shrapnel
in her aunt's head and it was not until years later, after little
Anna had immigrated to Canada, that she realized she too
had been injured, left deaf in her left ear.

"When I came to Canada, I found that if I held a phone to
my left ear, I couldn't hear," she says. "All those years before
and I didn't know, didn't realize."

Her other memory is of the war's end, the Germans gone,
her Aunt Anna hiding under a bed as three drunken
Canadian soldiers came, seeking wine, food and trouble.

"My grandmother was very fierce. She hit them and yelled
at them and pushed them out of the house. Thank God they
went away," she recalls. "But we were very frightened
because our men were still at the war, and very bad things
could have happened."

Meanwhile the Riccis fled northward: Mario's mother,
Erene; father, Arcangelo; brothers Antonio, Beneditto,
Tomaso, Franco, and their sister, Anna, seeking the relative
safety of Lombardy, in the town of Cremona, near Milan.
But the war eventually caught up with them there, too.

"I remember it was the eleventh of July, 1942. We were
sleeping in tents when the bombing started," recalls Mario,
then about twelve. "The target was only 1,300 meters from
where we were. The lights had been shot out, and the bombing that night, it continued for an hour and a half. An hour
and a half we stayed there, listening to the bombs and wondering if we would live through it.

"When it was over, we went out and it was a terrible thing
I saw. One girl, she was only thirteen years old, was lying in a
ditch and she was dead. It was such a terrible, terrible thing
to see for a boy, and I will never forget it."

A more pleasant memory for young Mario came out of the
chaos of the final stages of the war when a young Italian sol-
dier showed up one day at his parents' door.

"He wanted to know if we could give him a change of
clothing and my parents asked him what his name was," says
Ricci. "He said it was Ricci and he came from Florence. My
father told him that was our name, too, and asked him what

his first name was. He said, Mario, Mario Ricci from Florence. It is one of the strange things that come out of a war. I never saw him or heard of him again, but I remember him standing there, at my parents' door. Mario Ricci from Florence."

After the war, Mario became a bricklayer, but his love was soccer, and he started playing semi-pro at fifteen. A feisty, hard-driving defender, Mario's ambition was to be a pro in the Italian First Division and he spent years paying his dues, waiting for his chance. He might have made it, too, except that he met Anna first.

"I'd been playing for Pontecorvo when the league went bankrupt, so I went for a tryout with Ceprano. I remember I punched a player, got a red card and they put me out of the game."

Anna recalls those first impressions of her future husband: "He didn't just punch the player. He kicked him, too, and sent him to hospital," she says. "He was a wild man. I was there with some friends, we always went to the soccer, and everybody was talking about this Ricci. Ricci, Ricci, Ricci. That's all I heard. Who is this Ricci? I thought. Is he God?

"I didn't like him at all. He was too much of a fighter. I knew he was very bad. But he came and introduced himself after the game and I just laughed at him. We thought he was a crazy man."

The beautiful Anna was just thirteen at the time, and Mario, twenty-two, but neither their ages nor her bad opinion made the slightest impression on him. No matter how sharply Anna rebuffed him, Mario simply kept coming back. One day, after saving the winning goal for a thrilling victory, the league president kissed Mario on the cheeks. Then, spying Anna nearby, he was at her side instantly.

"Why don't you kiss me, too?" he demanded. In fact, it was almost three years before Anna kissed Mario and even then it was over the dire warnings of parents and friends.

"My mother told me again and again, 'Don't ever marry this guy, he's going to beat you up.' I had no intention of marrying him, either. He was always fighting. And every

time I turned around, he'd be there. He was always bother-
ing me, wherever I went.

"Once he came to my school and told the headmistress
she had to come and get me because my mother had sent
him with a message. Of course I came out to see him and
there was no message. I told him, 'Don't ever do that again.'
But no matter what I said, he wouldn't go away."

Even now, twenty-three years later, she smiles, then
shakes her head in exasperation. Mario smiles back, then
gives a shrug.

"It worked," he observes, and so it did. They were married
when Anna was sixteen and Mario, twenty-five, and almost
immediately they moved to France, where Mario played for
the French First Division and their first two sons, Maurice
and Bruno, were born. But the pressures of family responsi-
bilities caught up with the talented player and Mario decided to turn away from his soccer dream. They came to
Canada in June 1965, and Mario found a job as a steelwork-
er. Anna, an expert seamstress, began working, too, and
together they started building their new life. Their third son,
Michael, born October 27, 1971, at Scarborough General
Hospital, weighed nine pounds seven ounces, and his father
claims that from the first you could tell he was a Ricci.

The population of Craik, Saskatchewan, numbers about 500
souls and boasts a small creek that meanders sluggishly
through the town. The creek may have a name, but if so no
one remembers what it is. The Craik Dam gives the creek
enough depth that the brave and foolhardy can swim there,
although Marcia Katelnikoff, for one, would not recommend
it.

"I did swim there a few times when I was a kid, but I'd
always get the itch from the water, so I quit," she recalls.
"The water had lice in it, so it's a good place to stay away
from."

The village where Tracey Katelnikoff's mother, Marcia
Jones, and her future husband, Fred Katelnikoff, were born,
does have other things to recommend it, although Marcia

would be the first to admit she is not the greatest booster of her hometown.

"It's been years since I've been back there," she says. But, let's see, there was Charlie Fox's movie theatre where you could watch a picture twice a week. When she lived there, there were seven grain elevators, the tallest buildings for miles around. Craik is a place where agriculture, wheat farming in particular, is the lifeblood, as it is for hundreds of similar villages spread across the prairies. But if wheat is the lifeblood, the heart and soul is the hockey arena, designed by Marcia's uncle, George Archibald.

"It's a big arena, a very nice one," she says, and her face brightens at the thought of it. "There was no glass on the sides, so you could lean over the boards and yell. You could almost get right into the game that way and I loved those games at the Craik Arena."

Her warm feelings were chilled only slightly by the cold.

"It was natural ice and I think it's still natural ice," she says. "That's another thing about Craik: it's so cold that you don't have to worry about artificial ice. Winter's always cold in Craik."

Marcia is one of the ten children of Donna and Mel Jones; Fred, one of six children of Fred and Julie Katelnikoff. Marcia recalls that her future husband used to hang around with some of her brothers, and she was friends with one of Fred's sisters, but she steered clear of Fred himself. In fact, as Marcia remembers, she didn't even like Fred when they were kids.

Fred went to school, played hockey, grew up, joined the army and moved away from Craik, all to the vast indifference of Marcia. And it might have stayed that way forever, had not Fred showed up at a New Year's Eve party, fresh out of the army, three and a half years later, in the winter of 1964–65. Fred hated the army so much that he seldom talked about it afterwards, but Marcia had the impression that for a goodly part of his time in the service he was either AWOL or in the lockup. However, because he was a good hockey player, the army wanted him more than he wanted it, inviting him to

play for a national team then in formation. When he found
out the price of the invitation, re-enlistment for three years,
Fred refused. By the time it was all sorted out and he'd been
discharged, he'd served an extra six months beyond his hitch.
That extra half year cost him a chance to join the Victoria
Cougars and a possible tryout with its parent club, the
Boston Bruins. So Fred came back to Craik and became
reacquainted with the pretty Jones girl.

"Well, I guess I must have liked him better then," says
Marcia, laughing at the foibles of love. They were married
five months later, on May 21, 1965, Fred spiriting both of
them away to Regina. There, three years later, Tracey was
born. Fred's job as a truck driver took them from there to
Winnipeg and Calgary, where Trevor and Tricia were born in
their turns. Then, when Tracey was nine, they settled in
Blackie, Alberta, population 329, forty-five minutes' drive
south from Calgary. It had four grain elevators, and was similar to Craik. It had no movie theatre, but it had the High
River Pool where kids could swim in summer, and a big old
beech tree where they built a playhouse. Most importantly,
of course, it had a rink. And through it all, from the moment
of Tracey's birth—2:38 p.m. on July 21, 1968—through all
the moves, the hard times and the good, the laughter and the
tears that bond any family, Fred Katelnikoff was sure of one
thing. Never would a son of his be forced to abandon a
dream because he couldn't pry himself loose from the goddamn army.

Pierrette Lessard, who would become the mother of Patrice
Brisebois, was raised in le Plateau Mont Royal, the eldest
child of Rachel and Roméo. She was separated by a year
from her sister, Gertie, by two from her brother, Jean-Guy,
and they lived in a second-floor apartment on rue Messier.
There would very likely have been many more brothers and
sisters, except that Roméo died when Pierrette was ten. Her
memory of him is hazy.

"What memory I have is of a man who laughed a lot, who
took us to the park, played games with us and told us jokes,"
she says. She recalls that her father had a weak heart and

that after an illness of six months, he passed away, stricken by a cerebral hemorrhage. There was enough insurance money that the family was comfortable, and Rachel augmented it by cleaning houses while the children were at school. She attended school, from Grades 1 to 10, at the nearby École Ste-Véronique, where the nuns taught her the art of embroidery, among other things, something in which she has taken great joy ever since.

One of her fondest childhood memories is of the summer afternoons she spent with five or six playmates on the second-floor balcony at Number 4377, watching life in the street below, chattering gaily about their dreams and working their intricate designs.

"We were such good little girls," she says, and her eyes twinkle. "So good, it is hard to believe. We were, how do you say, *incroyable*." When not doing embroidery, the girls would knit or draw and Pierrette's pictures expressed her feelings about the things she knew best: objects in the house, her family, the street below, the sisters of Ste-Véronique.

"If my father had not died so young, I would have gone into some kind of art career," she says. Her voice is wistful, but it passes in an instant, because Pierrette Brisebois is not one to mourn what might have been. Instead, her memories are filled with happiness, the children the centre of a family filled with almost countless cousins, nieces, nephews, aunts, uncles and grandparents. In fact, her other most joyful memory is of New Year's Day, which in Quebec exceeds Christmas as the time for family celebrations. Her maternal grandmother alone had eighteen brothers and sisters, so there was no shortage of celebrants when the magic day arrived.

"Grandfather would say the benediction, and then we would start to eat," she says. "And what feasts they were." Her favourite dish of all, and a favourite of Patrice still, were the huge tortières made to her grandmother's special recipe, called *ci-pâte*. There would be five or six of them on the table at once, made of hare and lamb, pork and beef; but that wasn't all. There were turkey and ham, the ham rinds cut, salted, crisped and passed around to get the appetites started. And there were roasts of beef, three of them: one rare, one medium, one well-done. There were candied yams, turnips, glazed carrots, mashed potatoes and gravy. There was a deep, rich, dark fruit pudding, there were doughnuts, cakes and tartes. There were homemade chocolates. There were grapes, white and blue, mandarin oranges, a kind of russet-coloured apple that one of the uncles got from a farmer late each fall. After the meal someone would play the fiddle and people would dance, those who could still move.

Pierrette and her friends would romp the streets of Ville St-Michel, sometimes as far as the Parc Lafontaine to the south, boulevard Rosemont to the north.

It's interesting to wonder whether on a foray to one of the parks straddling the boulevard, little Pierrette might have walked past or spoken to young Jean Brisebois. More likely, if she ever saw him, she would not have noticed, because he was five years younger and that is a much greater difference at twelve or thirteen than it is later.

Jean Brisebois lived just north of boulevard Rosemont, on rue Garnier near the intersection with rue Belanger, not far from Jarry Park. Jean was the only boy and the youngest in the family. As a result, his sisters, Thérèse, Lise, Célène and Lilliane, indulged him in nearly all things and on the rare occasions when they did not, his parents, Antoinette and Henri, made up for it. Naturally, he sometimes tested both their patience and their nerve. A hyperactive, quick-witted boy, much like Patrice years later, Jean had a talent for mischief. He was such a pest sometimes that once, while Henri was relaxing with a few beers, he gave his son a hammer and a can of nails so he'd stop being bothersome. After a while, Henri realized the hammering and nailing had gone on for a very long time, and came to investigate.

"Everything was nailed," says Jean, still taking considerable glee in the memory. "There were nails sticking out of the floor, like quills in a porcupine. There were nails in doors, in windowsills, in walls. Anywhere there was a space, there were nails. I used up every nail in the can."

Pierrette and Jean finally did meet somewhat further afield, because both families had summer chalets in the woods near the village of St-Hippolyte in the Laurentides, north of St-Jerome.

"When I first saw Jean, I thought he was very handsome, very well made," says Pierrette, and then explains how she, not he, made the first move. "I knew he was younger and of course he was shy with girls, so I asked him out the first time. I found he had never heard martial music and they had concerts at the Parc Lafontaine. So one Sunday, he picked me up at my apartment. We walked to the *parc* together, and that was our first date."

They were married on June 11, 1960, not far from Pierrette's home, in the church of St Pierre Claver, crowded with 125 guests from the families of Lessard and Brisebois. Their first child was a daughter, Lynne, followed by Jean-Pierre, Stephane, and finally, at the Hôpital St-Michel, at 1:25 p.m., weighing eight pounds five ounces, their last child, Patrice.

When, at the age of three, Patrice began to show an interest in hockey, Jean Brisebois made it clear that he was different from most other fathers in at least one respect. Although he was a caring father, he would have nothing to do with the sport. He'd buy sticks and gloves and skates; he'd pay the fees; but never once did he take Patrice to a game. Fred Katelnikoff lived his son's dream, as to one degree or another did Rick Lelacheur, Gord Tanner, Mario Ricci, and Claude Audette. But to the bafflement and sometimes the resentment of his son, Jean Brisebois never took any real interest in hockey. He has seldom seen Patrice play the sport his son loves so much.

○ 4

The families of Mike Ricci, Tracey Katelnikoff and Donald Audette are ones in which hockey is encouraged. As a result each of the young men pursues excellence. It's as if Mario Ricci, Fred Katelnikoff and Claude Audette decided that they would extend their own quests for excellence through their sons. Mario aspired to be a top-rank soccer player; Fred and Claude had the same notions about hockey. And those are goals most of us share, that our children will be somehow better, or somehow happier or somehow more successful.

The Lelacheur, Tanner and Brisebois families are a little different. They seem like families in which cause and effect are reversed. The pursuit of excellence is encouraged and hockey is the result. Although his father, Rick, was a talented athlete, Rob Lelacheur didn't start to play the game until he was nine and it wasn't until his rookie year with the Blades that he finally accepted hockey as more than a pastime. His father, grandfather and great-grandfather were all successes in business, so it was always clear to Rob that hockey was just one of an infinite number of ways to achieve excellence.

John Tanner discovered hockey through his father, who played strictly for recreation. John's mother, Jeanette, always viewed the game with suspicion, hoping her son's preoccupation would pass. When it didn't, her suspicion turned to dismay. She knew her son had an outstanding mind and she believed his devotion to hockey was an insupportable waste of it.

And although Patrice Brisebois loved and lived hockey almost from the moment he learned to walk, his father, Jean, has until this day maintained his determined policy of non-involvement. All six players, however, came to hockey as a goal because, in the end, that's what they wanted to do.

Gord Tanner, known to friends for no particular reason as Jim, is a tall slim man with a laconic way of talking, which is, until you get to know him, a little reminiscent of Gary Cooper in *High Noon*. He was born in the southern Ontario city of Brantford and has lived in that area all his life. His father, Howard, and his mother, the former Violet Eaton, farmed near the village of Ayr, and that's where Jim Tanner grew up, played defence up to the Junior C level and went to school. His sister, Joyce, is eight years younger than Tanner, who's fifty-seven now. He completed part of Grade 13, then went to work on his father's farm until it was sold in 1957. After that Tanner started work for Canadian General Tower Ltd. in Cambridge, and stayed there until he retired thirty years later, in 1987.

"I met Jeanette for the first time at the wedding of a mutual friend and I don't think I made all that good an impression," says Tanner. "I didn't see her again for quite a while, but one day I called her up where she worked in Toronto, asked her for a date, and that was that."

But, as usually proves to be the case, there was more to the story than that. His soon-to-be wife, Jeanette Tamboer, remembers the phone call and remembers how he raised eyebrows at the friend's wedding, both with the guests in general, and with her father, Jan, and mother, Jennie, in particular: "My mother thought he was terrible. She didn't like him at all," says Jeanette. Jim Tanner was not only a divorced man, which made him suspicious to staunch members of the Dutch Reformed Church, but just as ominous or even more so was the fact that he rode a motorcycle. The Tamboers, who had immigrated from Apeldoorn in Holland in 1948, where Jeanette and her elder sister, Mary, were born, were not happy at the prospect of a divorced Canadian whisking their youngest daughter off on the back of a motorcycle.

So while the parents fretted, Jeanette, now a receptionist at the Workers' Compensation Board in Toronto, took the fateful phone call from Jim Tanner and accepted the fateful date.

"I thought, 'Boy, a divorced man who rides motorcycles. What a challenge,'" recalls Jeanette. They were married July 16, 1966, at the home of friends after the Dutch Reformed Church found Jim's divorce an insurmountable obstacle and forced the couple to consider a civil ceremony at City Hall.

"I was staying with a lady in Oakville at the time and I told her about the problems we were having," recalls Jeanette. "In fact, that lady—her name is Clara Shime— turned out to have a great influence on my life. She was a Jewish lady, with two sons of her own, but she made me feel as if I belonged with them. She was understanding and kind.

"And she said, 'Well, people used to get married in someone's home. Why don't you do that?' So that's what we did."

Presented with the imminent event, her parents capitulated and both families were present as the sunny-eyed girl from Holland married her quiet man with the suspicious taste for speed. They bought ten acres of gravelly land near Cambridge in 1969 and over the years built it into a prosperous apple orchard. They have 1,700 trees now, and on a good year they'll have a yield of 500 bushels per acre.

They built their home there in 1971, and later that year, on March 17, the same time of day that Donald Audette was born, at fifteen minutes to midnight, John Tanner was born at Cambridge Memorial Hospital. They gave him the middle name of Patrick because it was St Patrick's Day. John, for no reason he can think of, hates his middle name to this day. His sister, Mary, was born three and a half years later, at about the time John was putting elbow pads on his knees and flicking a sock at the wall with one of his first hockey sticks.

Even when John was still a baby, it was clear to Jeanette

that this son of hers would be able to achieve great things, just by the stunning power of his mind. Circumstances had limited her own education, but she was determined that nothing would fetter the mind of her brilliant boy. And so it was first with annoyance, then frustration and dismay, that she watched his growing preoccupation with what to her was no more than a game.

"I would argue. I would lay down the law. I would cry. I'd get angry," she recalled later. Eventually, driven by her immense pride in John and her love for him, she reached an uneasy truce with the sport.

"I used to get so angry at hockey," she says. "It seemed like hockey was such a waste of a mind."

And even today, deep in her heart of hearts, truce or no truce, she has her reservations.

The Lelacheur family, by marriage, can trace its roots to the pioneer beginnings of St Albert, a city of 40,000, five miles north of Edmonton. St Albert was founded in 1861 by Father Albert Lacombe, an Oblate of Mary Immaculate from the diocese of St-Sulpice in Montreal. Many residents take pride in the belief that St Albert, named after Father Lacombe's patron saint, was the first mission town in Alberta.

In 1862 Lacombe built his residence on Mission Hill overlooking the village. You can stand in front of that residence today and understand why, for this is the best view in town. The hill drops in swooping terraces for a quarter mile to the Sturgeon River. Children are drawn there in the winter, as they have been for generations, with their toboggans and sleds. Rob Lelacheur, Kevin Lovig and Chris Larkin risked their lives on the slope more than one hundred years later. From the hill you can see the latest version of the first bridge to be built west of the Great Lakes. It was constructed the same year as the Mission residence, and workers were paid one beaverskin a day, or an equivalent value in goods.

Into this outpost of civilization came Silas Lelacheur, Rob's great-grandfather, in 1905. He arrived from Prince

Edward Island and established Western Moving and
Storage, the family business. He met and eventually married Mildred Latimer, who at ninety-five takes fierce pride
in the fact that Rob, her great-grandson, represents the
fourth generation of her family to be born in St Albert.
Silas's son, James, known as Big Jim, took over the business
as Silas grew old, but sold it just after the Second World
War, when he became convinced another depression was
imminent. When the depression didn't come, he bought it
back, although it took him until 1965 to come up with the
money. Rob's father, Rick, and his brother, Ted, now own
the business and have expanded it from Vancouver to the
Maritimes.

While Rick, son of Big Jim and Shirley Lelacheur, was
growing up in Edmonton, so was his future wife, Faye. Her
parents, Evelyn and Jake Greenwald, had moved there from
Saskatoon when she was three. Her sisters Donna, Sharon
and Gloria and her brother, Gary, were born after the move.
She first met Rick in Grade 11, during a dance at Ross
Sheppard High School, and it wasn't exactly love at first
sight.

"I remember thinking, 'Oh, so that's Rick Lelacheur,'"
says Faye, recalling that night. "Rick was a jock at school
and of course I'd heard a couple of friends, Connie Hanson
and Pat Killips, talking about him. But I was with a date that
night, so we didn't dance or anything. Connie and Pat introduced us and that was about it."

Their next contact was more than two years later, when
Faye was a student nurse. Rick telephoned, inviting her to a
hockey party with some of his Edmonton Oil King teammates.

"Well, I'd never been to a hockey game, much less a
hockey party, but I said I'd go," she says. "The night came
and I was dressed and waiting and waiting, but he never
came. My parents thought it was a riot, because none of my
dates had ever stood me up before."

That, she thought, was the end of Rick Lelacheur, and
good riddance, too. But the next day brought flowers and an
apologetic note explaining he'd forgotten an out-of-town

game. He never did explain why he'd forgotten to tell her, but he seemed contrite and they began dating steadily, although the romance still had its downtimes. Once, for instance, Rick asked if she'd like to come home with him to see his trophies.

"I hadn't even gotten my coat off when a light flashed through the window and a car came into his parents' driveway.

"'Oh, my God, my parents are home!' he says. 'You'll have to leave!' I couldn't believe it. He showed me out the back door, into an alley and there I am. No money and I start to walk. I'm thinking where am I going to find a phone to call my dad to come and get me, and how am I going to explain it when he does? Just then a car comes inching along and there's Rick, the most sheepish look on his face, and he asks me to get into the car. I told him I wouldn't get in if he was the last person on earth. But he told me he wasn't allowed to have visitors home when his parents weren't there."

She remembers thinking, God, we're both nineteen, what's he talking about? But she allowed him to drive her home.

"When I got home, I told my friend what had happened and I swore I'd never see him again," says Faye. "She just laughed. 'You know, you're going to marry this guy,' she said. 'He stands you up, he pushes you out of his house, he causes you nothing but grief, and you're going to marry him. Just you wait and see.' I just looked at her as if she were crazy."

Faye and Rick were married May 17, 1969, in St James United Church, Edmonton. The previous fall Rick had attended a Detroit Red Wings' training camp, where he was one of the last wingers to be cut. They invited him to join their farm team, but he declined, playing out his season with the Oil Kings and going to work for Big Jim after the marriage. They moved to St Albert shortly before Rob was born, on October 28, 1971, at 3:36 a.m.

Sixteen years later, Rob Lelacheur stands outside the boards at Brandon's Keystone Centre, two hours before his very first Junior A game. The Blades have just spent more than seven hours riding the bus from Saskatoon on a gloomy, raw fall day, and they are tired and subdued. At 7:30 p.m. they will play the Wheat Kings in an exhibition game and coach Marcel Comeau has told Rob he'll be one of the rookies who'll see ice time.

"My dad played for the Oil Kings, but he didn't make it to the big leagues," says Rob, looking out across the ice surface and glancing up to the still empty seats. He speaks quietly, his words meant mainly to heighten his own sense of occasion. "He had his chance," he says. "And now it's mine."

Thirty-five miles southeast of Quebec City, close by the village of St-Isadore, the land of the Compté Beauce Nord is flat and fertile. There, starting with just four arpents of land, *La famille Gagné*, the family of Donald Audette's mother, Véronique, have farmed for generations. An arpent is an ancient land measurement still used in a few places, such as Louisiana and some former British colonies, but especially in Quebec. One arpent equals 0.85 acres, and the original four of the Gagné farm have grown to about 80 over the years. Just as well, since this black and fertile land south of the St Lawrence has had to support some very large families. That of Antoinette and Joseph Gagné, for instance, has fourteen children and Véronique was born into it forty-nine years ago. Her eldest brother, Raoul, now sixty, still operates the farm, but most of the children have left, settling in other parts of Quebec. Véronique moved away at fifteen, taking a job at a patisserie in the nearby village of Ste-Marie de Beauce. At nineteen she moved to Quebec City and worked in a restaurant until she was twenty-four.

She met Claude Audette during a concert at Port St-Jean during Quebec Carnival. Claude was the manager of a band, and when the dark-haired girl from Eastern Quebec showed up in the audience one evening, she immediately caught his eye.

"After the concert, Claude asked me if I would come and have dinner with him, so I did," she says. A few days later he called to ask if she'd like to come see him play hockey, and once again she accepted.

"Another guy in the band saw her, too, and we talked about who was going to ask her to this party at the Château Frontenac," says Claude. "I bet a hundred dollars that she'd end up going with me, so while the other guy was thinking about it I acted. I won the bet and I've been winning ever since."

Shortly afterwards, Claude lost everything he owned in a concert promotion gone sour and that was the end of his career in show business. He returned to Montreal, got a job in radio advertising, and hitchhiked to Quebec City most weekends to be with Véronique.

"I lost my car and I lost my money, so for a while all I could afford was to hitchhike," says Claude. "Once, I hitch-hiked all the way to Quebec City and the car let me out near the city limits. I was just getting out when I looked up and there was Véronique driving past in her car, heading in the direction of Montreal.

"Well, she didn't see me, so I went in to where she worked and they told me, 'Oh, she went to see you in Montreal. She wanted to surprise you.' So I hitchhiked all the way back and then, when I got there about midnight, I couldn't find her. Montreal's a big place. She hadn't called my parents' house because she thought it was too late. I checked with friends, but they hadn't seen her. Finally I found the hotel where she was staying, at four in the morning."

Claude, his five brothers and two sisters, were raised on avenue Chambord in the Ahuntsic district of North Montreal and money was often scarce. His father, Rosario, died of a heart attack before he was fifty, after having suffered poor health for years before. Both Claude's father and his mother, Marguerite, worked long hours: he to earn a living, she to raise the children.

"My dream was to be a professional hockey player, but my parents had no time to take me to games like some of the other boys," says Claude. "I had to do what I did on my own."

He and his brother, Jacques, took hockey seriously, but they were alone in that. Their sisters Raymonde and Claire, thought hockey a somewhat tiresome game. Their brothers Pierre, Gaétan, Ivan and François were never interested. Then, when Rosario died, the family began to grow slowly apart and Claude was even more isolated in the pursuit of his dream. A tough little left-winger, he played for the Junior Canadiens of Montreal North and for the St-Jérôme Alouettes. One of his teammates was Maurice Richard, Jr, known as the Junior Rocket. His dad, the great Rocket Richard, was one of Claude's heroes, along with other Canadien giants like Jean Beliveau and Pierre Pilotte.

"I always tried to skate like Pierre Pilotte," recalls Claude. "I couldn't play like him, but I tried to skate the way he skated."

The Rocket lived on avenue Peloquin, only four blocks west of avenue Chambord, on the expensive west side of Ahuntsic, and he'd often come to the Junior games.

"He'd give me tickets to The Forum," says Claude. "And I'd go there alone. And I'd watch the Canadiens play, and I'd dream."

But it takes more than fierce desire to make a hockey player, and as Claude got older he began to realize he would never skate onto the ice of The Forum in an NHL uniform, brandishing his stick to acknowledge the cheers.

"In those days, you had to be better than good if you were French Canadian and hoping to play in the NHL," says Claude Audette and there's an echo of an old anger in his voice as he muses on the unfairness of it. "It still happens today and you can see it when the Junior players are drafted. If you have an English-speaking player and a French-speaking player and both are about equally talented, the English player will be drafted first. The French player will be drafted long after."

Claude admits, looking back, that he would never have made a top-flight player, but it still hurts when he sees the same old double standard being applied to his sons. Still, he had done what he could, gone as far as his talent allowed. Although it's always painful to turn away from a dream, it helps if you know you've done your best. Besides, there was

Véronique, and Claude's feelings for her helped soothe the pain, too.

"Time passes and other things become important," says Claude. "When I met Véronique, I thought, 'Ah, *très belle,*' and my heart beat a little faster. When you meet a woman and you like her very much, then that's what happens."

They were married on May 20, 1967, at St-Gilles à Pont Viau in Laval, the Gagnés from St-Isadore and the Audettes from Montreal filling the church. Their first son, Richard, was born a year later and the hockey dream of Claude Audette took on new life as well. Richard eventually played for the Junior Canadiens, but like his father, he wasn't big-league material. Then, on September 23, 1969, at fifteen minutes before midnight, in Montreal's Hôpital Jean Talon, a second son, Donald, was born. And the dream of Claude Audette burned with an ever brighter flame.

○ 5

Driver Dennis Zatylny eases the big Saskatoon Blades' bus through the blue security door of SaskPlace at 8:30 a.m., on time as usual. This is the first real road trip of the pre-season, seven hours to Brandon, Manitoba, for a game against the Wheat Kings this evening. It is one of those perverse prairie days that is alternately sunny in a cold, unfriendly way, then drizzly rain, then wet wind, then a stingy kind of snow. Then sun again, in the same cold, unfriendly way. It is the kind of day that true prairie-dwellers, who are sometimes as perverse as the weather, affect to glory in. This is nonsense, of course, but it doesn't stop them regaling newcomers from more favoured latitudes with endless examples of weather-based prairie humour.

Jason Christie, the feisty little right-winger from Gibbons, Alberta, has an apparently endless supply of weather stories, which he insists on telling. Rookies like Rob Lelacheur, even though they may be prairie boys themselves and have heard the stuff before, suffer silently, a captive audience for reasons we will get to later. Dean Beattie, who comes from Lloydminster, Alberta, and is a rookie as far as the Blades are concerned, breaks into laughter occasionally because that's all you can do with seven hours to kill. Harri Leskinen, who comes from Sweden, is the only one spared because he understands almost no English.

"You think this is cold. This is the tropics, man," says Christie. "Wait till it gets really cold. It gets so cold you have to carry a blowtorch in case you meet a girl. Nothing like a warm jockstrap to turn on a prairie girl."

Someone else chips in with the news that, speaking of jockstraps, they should always be pre-heated just before a game. The rinks get so cold on the prairies you could seize up in the middle of a match. Someone—it sounds like Ken Sutton—has the temerity to try sidetracking things by saying he's heard that in Saskatchewan, rapid transit is a set of snowshoes and a half-hour's head start before they turn loose the wolves. This sally is met with a huge disapproving silence because Sutton is not only a rookie and thus expected to keep silent, but he comes from Calgary. And furthermore, he lived in Pickering, Ontario, until he was ten.

Cold-weather lore holds that when travelling by bus, like now, you should always carry dry wood, a blanket and lots of matches. You never can tell when you might want to call home. And when you order dinner in a restaurant, did you know the wine comes frozen on a stick? And when this bus blows a tire, you rooks stay right where you are. Let Denny change it. He's the driver and he knows how to do it fast. Those things that look like stooks by the side of the road? They're not stooks, they're tombstones—rookies who thought they could change a tire on the prairies.

Eventually the weather jokes peter out and the team, minus the rookies, starts to break up into groups of four. Boards are extracted from the overhead racks and set in the aisle, supported by the seat armrests to make a table for each group of four seats. The cards come out and the hearts games begin. Mile after mile of hearts games, with the four-somes being formed in a kind of team pecking order. At the top of the order on this trip is a quartet made up of Daryl Lubiniecki, the general manager; Dennis Beyak, the assistant GM; Marcel Comeau, the coach; and Jeff Thomas, the trainer. Actually, Thomas is officially the team's athletic therapist, but at some point he has made the mistake of letting team members know he prefers the term "athletic therapist" to "trainer." The Blades, always sensitive to such preferences, naturally refer to Thomas as trainer without fail after learning this.

Thomas is at the low end of this high, non-player pecking order, partly because this is his first year as, um, athletic therapist, and partly because he is the worst hearts player on the bus. Comeau, Beyak and Lubiniecki are all experienced hockey men with years and miles of bus trips behind them and concomitantly high levels of hearts-playing ability. They make no attempt to hide their disdain for Thomas's lack of expertise.

"Jeez, Jeff, you'd think you could learn to count," grumbles Beyak. "Just try to remember. Ten fingers and ten toes. Try to remember the value of the cards. How many times we gotta tell ya?"

Thomas lets the criticism wash over him with the restless tide of sound that surges through the bus. Comeau is amusing himself with variations on Lubiniecki's name. The name is properly pronounced Loob-in-icky, and his nickname is Looby, but Comeau is bored with those alternatives, so he makes up his own.

"Hey, Loobanitchy, whattayou hiding, there?" says Comeau. "Looberooly's sitting there looking like he's got a hand full of nothing. Probably got a fist full of aces."

Beyak peers over his hand and smiles.

"Bullshit," he says. "Looby looks like he's got nothing because that's what he's got."

Looby remains silent, simply dragging on his cigarette and smiling what the players call his E.T. smile, one that goes ear to ear, threatening to split off the top half of his head.

"Oh, I don't know," says Comeau. "Looberatchi here can do more than play the piano. He's a tricky cuss, aintcha, Loobalosky?"

Looby puts down the queen and Comeau has to take the trick, to the groans of the other three.

"You had to do it, dintcha, Looby-dooby-doo?" says Comeau. "Sit there and smile and smile and then zing it to us. Our Looby-nasty."

Through all this chatter, every once in a while a chant comes from players at the back of the bus.

"Red Rover, come on over. . . ." Then it stops and there is raucous laughter from the veteran players. A few minutes pass, five or ten maybe, and then it starts again. "Red Rover, come on over. . . ."

The words are chanted in a teasing sing-song lilt and each time they hear them, the rookies seem to shrink lower into their seats, staring fixedly at the ceiling or out the window, as if just by looking they can transport themselves else-where. But nothing seems to develop beyond the sing-song refrain, certainly the four card players take no notice, and the game goes on. By this time, Beyak, who is much in demand as an after-dinner speaker, is testing some of his jokes on the captive audience.

"You can always tell a tough hockey player, but not much. . . . A tough player's the kind who gets called names in the bar. One guy heard himself called a wimp. He turned around and five punches later the poor girl still didn't know what hit her. . . ." There had been a few scattered smiles, to acknowledge the earlier jokes, but this one brings a chorus of boos. Beyak persists.

"Years ago, Johnny Bower, the great Leaf goaltender, took Foster and Bill Hewitt out for dinner. There they sat, the father, the son and the goalie host. . . .

"Then there was the goaltender who had two bad games in a row. Eleven went by him one night and nine the next. He was so depressed he tried to commit suicide. But when he jumped in front of a train, damned if it didn't go through his legs. . . .

"I'm going to tell some Ukrainian jokes. Are there any Ukrainians here?"

"Ye-e-es," chorus the players, many of whom are listening now.

"Then I'll tell them slow," quips Beyak, as the players groan.

"And here's one for all you guys heading for the big leagues. All you guys shooting for the big buck. It's about a divorced player who thanked his wife for making him a mil-lionaire. Before the divorce, he had two million. . . .

"A guy in Ottawa comes out of a shopping centre and spots this dog howling in a car. The owner finally shows up and explains the dog's a Roughrider fan and he howls every time his team is losing. 'Well, what does he do when they win?' says the first guy. 'Don't know,' says the owner. 'I've only had him ten years.'"

It is around 12:30 now, and as the bus passes the turnoff for Springside someone glimpses a sign that says, "Yorkton, twenty-four kilometers," which seems to trigger a basic urge.

"When are we gonna eat!" someone hollers and then everyone takes up the cause.

"Yeah, it's about that time. Let's get this show on the road. Time to eat! Time to eat! Dennis, when the hell we gonna eat?"

Beyak, whose multitude of duties include making meal arrangements during road trips, at first accords this mini-rebellion the disdain he feels it deserves and simply continues with his hearts game. "Geez, what a pack of wolves," he mutters, dealing another hand. But what began as rebellion turns within seconds into a feeding frenzy. Finally, Beyak throws down his hand and stands up to face the hungry oppressed.

"Shuddup, you guys, and listen." The noise abates only slightly. "There is not gonna *be* any stop this trip for meals."

This statement brings instant silence, the rookies staring at him aghast, the vets, wise to the Beyak sense of humour, watching with quizzical smiles. "You've all heard of lean and mean," he says straight-faced. "Well, you yahoos are gonna be lean and mean when we meet the Wheat Kings. We've decided no break for meals, nothing till we get to Brandon. Then we've laid on a nice light meal of soup and crackers when we get to the motel. Besides, we're already running late this trip and we don't have time for stopping."

Beyak is immediately engulfed in a tide of imprecations: real annoyance from the rookies, feigned anger and obscenities from the veterans. The argument rages for several kilometers, the rookies doing most of the complaining, the vets now sitting back with knowing smiles. Then, entering the outskirts of Yorkton, Zatylny the driver, smiling broadly through everything, swings into the Holiday Inn.

"Shit, he was just having us on," says a rookie, and within minutes the bus is parked and twenty Saskatoon Blades stampede for the restaurant. There are rolls, soup, mashed potatoes and gravy, fried chicken and caramel custard, all waiting buffet style. Jugs of Coke wait on the tables. Comeau, moderate in most things, is a Coke-aholic and pours his first glass even before he sits down. The players fidget impatiently in line. The team pecking order is even more strictly adhered to at mealtimes. They do not allow themselves to be served or seated until Looby, Beyak, Comeau and Thomas have loaded up; then they fall in behind. Veterans are served first, rookies watching critically, fearful that the choicest pieces of chicken and the biggest portions of dessert will be plundered before it's their turn. But there's plenty to go around and the ritual of getting seated goes ahead. Veterans keep a lookout for rookies who show unseemly haste in choosing seats. The dialogue always follows roughly the same format.

"Move, rook, you're in my seat," says the veteran.

"No, I'm fucking not," says the rookie.

"Yes, you damn well fucking are," says the vet. The rookies always put up a token resistance, but they always move because they are rookies and expected to defer to everyone.

This pecking-order business, though it is sometimes random in its manifestations, is not random in its purpose. The hierarchy of management, veteran, rookie, is part of a bonding process. It is part of a hazing system that many clubs—the Blades, the Petes and the Titans among them—regard as important in developing a team out of a collection of individuals. The same idea has been used throughout military history. A bond is formed by wearing a uniform and forcing recruits to undergo various demeaning tests of one sort or another. The result is that when the ultimate demeaning test is demanded, that of unquestioningly offering your life simply because you are ordered to do so, the recruit will not turn and flee as his rational mind urges him to do. Instead, he stands and fights, even dies, because dying is preferable to breaking that bond.

Though on a hockey team the ultimate sacrifice is obviously less drastic, the purpose is the same. Much as in the military, the officers, who are the coach, GM, etc., turn a blind eye while the hazing goes on around them, conducted by the veterans. Thus, at this meal, there are cries of "Shoe check! Shoe check!" followed by much laughter and just as much moaning and groaning. Someone, usually a vet, ducks under the table armed with mustard or ketchup bottle and dumps it over someone's shoe. While he yells, "Shoe check! Shoe check!" each nervous rookie inspects his feet, hoping it isn't him. Aside from shoe checks, this particular meal is uneventful. A couple of buns are thrown at rookies and one or two spoonsful of soup, but that's about it. About thirty-five minutes after the meal begins, the players are back on the bus and Zatylny is pulling onto the Yellowhead Highway.

"Jason, you count the players," says Comeau to Christie, whose nickname is Smurf. "There should be twenty."

This directive of Comeau's moves one wit to express his concern.

"Geez, Marse, twenty? That's a lot of guys, I don't know. Smurf only went to Grade 10."

The bus crosses into Manitoba around 1:30, passing the sign to Langenburg where the Yellowhead dips into a deep coulee. This valley has been worn over the millennia by the Assiniboine River and it's the only relief from the prairie flatness between here and Saskatoon. Beyak remarks that there have been reports of UFO sightings around Langenburg, speculating that maybe a little something extra has been getting into the local water. Nobody comments further, but eyes narrow intently, looking for signs in the sky, just in case. They see nothing of green men, or man of any other colour, but as the bus grinds up onto the Manitoba flatland, players look out at a copse of maples blazing red. The valley and that splash of colour are both rare, at least on this stretch. The trees of the southern prairie seem mostly to be small poplars or aspens, so their leaves turn to pale yellow, fading to drabness under the pale sun.

The players doze or read or both for the next two hours, and even the card players have folded their games. The road

stretches straight and flat, mile after sleepy mile, and Rob
Lelacheur makes an entry in his diary:

> What do you do when you feel two ways at the same
> time? There's part of me that doesn't want to be here.
> And there's part of me that does. I want to play Junior
> A, but today I feel so lonely I wonder if it's worth it. I
> want to make my parents proud and myself, too. But it
> is really hard and sometimes I just don't know. Oh,
> well. I've felt like this before and it has passed, so this
> time probably won't be any different. But it's still very
> hard when you feel this way.

Rob is drawn away from these musings around Shoal
Lake, where Zatylny draws attention to the brightly blinking
lights of what may be police cars in the distance. As the bus
draws close the team can see police vehicles ranged across
the highway, blocking it. There is intense curiosity about
why the Mounties are blocking a highway and plenty of
guessing. A sign says there's an airshow nearby, so the players speculate that perhaps they are using the four-laned
highway as a runway. Or maybe there has been a crash. The
crash theory, with its connotations of doom and drama,
quickly gains favour as the bus slows to take directions from
the Mountie on traffic duty. Zatylny leans out the window to
confer, and when he closes it and turns into a detour, he is
bombarded with questions.

"Why they got the road closed, Dennis?" Their curiosity
at the breaking point, everyone hangs on his answer.

"I don't know. She didn't say," says Zatylny, smiling. There
are gasps of purest disbelief.

"Whaddya mean, she didn't say?" says someone else, and
Dennis smiles again.

"She didn't say, because I never asked her." Players and
team executives slump into their seats as if broken by the
vast implications of this incomprehensible lack of curiosity.
How could he not ask?

"Dennis never asked," says Lelacheur to a player sitting
behind him. There is wonder in his voice and his tone

suggests that he has just announced the loss of an irre-
deemable opportunity. "A nice-looking girl Mountie, too."

"*Je*-zus," intones another player, shaking his head. "Now
we'll never know."

The players settle into silence, sharing a frustration no
one really understands, and this lasts the final two hours to
Brandon. As the bus bears down on the Red Oak Inn,
where the team will spend the next two nights, they slowly
stir out of their silence and begin reassuming the personae
of hockey players again. Ties are put on, collars straight-
ened, mustard remnants wiped from shoes, hair combed.

"Listen up, guys," says Comeau, standing at the front of
the bus. "I want you to get an hour of rest in your rooms,
then back in the lobby for 5:15. That's in your rooms, an
hour of rest, then in the lobby at 5:15. That's all, guys."

The big bus trundles up to the door of the Red Oak and
the Saskatoon Blades file off; ties straight, hair combed,
every mother's perfect son, looking sharp and lean and
mean.

Tracey Katelnikoff stands with his brother, Trevor, his little
sister, Tricia, and his mother, Marcia, at the side of his
father's grave in Calgary.

"Ashes to ashes, dust to dust," he hears the minister
intone, and he feels a flush of anger at the words. That's
wrong, he thinks. People are more than that. My father was
not ashes when he was alive and he is not ashes now. He
was a man I loved, a man who loved me. He was my father
when he was alive and now that he has left us, he is not dust
or ashes, whatever they say. He is still my father.

He looks down at the coffin, his sense of loss like a stone
on his heart. He senses his brother and sister beside him
and hears his mother weep.

○ **6**

The Laval Titans' bus trip to St-Jean-sur-Richelieu, south of Montreal, is only about an hour long, but the veterans are making certain the rookies won't find it boring. Patrice Brisebois grimaces as a particularly anguished shriek comes from the small toilet where five rookies are enjoying the initiation rites that will make them fully-fledged members of the team. Five of them have been stuffed and pushed and pried into the space, which measures a little more than three feet square. The five have been selected more or less at random, forced to strip naked, then stuffed into what is called simply *la boîte*, the box. Their clothes are jumbled into a pile, then knotted together, knots on top of knots. When the pile looks hopelessly snarled, the toilet door is cracked open just wide enough for the clothes to be shoved in. Someone's arm is forced through, too, holding a can of Coke, and the sticky soft drink is poured over the howling rooks. The door slams shut again and the veterans wait gleefully, imagining what is happening inside. Three of them are guarding the door to make sure no one inside makes a break for it. The rookies must untie the knots, sort out their own clothes and dress. If someone emerges wearing the wrong clothes, he is pummelled back into the box. When all are dressed, they are allowed to return to their seats. Each gets a resounding cheer, and each rookie tells his tormentors about the various things they can do with their cheers.

The identical scene could be taking place on the Peterborough Petes' bus or the Blades' bus, the dialogue much the same. The Petes call it "hee-baa" for no particular reason, and the Blades, with their Red Rover shenanigans, take it a step further. Of course, they have longer bus trips, more idle time and more chance for the devil to take a hand.

In Red Rover, depending on the mood of their tormentors, the last two out of the box are sometimes given one further opportunity to show how serious they are about this business of team bonding. One vet draws a line on the floor and the rookies stand on each side of it. They are given a length of string, told to tie an end to each of their penises and then start pulling. Winner of the tug o' war is exempted from rookie harassment for a specified length of time.

Patrice Brisebois takes little part in harrying the rookies, although he can't help smiling at the expressions on some of the faces. Many veterans have experienced the same treatment in their rookie seasons, although Patrice himself favours practical jokes over *la boîte*. As the furor subsides he thinks of his rookie year, when the veterans set various tasks for the rookies, vying to come up with the most embarrassing. His task was to approach his coach at the time, Claude Terrion, during a bus trip and tell him he didn't feel like playing that night, so he wasn't going to play. The veterans were most specific about the choice of words. He had to say them precisely, or they would think of something worse to do to him.

"*Coach, ça me tente pas de jouer ce soir. Je ne me fend pas en soixante-dix.*" Those were the words Patrice was to use, no deviation allowed. Rough translation: "Coach, I don't feel like playing tonight, so I'm not going to bust my ass." Those would be seditious words to any coach and to Terrion in particular. Terrion, known for his iron discipline, was capable of trading a player for less insubordinate conduct and Patrice still remembers his fear vividly. He'll bench me for a week, even if I'm lucky, thought Patrice. More likely he'll make my life so miserable, I'll have to ask for a trade.

Terrion's reaction is even worse than he feared.

"You don't *feel* like playing?" he roars. "You don't wanta bust your ass?" Red-faced with rage, Terrion orders the bus to stop.

"*Arrêtez le bus! Arrêtez le bus!*" he screams. The bus stops and he tells Patrice to get off, get off *now*.

"You don't want to play, get off the bus! Get off the bus!" As Patrice makes to get his coat, Terrion shoves him towards the door. "Never mind your coat. Just get off this bus! Get off the bus!"

Patrice steps out into the cold dark night, feeling more abandoned than he's ever felt in his life. "I felt like breaking down. I felt like crying," he said later, describing the horrible moments as the red taillights shrank into the distance. Then, just as the bus was about to disappear around a bend in the road, he saw the brake lights come on and the bus stop. He remembers running towards it, feeling like he had seen death and been passed by. As he climbs aboard the whole team is laughing and clapping, Terrion with them. The veterans had filled him in about the whole escapade; the rookie had been set up.

Now, listening to the chatter around him, Patrice thinks maybe *la boîte* would be easier on the nerves after all.

A couple of seats away, Donald Audette remembers his initiation rite, too. He and the other rookies were required to play five-a-side, wearing only their jockstraps. What made it really excruciatingly embarrassing was that they had to do it in the parking lot of Carrefours Laval, the biggest shopping mall in town. Nobody called the cops; at least they had that to be thankful for. In fact, the onlookers seemed to enjoy the spectacle immensely, the women laughing and blushing, the men making rude remarks.

No rookie, it seems, is immune from this sort of initiation rite. Even the Great One, Gretzky, when he played for the Soo Greyhounds in the 1977-78 season, got his chance to become one of the boys. Ted Nolan, then a veteran defenceman, now coach of the Greyhounds, recalls that incident well.

"There was Wayne and I think another rookie named Jeff Mitchell. Craig Hartsburg was there and I was there and my friend Donny Roach," says Nolan. "We waited for a nice cool September night, then we took them to Bellevue Park."

There they ordered the two rookies to strip, then streak the park.

"Gretzky breaks out of the trees, Mitchell behind him, running like hell for the street at the other side. Just as they get there, make the turn to head back, two police cruisers turn on their lights and sirens and hell breaks loose. They nab Wayne and Jeff, arrest them, put them into a paddy wagon and cart them off to jail."

After the embarrassed pair spend an hour worrying about whether this is going to get in the papers, what they'll tell their parents, how they're going to, for God's sake, even show their faces on the street again, Nolan and Hartsburg and Roach show up, real comedians, laughing like crazy. The cops have a good laugh, too, while Gretzky and Mitchell put on their clothes, realizing, finally, that the whole act was set up ahead of time.

But now it is another cool September day more than ten years later and Patrice Brisebois's thoughts begin to drift away from these rites of passage. He thinks of how this question started for him and after a while takes a small journal from his duffel bag and begins writing down his thoughts:

> I began in Atom and even when I was little I was pretty good. I was always the tallest on the team, always the captain, the leader, and I liked to win. When you're chosen captain of the team, you have the responsibility of the team and that's a lot of fun. Even though I was a defenceman, I played offensive, I was on the puck, always since I was little I was on the puck, so that's nothing new. I like to get goals. I was never big in terms of weight. Always taller, but never bigger. *Il faut prendre un peu de poids.* You have to put on a little weight, you have to put on a little weight. It's true. You need that extra muscle mass. That's where I'm a little weak.
>
> Here's a joke that happened to me when I was small. I had a practice in the morning and it was an important one. *Elle coutait ben bonne, celle-là.* It was going to count big. The practice was at eight so I got up about six and my father got up the same time I did. It must

have been 30 below outside. So I finished my breakfast and my father was having his coffee. It was time to go to the arena. So while I was getting ready, my father was watching me. I put my bag on my shoulder and he just looked at me and said, "Have a good practice."

I didn't know what to say. I wanted my father to drive me, I hoped he would, but he never drove me to a practice. *Jamais, jamais.* I went all the time on foot or on the bus. I was the only one of my team who did that. When I think of all the sacrifices; that hockey bag was heavy on that bus, walking in the wintertime when it was so cold. I am really proud of having done that.

My mother knew I had potential. She always encouraged me. She knew I could do something good in life. She knew I could go all the way. But my father didn't encourage me and he didn't say much, either. Still, he always paid for the hockey, even though it was sometimes difficult. When I was sixteen, my parents moved to St-Donat, in the Laurentians, on Lac Croche. I lived here and there, because I stayed behind to play hockey. I stayed at my brother's, I boarded, and this past year, I stayed at the house of *ma p'tite blonde*, Michèle. The one that helps me the most in my everyday life is my brother, Jean-Pierre. He is like my second father. All the little things he did for me, I appreciate and will never forget. My brother's the one that helped me the most in my hockey career.

Memories. The Peterborough Petes are only about half an hour into their trip to Belleville where they'll play the Bulls, but John Tanner has tuned out the no-brainer showing on the VCR, *Rambo XXIII* or something like that, one of the high numbers, anyway. Although he found the first Rambo movie entertaining as pure escapism, he wonders why they bother with the rest and thinks idly that if he put his mind to it, he could do better. He may be right for his ambition, if he does not become a major-league goalie, is to be a writer, and there is little doubt that he has the talent. His mother has saved one of his first short stories, entitled "In the War", completed when he was in Grade 3. It won first prize in the North Dumphries Township school fair creative writing contest. Now, as the bus counts off the miles, John Tanner smiles to himself as he recalls his mother showing him the story again after treasuring it for all the years. He understands that she reminds him of such things because she fears his intellectual gifts will be wasted in his preoccupation with hockey. She believes hockey is the waste of a great brain and he knows her fears hurt her.

Don't worry, Mother, he says to himself, at the same time knowing she will worry anyway. He is suddenly struck with a feeling of tenderness, because he loves her very much. Someday, you'll be very proud, he vows to himself, promising her. Someday . . .

Mike Ricci sits across the aisle, and now that the no-brainer is over he starts to clear his mind before the game. He lets his thoughts wander wherever they will, lets his daydreams take him.

He thinks for some reason of a time when he was about six and his big brother, Bruno, is pushing him around in a kind of hybrid go-cart that someone, his dad, probably, has put together for him. He loves to play in the thing, especially when he can get his brothers, Bruno and Maurice, to push him. He has a thirst for speed and when he is being pushed in the go-cart he can almost imagine he is on skates, they get moving so fast. The speed and the sense of danger exhilarate him and he screeches with joy while Bruno whoops behind him.

They are zinging along, Mario Andretti at the wheel, getting every last revolution out of his two-cylinder Bruno engine, bearing down on the finish line, bearing down, the hungry dogs behind him. The only thing between Mike Ricci/Mario Andretti and victory now is an imaginary A.J. Foyt and he's gotta squeeze past him, just enough room to jam himself in there past the starting gate with a half-inch, a quarter-inch, lots of room, to spare, if only Bruno's legs hold up for another ten feet. He is past A.J., the wind whipping his face, gas fumes in his lungs, he is at the starting gate and then there's this god-awful sound as he hits the post of the gateway. Bruno is shoving full-bore, all his strength directed at forcing him through a hole one quarter-inch too narrow when a wheel comes off. The front end grinds into the pavement, the wooden axle breaks, and suddenly there is no more Mario Andretti. He's long gone at the instant of disaster and there's just little Mike Ricci left, picking himself up off the cement and blinking through his tears.

"You stupid . . . ," he rages at Bruno, searching his experience for a suitable swear word but failing to find one bad enough. "You broke my go-cart!" Bruno reddens angrily at the monumental unfairness of this accusation from his speed-demon little squirt of a brother.

"You little jerk," he says. "I didn't make you break your stupid go-cart; I was just trying to make you go fast. You said you wanted to go fast, didn't you?"

Mike can think of nothing to say to that because it's true. But his beloved go-cart is ruined and he'll probably never have another. His instincts are right about that. He starts to bawl in earnest then and Bruno tries to console him by patting his shoulder.

"Aw, I'm sorry," says Bruno. "We'll take it home and get it fixed up as good as new." Bruno pats him again, but Mike shrugs him off, still angry. He has no faith in what tomorrow will bring, and not much interest in it either. What he wants is the go-cart whole again and it angers him that nothing he can do will make it so.

His period of mourning the go-cart lasts for about an hour, until a few of the guys show up at the door, looking for a road-hockey game—Marco Sachetti, Chris Kyriakou, Mike Ferguson—waiting patiently for the star player. No road-hockey game is complete without Mike. He dominates every game even though the other players tend to be two or three years older. In fact, as word of his ability gets around the neighbourhood, it's no longer as easy as it once was to get opposition without giving away goals as a handicap. Mike finds it slightly annoying that whichever team he's on is expected either to give away goals or to play shorthanded. It's always something. What it means is that even at six, they're scared to play against him. That makes him feel okay; he doesn't mind that, them being scared. As time passes, a thought becomes central to his life..

I want to just play, he thinks. No giving up goals. No giving up players. Just play. Then he smiles. I guess that would show how good I really am, he thinks. And that thought pleases him very much.

o 7

It is an hour and a half before game time, and the Keystone Centre, where the Blades will meet the Wheat Kings in this exhibition match, is still empty. It always seems to Lelacheur that, on game nights, there is something a little troubling about an empty hockey arena. At other times, such as during a practice, empty arenas are O.K., but on game nights there is something sad about them, something incomplete. At least it's a temporary condition and already there are hints of a quickening heartbeat. Somewhere a door slams, a light is turned on, somewhere somebody shouts.

Lelacheur leaves off his musing because now it's time to start his own pre-game rhythm. He gets the blowtorch and carefully heats the blade of his spare stick, adding a little extra curve. He feels the pleasure hockey players feel in the job, moulding the blade under the heat. Then he tapes the game stick and the spare. He prefers the Canadien, and it is a continual annoyance to him that Jeff Thomas, the trainer, is always foisting off Titan sticks on him. Lelacheur hefts the game stick in his hand, briefly admiring his taping job, the curve of the blade, the blue and silver bands on the white shaft, the grain of the wood. He flips a couple of imaginary pucks with it, making a quiet "pow" sound with his mouth, like a boy imitating the noise of a gun. He speaks little but the ghetto-blaster is on loud, and he lets the pre-game sounds swirl around him.

Jason Christie, Brian Gerrits and Drew Sawtell, all forwards and all veterans, are making a production of getting into their cold longjohns, professing to hold the rookies responsible.

"Fucking rooks, these longjohns are gonna give me fucking chilblains," says Christie, while Gerrits smiles in his deadpan way and Sawtell, who seems to find the pronouncement hilarious, for reasons lost on Lelacheur, breaks up in guffaws of laughter. Christie, basically good-natured and well liked on the team, nonetheless never needs much encouragement when it comes to needling rookies.

"Didn't nobody tell you you rooks are supposed to get this stuff warmed up before we put them on?" he says. "You're supposed to unpack them first thing and sit on them to get them warm. That's a rookies' job. My ass is gonna be cold halfway through the first period."

"Shit, the way you play, your ass'll still be cold by the end of the game," someone hollers.

"The only thing worries Smurf is his dong is gonna be cold by the end of the game."

"Yeah, Smurf's girlfriend said."

"That's a lie. Smurf don't have no girlfriend. That was Smurf's boyfriend you were out with."

"Get off my case," says Christie, who enjoys the heckling, even when it's at his expense. "And I wouldn't talk if I was you, DooBee," he admonishes Sawtell. "You don't know the difference anyway; that's what I think."

The witticisms continue as the players work their way closer to game time and then, about half an hour before, someone, maybe Christie again, remarks on the looseness of the atmosphere. The other veterans pick it up.

"Time to get serious, guys. This is an exhibition, but we still want to win. Let's get a little serious in here."

Although Lelacheur and the other rookies participate only on the fringes of this ebb and flow, it has its effect on him, taking him first into the team, helping to make him part of it, then in the near silence that follows, carrying him into the game to come. He recedes into himself and so the other players with him, each envisioning the sort of game they'll have. Rob goes over in his mind what he knows of the Kings' players, ticking the facts off in his mind like items on a checklist. He visualizes different situations, imagines how the play might go, examines the various scenarios of how he can better play his man.

Comeau enters the room, says, "Listen up, guys," and right away, at least two veterans are on their feet saying the same thing, "Yeah, listen up, guys." They sound like parrots, thinks Lelacheur with sudden annoyance. Comeau goes over some of the strong and weak points of the Kings, emphasizing that they are big and tough, which, when you boil down all he says, seems to be their major strong point at this stage of the pre-season. Although he doesn't spell it out, he does offer hints about how they should receive the expected violent play, whether to retaliate or try to avoid penalties. He mentions he will be using the rookies a lot—"counting on you rookies," is how he puts it—and Lelacheur, digesting it all, takes this to mean that he doesn't want to see dumb penalties, but he doesn't want them putting up with crap either. A dumb penalty, in Comeau's or anyone else's view, is one where a player succumbs to the provocation of constant jabbings and boardings and surreptitious elbowings to retaliate just at the moment when the ref is looking his way. That's a dumb penalty, getting caught, and he doesn't want his players getting caught and sitting on their asses in the penalty box and making a power play possible just because somebody's fucking feelings are hurt.

Well, everybody apparently agrees with this, every word, all nodding sagely. Who, us? Retaliate? Geez, he think we're stupid? Lelacheur nods right along with the rest, knowing full well that as a rookie defenceman, the first time anyone does anything out of line, *anything*, he is going to do his best to knock him over the boards and into the third row. He does not *like* fighting, exactly, but he doesn't hold back either. At five foot eleven and 180 pounds, he looks small in comparison to many of the bruisers he meets, but he's deceptive and quick and strong, smart enough already in the ways of hockey to try and make the first punch count, to devastate the guy before the sucker knows things have gotten serious. He also knows that unless you are an astoundingly talented player, demonstrating a willingness to fight is the quickest way to get respect from the opposition team. Even more important for a rookie, it also gains you respect from your own team. The benefit is that opposing players stop whacking and hacking at you every time the ref isn't looking, and your own players stop their constant harassment of you every practice as they try to decide how much "character" you've got. He has already established his own credibility with his teammates by coming out on top of a fight with veteran Kevin Kaminski, which took place during his second or third practice in Junior A. The tough centre, nicknamed Killer, had let it be known he intended to test Lelacheur, goading him in practice, crowding him, jamming him into the corners.

"C'mon, let's go. Let's see if you can fight," he said and Lelacheur, knowing the challenges would continue until he accepted, decided now was the time.

"Okay, let's go," he said, dropping his gloves, and, as is the custom in the Western Hockey League, ripping off his own helmet. His first punch, a hard, straight, overhand right, caught the Killer flush in the mouth and dropped him to the ice. The fight was over almost before it had really started. After that, Lelacheur recalls, the team more or less leave you alone to do what you came for, play hockey. So although Rob Lelacheur doesn't like to fight, if he has to, he will.

Lelacheur is not in the first shift, so he stands at the bench facing the end of the arena where the Canadian flag has been dropped into view on a pulley system. He fidgets slightly, silently mouthing the words, as "O Canada" blares through the speakers. On the first note of the final bar, the starters for both teams observe the unwritten law of abandoning respectful formality to break into motion. If anyone ever stayed at attention until the music actually ended, it would be a world-first, thinks Lelacheur. Long before the music has ended the players are skating around, every fan has taken a seat, and the ref is waiting to drop the puck.

Comeau's estimation of the Kings' disposition for violence is soon confirmed. At 1:51 Brandon gets a roughing penalty, but before the power play gets in gear the Blades are caught slashing. That's the way it goes: pushings and shovings, insults and curses, while the penalties mount. Paul Sutcliffe gets the first Blades' goal and then for a while the ill feelings simmer. The simmer, though, is gradually approaching a boil. A Blade is charged from behind. A Wheat King is slashed. There's another roughing call, another slashing. You can imagine steam forming at ice level. This is not helped at the eleven-minute mark when the Kings are caught sleeping. One moment, they have the puck at the Blades' net, boring in. The next moment, goalie David Bell clears it to Christie; Smurf gives it to Kevin Yellowaga, and the fast right-winger scores for the Blades.

Lelacheur, who has been playing well but uneventfully, contributes to the inevitable boilover during the play that leads to the Kings' first goal. Seconds earlier, while he's carrying the puck, he is hit from behind and smashed into the boards. He doesn't know who hit him, but someone is going to pay. As he picks himself up, the first person he sees is Greg Hutchings, a right-winger who's four inches taller and fifteen pounds heavier. He whacks him with his glove.

"You wanna go?" says Hutchings.

"Yeah, let's go," says Lelacheur. They throw gloves and helmets on the ice and start in, but this is not one of those satisfying fights where much is decided. Hutchings grabs Lelacheur and hangs on while Lelacheur pummels him, or tries his best, with his arms hampered. They fall to the ice, still churning away at each other as the referee and linesmen break it up. When it finally is sorted out, Lelacheur gets a game misconduct and he's through for the night. Teammate Geoff McMaster gets a roughing penalty and Hutchings gets a game misconduct, too.

From then on, just about everybody gets into the act, with each side collecting four more game misconducts, all for fighting. There is the usual complement of holdings, slashings, chargings both from behind and otherwise. There are several unsportsmanlike conducts. There is even a bench minor as Kings' coach Doug Sauter waves a fist at the referee.

The Blades win 6–5, and after the game, while the players nurse their various contusions and abrasions, they can barely

contain their glee and satisfaction. Actually, it is not contained at all.

"Did you see what we did to those poor fuckers?" somebody asks of no one in particular. "Shee-it, did we kick ass?
They'll be phoning home to mommy tonight."

Comeau comes into the dressing-room and peers about
him sternly as the room falls silent.

"Well, it wasn't pretty, guys. But we'll take it," he says
deadpan, then leaves the room. Lelacheur accepts the congratulations of teammates, vets and rookies alike, smiling
quietly, proudly, despite his protestations that "It really
wasn't much of a fight." His mates, moving a step closer to
fully accepting the rook, will have none of it.

"You cleaned his clock, Lolly," they say. "You worked him
over good."

"Naw, I didn't," says Lelacheur, trying to be modest, but
very much aware of the fact that the team has just assigned
him a nickname. Later, as Lelacheur gets on the bus and
takes his seat, he just can't stop smiling. Lolly, he says to
himself, liking the name and getting used to it. Lolly, he says.
He sits in his seat and the smiles keep coming. He just
smiles and smiles.

Tracey Katelnikoff spent seventeen days in his Midget year
on the greatest adventure of his life to date, on what he still
refers to as the China Trip. He was a member of an Alberta
under-seventeen team that toured Beijing, Harbin, and even
the remote northern closed city of Qiqihar. He knows that
although life will hold other adventures, none is ever likely to
make this one fade from his mind.

Now, as he heads back to the Washington Capitals' training camp after his father's funeral, he looks down on the
prairie from 32,000 feet and thinks this is how some of
China's open lands would have looked to him, if he'd ever
gotten to fly over it in a plane. Harbin to Qiqihar, particularly, although he'd made the trip by train, would probably look
like this from the air. The notion sets in motion a sequence
that carries him again through some of those seventeen days.
Crowded, uncomfortable hours on trains, strange and, to

Canadian tastes, simply unpalatable food, incomprehensible attitudes and customs. Although people say they long for adventure, Tracey knows that when one is actually happening to you, it's always a matter of enduring some kind of discomfort or uncertainty, even danger, with your dominant thought being something like, Lord, let it end. It is only later that adventures can be enjoyed in the retelling, survival endowing them with grandeur.

He wonders if time will endow this new adventure, this tryout with the Capitals, with any kind of grandeur. He knows the sense of excitement will return, that he'll regain the feeling he had before his father's death intervened. He knows that much because he's enough of his father's son to recognize that no sort of depression or sense of loss can keep him from working towards his dream. Just for now everything is muted, or not really happening yet. He feels he is caught in a sort of trance, knowing he's caught in it but unable to wake up and escape. Tracey knows his dream has been dealt a blow partly because he has had to miss a week of training camp. His difficulty of making an impression on the coaches and scouts will be vastly increased, now that all the other players are a week ahead of him. At a time like this a week might as well be forever.

Well, hell, he tells himself. I haven't gotten where I am by thinking this way; I got where I am by facing up to what the problem is. Decide what the problem is, then get on with it. Tracey can hear his father's words as clearly as if Fred were sitting in the seat beside him. Don't whine about it. Don't whine and don't quit. Just do the best you can do. Do the best you can do and no one will ever criticize. No man can ask for more. Just go out and do it, Tracey. It's up to you. You can do it if you want, do whatever you want.

Tracey recalls his anger and fear in the first shock of Fred's death, and realizes with a sense of relief that his feelings were wrong. His father is gone but he has not deserted his son. He knows, somehow, that Fred will ride beside him until he is strong enough to ride alone. His memories encourage him, urge and reassure him. Simple words, maybe overly simple. There is nothing you cannot do,

Tracey, the familiar voice tells him. Nothing you cannot do. The words may be simplistic but Tracey is comforted by them.

By the time the aircraft lands and the van shuttles him to the Holiday Inn in Alexandria, Virginia, his flagging confidence has returned. Devon Oleniuk claps him on the shoulder as they line up for supper and all of a sudden Tracey is fearless, indestructible, ready to pick up where he left off a week ago. Ready to meet whatever comes.

○ 8

The national anthem winds down and the announcer immediately starts to introduce the starting lineup for the Peterborough Petes as the fans in the Quinte Sports Centre, home of the Belleville Bulls, mutter and buzz. When he hears his name, John Tanner skates three strides forward, acknowledging the routine boos of the homers and the smattering of applause from a small Peterborough contingent. This will be his first start away from home in the pre-season exhibition series and it takes place, coincidentally, on the same day that Rob Lelacheur tests his boxing technique with Greg Hutchings in Brandon.

Mike Ricci takes his seat on the bench, but waits nonetheless intently for the puck to drop. At centre for the opening shift that would normally be his is Dave Lorentz. He normally plays left wing. Lorentz is a veteran in his last year of Junior eligibility, a solid team leader who was named captain just two games earlier. He is on a line, at least for the opening face-off, with Mark Myles and Paul Mitton, both nervous but talented rookies. Dick Todd, watching from behind the bench, can sense their jitters by the way they keep moving in on the puck, anticipating referee Jim Houston as he prepares to make the drop.

Tanner, setting himself at the net, can feel the nervousness, all right, but what he feels within himself is even more ominous. It's a feeling familiar to every goalie. Ron Hextall, the great and in some minds controversial goalie of the Philadelphia Flyers, says it is hard to describe, but goalies know, in the warm-up, the signs of a long game in the offing.

"I don't know what it is," says Hextall. "You get a kind of flat feeling. You may stop everything they throw at you in the warm-up and in other ways feel hot as a pistol, but if you get that flat feeling kind of laying there over everything else, then you know you could be in trouble."

Sometimes the flat feeling evaporates with the opening face-off or the goalie can simply work himself out of it, but at other times it sits there waiting, like a monster conjured up by Stephen King. And although he has never compared notes with Hextall, that's the way it is now for Tanner as he watches Lorentz win the face-off, then sees the first of what will be many passes this night, either intercepted or somehow not completed, simply gone wildly astray. But the flatness, his own flatness, worries him the most.

Even before he takes his shift, Ricci feels the flatness too. He senses it more as a general malaise; if his team plays poorly, no matter how brilliantly he himself may perform, he feels himself diminished by the whole. That's the kind of player he is—capable even at sixteen of transcending whatever his team does, of uplifting them, but always being part of them.

John Tanner is also a team player, in his way. But for him the flatness is a personal monster. He is a goalie, and goalies are not like other players. A goalie knows that every team member's contribution is important, but he also knows that every other team member can miss a play, or even have a bad game, without dire results. The goalie alone, or so he thinks in his heart, must be perfect. He is like the surgeon, whose every mistake is potentially fatal, the results appallingly and publicly obvious. His task is an impossible one: to achieve not just excellence but perfection. The knowledge that he must attempt the impossible puts him under extraordinary psychological and physical pressure. He commonly goes to equally extraordinary lengths to deal with it.

Hextall, for instance, sleeps twelve hours a day, not necessarily at a stretch, and follows a careful off-ice regimen, balancing his diet and exercise and periods of relaxation.

"The pressure is always there," he says. "You have to deal with it, because if you don't you will have a short career in the big leagues. The best players deal with their pressure. The ones who don't, disappear.

"The most difficult thing a young goalie has to do is deal with the pressure," says Hextall. "As long as you play, it will be there, waiting to get to you. You can't hope it will go away; it never will. You learn to accept it, and I think that's the key. Pressure is your enemy, as a goalie or as anyone else. By accepting it, you turn it into, well, maybe not your friend, but something that works for you, not against you."

Ron Hextall's experience is germane to the case of John Tanner because, of the six dreamers, none has more riding on the outcome of his struggle with his own psychology. Roger Neilson, one of hockey's most cerebral of critics, summarizes the danger facing Tanner. Neilson, now coach of the New York Rangers, knows the talented goalie well. He maintains a summer home just north of Peterborough, and ever since his days as coach of the Petes he has kept up a close relationship with the team.

"John is very talented," says Neilson. "He's big. He's very fast. He has all the tools to be a success in the NHL. The thing that could stop him is what goes on in his mind."

It's this common struggle that accounts for goalies' reputations as the magnificent eccentrics of hockey. The struggle is heightened by the fact that, in their attempt to achieve not just excellence but perfection, they must face and conquer the unknown. The goalie cannot predict precisely at what angle a puck will come hurtling at him, or at exactly what instant it will come dribbling his way through a confusing cover of tangled legs. He knows only that it will come. If, when it comes, he stops the puck, he has for that instant achieved perfection. If he gets only a piece of the puck, then the goalie believes that he has had perfection in his grasp and he has let the opportunity elude him.

"If I can get a piece of the puck, I should be able to get it all," says Hextall, and most goalies, and certainly John Tanner, would agree.

If a goalie misses a shot entirely, his first thought is, what did I do wrong? What should I have done? He knows, even as he asks himself these questions, that often there is nothing he did wrong, nothing he could have done, yet, still, relentlessly, he examines himself. Tanner, like many other goalies, can lose ten pounds during a game. This constant threat of the unknowable accounts for the sometimes arcane measures goalies adopt to help them deal with it. Hextall pounds the goalposts. During warm-ups he picks specific spots on the ice where he stands for a moment. If either a teammate or an opposing player happens to be standing in his way, he brusquely shoves him aside. His teammate Ken Wregget avoids talking to teammates on the day of a game and teammates do not talk to him. Patrick Roy, of the Montreal Canadiens, talks to his goalposts. Edmonton Oilers' Grant Fuhr plays thirty-six holes of golf every day of a play-off game.

John Tanner observes his own complex variety of rituals. As he skates to the net, he slaps his goalposts; right, left, right, left, right, repeating the process for each period. That's something he picked up from Hextall, whom he greatly admires. He dons his equipment in exactly the same sequence every game: right skate, left skate, right pad, left pad. If he's on a streak, he'll wear the same suit, the same shirt, tie, shoes, underwear, not changing or cleaning them until the streak is over. If he happens to have eaten, say, ravioli before a win, he eats ravioli before every game until the streak ends. If he slept in until ten o'clock, he'll continue to sleep in until ten. He tries to duplicate every aspect of the day. Phoning a girl at the same time, seeing the same movie.

"If something varies, like maybe you forget and put on clean underwear, then it worries you when you remember it later on," says Tanner. Before a game, if he's alone at home, he loves to crank up the stereo and listen to whatever's at hand: Otis Redding, Van Halen, Madonna. Although he's a loner and says little in the dressing-room, Tanner draws reassurance from those who do. Certain teammates say the same things before every game. Everyone expects it, everyone waits on the words and the role-players would no more forget their lines than forget their sticks or their skates.

"Hum now, guy," says Ricci to his friend Geoff Ingram, in a falsetto voice.

"Let's go, Ratdawg," comes the reply, basso profundo.

"Let's go, T.B.," says Ricci, falsetto, to Todd Bojcun.

"Let's go, Dawgs," replies Bojcun, basso profundo.

As "O Canada" plays, Tanner stands absolutely still, his feet rooted to the spot, hands at his sides, ramrod straight, his eyes fixed on the Queen's portrait. Everything controllable must be controlled in order to make up, somehow, for the many things that are out of control.

And on this night in Belleville, his efforts to control the uncontrollable, know the unknowable, are unsuccessful. The ice monsters swoop in to envelop Tanner and the team. The Petes' attacks fizzle, the defence falls asleep at the switch, seemingly never to awaken. Tanner's reflexes, at other times so sharp and crisp, are a split second off, uncertain, waterlogged, tentative. The Petes manage to hang on until, at 2:29 of the first period, Bob Berg opens the scoring for the Bulls. The game slides downhill from there as the flatness that Tanner had sensed earlier assumes control. If they were measuring this on an oscilloscope, he thinks, we'd get a straight line and they'd pronounce us dead. At 5:49 Jeff MacLeod scores for the Bulls, then the entire Belleville team begins to take turns: Berg, with his second goal, on a power play at 17:46; Gord Christian at 19:10. At 13:07 of the second, Ingram gets the Petes' first goal, but by this time they are trailing 6–1. Belleville's Scott Thornton scores at 13:34 to make it 7–1 before finally, at 13:52, Ricci helps set up a play that results in a goal by Lorentz. Ricci, who is capable of single-handedly jump-starting his teammates in situations like this, can't manage it on this night. He feels the flatness overwhelming them, and although he resists with some success it eventually affects him, too. He works with Ingram and Lorentz, trying to move the puck out, but somehow their passes miss or they're intercepted or the puck gets coughed up. He begins to feel as if he is skating through water. The soaring power in his skates has been drained, like a car on a low battery. He taps the face-off circle with his stick each time he passes, but even that trusted ritual fails him. As the game winds down he is overtaken by a dull anger at the way the Bulls keep throwing in their best lines, keep padding the score even though they have an insurmountable lead. The exhibition ends 11–5 and the Petes silently re-enter their dressing-room.

"Jee-zuz," somebody says, but there is almost no conversation. They are not dejected exactly, for this game means little, but they are uneasy. Sometimes the monsters strike and there is nothing you can do. And that is an uneasy thought, the stuff of all our nightmares: that when the monsters of all our unknowns strike us, our defences will be wanting and we will be helpless.

Many of us, hockey players or not, build support systems to sustain us through such times. We have wives, families, lovers, friends, homes where we can find safety and peace until our turmoil subsides. But hockey players at the Junior level don't yet have this sort of support. They often don't have the time for girlfriends; they are removed from their families; they live in someone else's home. Their family is their teammates. Their father is their coach. And if they are loners, like John Tanner, on such nights they sometimes have no one.

"Anything that had the remotest chance of getting by me got by," he says, hoping, through this small act of sharing, this offering, to trigger from his teammates a word of denial, some gesture of comfort to allay his doubts. But no word comes, no gesture, no help. And as the Petes take their seats on the bus, Tanner breaks into laughter. Secretly, he hopes the others will join him so that together their laughter can dispel their fears. But they do not laugh with him and John Tanner sits by himself, hearing the echo of his own laughter, listening to the silence.

○ 9

The Laval Titans go to some trouble to awaken Les Castors-de-St-Jean, but only as a learning experience is this exhibition match even remotely worth the trouble. Coach Bordeleau has decided to use a lineup consisting mainly of rookies and Midgets hopeful of making the team. It's a baptism of fire, with everyone excruciatingly aware that many roster cuts will be made based largely on the strength of what Bordeleau sees tonight. A handful of veterans is playing, although mercifully neither Donald Audette nor Patrice Brisebois are among them. Brisebois won't play because he's nursing a sprained thumb, and Audette and most of the other veterans are given the night off. They watch the game from the stands. It takes only a few minutes to demonstrate that while the evening might prove instructive for Bordeleau and the participants, it is going to be painful for players like Audette and Brisebois to watch. By the time the battered players skate off at the end of the third period, both sides are weary. Perhaps the Castors are less weary because they win, 10–2, but only slightly. Between them the teams have drawn penalties for a wide range of infractions in the rule book. Unsportsmanlike conduct, fighting, roughing, slashing, charging, tripping, high-sticking, spearing. Thirty-six penalties in all. Even Boris Rousson, the Titans' rookie goalie, draws a penalty for slashing following a pileup around his net. That is not unusual in itself, but it happens before two minutes are up and it sets the tone for the rest of the game.

Very little is said as Bordeleau joins the team in the dressing-room. The veterans regard the game simply as a learning exercise for the rookies, and beyond a few shrugs and raised eyebrows they make no comment. The rookies sit silently, eyes downcast, wishing they could become invisible because they know that although the match is unimportant to the team, their own performance has been scrutinized and in some cases found wanting.

"Losing is not such a bad thing, if you learn from it," says Bordeleau, words he would normally reserve for a loss in which the team had nonetheless played well. "Don't worry about it." But he knows they will worry, and with good reason. Partly as a result of what he has seen tonight, he will be cutting players tomorrow and it is this part of his job that he hates.

During the ride back to Laval, Brisebois reads over some diary notes he made during the game. Significantly, none of these thoughts relates directly to it, although he's strongly aware of what was at stake for the rookies:

> People are so important. You cannot do these things by yourself, support is essential. The person in hockey I admire a lot, in this way, is my agent in Quebec, Pierre Meilleur. [Meilleur is the Quebec representative for Toronto agent Don Meehan.] He calls me every day during the hockey season, asks me how I am doing and encourages me a lot. That's really good to have someone like that who encourages you, shows that he likes you. He wants you to succeed. Someone like that wouldn't waste his time if he didn't feel that you have potential to play in the NHL. And also my agent, Don Meehan. He is the biggest agent in national hockey. I chose him and I'm really happy with what he's done so far. I know he'll do good things for me in the times ahead. He's the biggest and I know he's going to do what's necessary for him to stay the biggest.
>
> I'm going to talk about my little friend, whose name is Michèle. Michèle, *ma blonde*, that makes two years and a half that I'm with her. *C'est une super bonne fille.* Super nice. She gives me massages, she makes me snacks, she makes me meals. She encourages me, she

gives me advice. She wants me to succeed, she knows that the effort I put in now will pay dividends later. She wants me to have every chance at success and she'll do whatever she can to make that happen. I feel so good when she is with me, I feel I know her mind. We went to nursery school together, you know, St-Noël-de-Chabanel, grew up together, so I think we know each other by now very well. I changed school for a year and I didn't see her. But one day her brother came to visit and she came along and that was my chance. She started talking, *merveilleux*, can you believe it? And that was my chance, I asked her to a hockey game, yes, a hockey game, what else? She goes to all my games, now, and she's seen all of them since Midget. What a friend, *ma super blonde*.

And Paulin, now there's a coach. He's a guy who knows his hockey. He's the tops, *un technicien excellent*, he can really show you how to play hockey well. He knows lots of things, *p'tits trucs*, to make your game better. It's important that a coach know how to make you work hard. When he first came, Paulin showed us how to play hockey—win. That's how to play hockey. You win. That's why we're going to the final this year, you wait. The Coupe Memorial, you wait. Paulin is a winner, *c'est un vainqueur*, he doesn't like to lose. When we lose, Paulin is so mad, *super fâché*. He always says if we lose well, it's not so bad and that feeling rubs off on the team. We do not like to lose.

One thing I reproach him a little for—and tonight reminds me—is not being strict enough with some of the Juniors. Players who goof off, *font des niaiseries*. He could yell at them a bit more, come down harder on them. Still, Paulin is the best coach I ever had. The other really good coach was Claude Terrion. He was my coach my first year of Junior. He wasn't a technical coach, like Paulin. He was aggressive and strict, the opposite of Paulin. He was strict, but he knew people well. He'd yell things at you while you were on the ice, tell you, "you didn't do this, you didn't do that." Paulin would know you'd done something wrong, but he wouldn't always say it, or he'd tell you afterwards. *On sait jamais ce qui était dans sa tête.* You wouldn't always know what he was thinking. They are the two best coaches I ever had in my career.

A few feet away, as the bus approaches the southern outskirts of Montreal, Donald Audette writes about the problems of being a small player trying to make his mark in a sport enamoured of size. He also writes about the importance of those who give him their encouragement and support:

I wasn't invited to try out for the Canadian Junior national team and I was very disappointed. But that taught me nothing in life can be taken for granted. I am simply going to show them they were wrong in not choosing me. It is nothing new, really, being overlooked because of my size. When I came up to Junior, they said, "Oh, you'll never make it in Junior because you're too small." I made it and then they said, "Oh, you'll never be able to score." But I worked hard and I showed them they were wrong there, too. Now, I'll have to work to get on the NHL's Central Scouting list. It's frustrating when I think of some of those on the list, while I'm not. It makes me furious when I think that they're big, but they don't work and still they're on the list. I work much harder than they, but I'm left off. I'm a little discouraged that I haven't been drafted, but then there are lots of people who have gone through the same thing. Stephane Lebeau, who plays for the Canadiens of Sherbrooke, was never drafted but saw beyond that and he has a good chance to play for the Canadiens one day. There are others—I think of Steve Duchesne who was never drafted but just signed a big contract. There are a lot of people like that. I tell myself, "Never give up." It's something I say all the time to myself. It's the best I can say today.
On the other hand, I have a great deal to be happy

about, especially when I look around and see that the people closest to me give me so much support. I know if I keep working, with this kind of support, I'll prevail. For instance, my older brother Richard and I are very close. This season, I've shared a lot both with him and my *entourage*. When he played Junior he played for St-Jean, the team we played tonight. I played against him from time to time, and although I would have preferred playing with him the circumstances were against it. It was a strange experience, playing against a brother with whom you're close. I remember one time he mistook me for another player in front of the net and he hit me really hard in the back. I had the bruises for quite a few days and I felt like giving him a few bruises to pay him back. He really laughed about that, although I didn't see where it was so funny at the time.

For me, my family is very important. We are united one with the other no matter what happens. I know I can always count on my family. My mother's character is easy to describe. She is a very simple person who rarely gets angry with us. She is there to encourage me in all that I do.

As for my father, he is tough with me because he knows I can succeed if I take the trouble. When I was little, he taught me lots of things in order to be the best. He always told us that, "One gets nothing for nothing, you must work to reap what you've sown." Whatever has happened in my life, he's been there to help. Even when he's mean to me, he does it to help, for my own good.

My brother, Rickie, is the best friend that I know, because he gives me his opinion in everything I do. We have always done everything together, even when we were small boys. I remember when I was about 10, we were supposed to be in bed asleep by 11. My mother worked nights and so there was only my dad in the house. We would sneak out, Rickie and I, and we'd go across the road to where there was a rink and we'd play hockey. We'd play until one or two in the morning and then, just before we knew my mother would be coming home, we'd sneak back into our room and go to bed. My dad found out about it, but he let us keep doing it and my mother never knew. It was not until long after that she knew and we did it almost every night for years. Playing hockey under a street light, Rickie and me.

I respect him very much, my brother. He has more experience than I so before making important decisions, I speak to him first. He is very different from me. He never gets angry for nothing, like I sometimes do. He takes life as it comes and he has heart. He hasn't been lucky with his hockey but he maintains a high morale. My brother, Rickie, is a good person.

My girlfriend, Manon Lachance, we've gone together two years now and it's wonderful how well she understands me. Before an important game she always encourages me. Sometimes, the evening before a game, I want to stay longer with her but she takes me home, knowing I need my rest.

The team is already getting very close. Of course, like anywhere else, there are people you don't like so much, but when you get to the rink all that is forgotten. The others are respectful to me because I am one of the oldest veterans. I am an example to them, the way I work on the ice. Since my physical stature is small, I have to work harder and that inspires them.

Paulin is a wonderful guy, *un gars merveilleux*. He treats us like his sons, or like he would want his sons treated by a coach. He shows us a lot of respect and even when someone isn't doing well he doesn't rub it in. He explains the mistakes instead of screaming at us. As a result, we learn from him without loss of confidence. He is the best coach I ever had.

Among the players, there are those I like more than others. There are guys like Eric Dubois, Patrice [Brisebois], Christian Larivière, Ghislain Lefebvre, Carl Mantha, with whom I get along better than the others, but I speak to everyone. I get along best with them because they are *très serieux*, the most serious players on the team. We hardly ever go out, even to a party, because hockey must always come first.

My family supports me, *absolument*. Sometimes there will be a dozen of them watching, uncles, aunts, cousins; my father, mother, brother. But my father is the one who takes it to heart, my being the youngest of the family. He even came to watch me in Chicoutimi [a five-hour drive]. When something isn't working, he gives me advice to help me. He's the one that started me skating when I was three years old, and he'd come with us, my brother and I. He'd show us many little things to do, so we'd get better every day. Oh, the efforts I made so that in spite of my size I'd be the best wherever I played. During my first year in Junior, I had to wait my turn to play—I hardly played and still I finished with nearly 50 points.

But it took hard work to arrive at that point. I skated long. When I got older I knew someone who worked at the arena [Centre Sportif Laval], and he let me skate after hockey was through for the night. I would skate for hours, but in the morning when it was time to go to school I couldn't get up and often I missed school. I began my own dryland training at 12. I did leg exercises like jogging and practised my reflexes by throwing a ball against a wall, so it came back very fast. In the summer, I would spend the whole day in the pool, building my strength. At the age of fifteen, I undertook my first long-distance cycling. I left Montreal and went as far as Quebec City, before turning back. It took me 10 hours, and I did other trips as well, four or five of them every summer, two hours there, two hours back.

When I look back, I know I will never forget my first game with the Titans, I thought I was dreaming. That first year, when I was 17, everyone said I wouldn't make it, but that only motivated me all the more. I wanted to show them my size made no difference.

When I put on the uniform for the first game, I couldn't believe my eyes—I could say I'd succeeded in making the team. But I told myself if I wanted to stay on the team I would have to work always at 150 percent in order to be better than the others, since I was smaller in stature. I know I talk often about this, but sometimes I think my size worries others more than it worries me. It is just height [5-foot-8] because my weight [fluctuating slightly around 180] is the same as others'.

When I think of other players of small stature, like Denis Savard, Mats Naslund, Theoren Fleury, Joe Mullen; they succeeded. Oh, you can't imagine what feeling I feel, *c'est super, c'est formidable*, about succeeding in the NHL. I feel, oh, all funny, *tout drôle*. I have ants in my legs, *j'ai des fourmis dans les jambes*, just thinking about going to camp with the pros.

I also think that if I don't make it, that will not be bad, *ça ne sera pas grave*, because I'll have nothing about which to reproach myself. I'll know for sure that I gave my all, *j'avais donne tout ce que j'avais dans le ventre*. I gave all that I had in my belly. I can say I tried everything, but the others were better than me.

The season awaits: 70 games for the QMJHL, 68 for the OHL and 72 for the WHL—every game leading inexorably to The Grail of Junior hockey, the Memorial Cup in Saskatoon. Before each game, six dreamers will recommit themselves to their dreams, in their minds and hearts and bodies. Mike Ricci will chew the front of his jersey as each anthem is played, tap his talisman at centre ice and hear the beat of his own rare drummer. John Tanner will bang his goalposts, banking the fires of his soul against the demons of the ice. Tracey Katelnikoff will skate through his warm-ups, then at the absolute last moment, tap the goalie on the leg pad, the chest, the elbow pad; an arcane code known only to him and the hockey gods. Rob Lelacheur will watch intently as his teammates file onto the ice. Scott Scissons, Dean Holoien, Collin Bauer; all step through the gate and only then does he follow, the power of his future and his youth secure. Donald Audette will wait until everyone is on the ice before he follows. It is written, *l'écriture sainte*, that the last shall be first, the follower, lead. And Patrice Brisebois says a prayer, secure in the knowledge that around the same time, just before every game, wherever she may be, his mother will say the same prayer.

○ Part 2

CHASE THE DREAM

o 1

Tracey Katelnikoff has never been able to analyze the feeling that comes over a player when he knows he can do no wrong. It is one of the mysteries of the game. Sometimes you have it, sometimes you don't, and it is not always apparent why. Sometimes the feeling is so strong and pure that you know, as surely as you know the eccentricities of your own body, that the game will go well, that you are an unstoppable part of an unstoppable force, the team.

It's the first game of the regular season, the Moose Jaw Warriors visiting Saskatoon, and the feeling is on him like inspiration. He had arrived back from the Washington Capitals' camp three or four days earlier, and now he feels rested, full of optimism, ready to make the most of the opportunities of this brand new season. The day has gone like clockwork—no jarring notes, no detail forgotten. One sock, inside out, on the left foot. A box of Kraft Dinner and four hot dogs at 1:00 p.m., followed by a half hour of TV. Sleep from 2:00 to 4:25; then up, dress again, go to the rink. In the dressing-room by 5:00, the first or second player there. Get undressed, tape the game stick and be in the trainer's room by 5:40. Grab a book and take a dump, reading through whatever it is, WHL or scouting stats or a magazine. In the toilet for ten minutes. Back to the training-room for a few minutes, relaxing, listening to music. Back to the dressing-room by 6:20; start dressing. Left sock first. Put the tape around the shin pad, always under the sock, never over it. Always plastic tape. Left elbow pad. Left skate first. Each item in its place, every movement in its sequence. Out to the pre-game warm-up, the pre-game huddle.

"One, two, three . . . Hungry dogs!" the players chant. Out of the huddle. Into the easy rhythm of the pre-game skate. Everything like clockwork. Nothing out of place. Everything right.

He's in the opening lineup, standing as always on the left side near the face-off dot at the blue line, his eyes glued unwaveringly to the top of the flag. As always, he spits on the ice just as the anthem begins to play. He knows things will go, he knows it. The game is his, is theirs, the Hungry Dogs'. The Warriors, as far as Tracey is concerned, are simply present as part of the ritual, are simply present so there can *be* a ritual. He feels an excitement in his gut, feels strength building within him, feels invincible. Really weird, he thinks. That's the feeling.

The puck is dropped. Linemate Kory Kocur wins the face-off, slaps it back to defenceman Dean Holoien, who passes it back to Kocur at the blue line. Kocur takes it across the blue line, with Katelnikoff on his flank and close in. A Warrior stick pokes the puck away from Kocur, but Tracey reaches back for it, feels it on his stick and lets go with a wrist-shot. It threads its way through three players and behind the Moose Jaw goalie, Tyler Wall, as if running on a track. Tracey looks at it with successive expressions of surprise and non-surprise rippling across his face. He looks up at the clock and it is 27 seconds into the period. His first goal, 27 seconds into the first period of his first game of the season. Now he knows the feeling is not something he is going to lose, not this game. It is his and it is now, and nothing can change it.

Nothing does. He scores again at 6:57 of the period, this time assisted by Kelly Chotowetz, with Kocur again feeding him the puck. The ice is his, his legs tireless, the skates wings, his body sings with the energy, the energy of the feeling. Brian Gerrits gets the Blades' third goal at 9:29. The Warriors score at 10:21, Wade Shutter getting his first of the season, trying desperately to grab the feeling from the Blades, turn it against them. But the Blades know, they *know*. Tracey knows that nothing, *nothing*, can stop them tonight. They own the feeling. It is theirs by gift, a divine gift, theirs for sixty minutes and maybe never theirs again. But thcirs now.

Tracey starts even faster in the second, scoring for his hat trick 25 seconds in, again Kocur setting up the goal on a pass from Holoien. Kocur passes it from deep in the Warriors' corner, passes it to T.K., who first fans on it from the near side, then takes it to the far side and gets off a slapshot. He half fans on it again, but he makes contact and although the shot doesn't go where he wants it, it goes in the net. It's as if the puck itself had no choice, as if no matter how many times Tracey fanned or how he hit it, the puck had to follow its destiny. Just as on this night Tracey has his destiny, the Blades have theirs and all are powerless, or perhaps all-powerful, in the grip of the feeling. Dean Sexsmith scores at 18:14 of the second, but the feeling has begun to wind down long before. It has not passed to the Warriors, just diminished, a protective blanket of warmth. At 18:11 of the third, Drew Sawtell wrings out the last drop of its substance as the game winds down, the final score, 7–1.

Still, as Tracey Katelnikoff lingers in the dressing-room after the game, the feeling remains in his psyche. So subtle is it that he is unsure, now, whether what he senses is the feeling itself, bestowing on him the last sweet measure of its gift, or just a memory. Perhaps they are the same thing, he thinks. Perhaps the memory calls the gift into being.

The feeling is working for Rob Lelacheur this night as well, but partly because of the nervousness inspired by the fact that this is his first-ever regular-season game in Junior A he is not so sharply involved in it. He plays well, doing his job on each shift, and this is enough. It is as if the feeling envelops those who are indispensable to the ritual and then drags the rest along in the wake of its power. Lelacheur is carried along on an immense feeling of excitement, but he puts it down to the fact that this *is* his first game, and his first experience of playing before a nearly full house.

There are 5,151 people watching, according to the scoreboard, mostly rabidly pro-Blades, and the sounds they make, caroming off the confining barriers of SaskPlace, act like a shot of pure adrenaline, music for the soul. He has never known anything remotely like the power of these fans, the power they have to uplift, to draw a player out of himself, out and away. He wonders for a moment what it would be like if that same power were turned against them and the thought brings a flash of fear, so he puts it out of his mind.

As he gets into the game, he begins to draw back from the fans. He is almost able to disassociate himself from them, making their sounds recede into a separate space warp. The sound still cascades around his ears, is still a physical force, but over it or under or through it he can clearly hear the sounds on the ice. The sound of his own skates, even the breathing of Collin Bauer when he is ten feet away. He hears the intake of breath as someone slaps a pass, hears the crack of the stick on the puck. He can see things, too, with preternatural clarity. The flex of a stick as he digs the puck out of someone's skate, the marvellous feel of his body as he leans into a turn, seeming to hang horizontal over the ice yet maintaining his balance.

"Man on, man on!" He hears Bauer's warning, glances over his shoulder, picks up his pursuer in the periphery of his vision, pivots and whips a reverse rim shot over to Bauer. He feels the bite of the ice chips on his face as he turns, the wind of his own passage.

"Move it! Move it! Move it!" He hears Paul Sutcliffe trying by force of command to ward off an attack on Dean Beattie. "Watch out for six!" Sutcliffe screams, as the Warriors' assistant captain, Jerome Bechard, moves on Beattie, trying to slash. The Warriors, frustrated, are using their sticks freely, slashing and hooking, but in this instance the referee is blind and Beattie skates away out of range.

"You speedbag! You're brutal!" growls Lelacheur, snarling at Bechard, who isn't normally so aggressive. "Who are you, anyway? You a tough guy, now?"

"Fuck you," Bechard snarls back, then skates away.

The Warriors fire it in, attacking, but as Lelacheur heads

for the corner someone grabs his stick, then jams him into the boards.

"Play it! Play it!" he yells to Dean Kuntz, the goalie, and Koonee obliges, moving behind the net and firing a pass out to Bauer. Lelacheur is aware of Bauer as he takes the puck up ice, and as he watches the way the veteran moves through the game his admiration for his defensive partner grows. Bauer, drafted in the third round of the previous year's Entry Draft by the Edmonton Oilers, has taught him a great deal in the few games they've played together. He still gets annoyed with Bauer in practice because he constantly badgers Lelacheur about playing angry. He and Kocur, a two-man band, always singing the same refrain at him, and he gets sick and tired of it.

"Go out there and get mad," they say over and over. "Go and show that guy who's the boss." Lelacheur can play just as angry as anyone, he thinks. But he likes to save it for a game. Why should he get angry at his own teammates during practice? But Kocur and Bauer never let up.

"Play mad," they say. "Give that guy shit." Over and over until he gets mad at them. They get him so angry he plays mad in practice, in spite of himself.

As the Blades skate off after the game, Bauer glides up to Lelacheur and thumps him on the back: "Hungry dog, Lolly. Way to play. Ya played mad. I saw ya. You had Bechard shakin'. He wasn't gonna mess with you. Way to go! Play mad, hoo boy! Now ya got it!"

He keeps this up all the way to the dressing-room, telling everyone in earshot about that Lolly, that sonofabitch, that *Tiger*, was playing mad, like *mad*.

"Jeez. Didja see the look on that guy's face?" Bauer is wound up, filled with pride at the strides made by his protégé, his *buddy*, that he beams from ear to ear, his eyes scanning the faces around the room, beaming. And Lelacheur, unlacing his skate, smiles a slow, bemused sort of smile as a feeling of warmth spreads through him. Bauer catches his eye and they grin at each other across the room, grinning like fools, as the feeling takes them all.

The Laval Titans begin their season in St-Jean-sur-Richelieu with the Castors in the Colisée. And although both teams feel the excitement of opening night and there is a suggestion now and then of that special invincibility, that special gift, neither side really captures its full power and turns it to their exclusive purpose. Both Audette and Brisebois get an assist each, but the Castors win 5–3 in a game where no one has played either very well, or very badly. Paulin talks to his team about the psychology of winning, and they listen raptly, drawing in his words, though they've heard it all before. He tells them that in order for a team to win, they must develop and maintain an absolute revulsion of losing.

"It is not enough to desire victory," he says. "Everyone *desires* victory. *Tout le monde veut la victoire.* We do not seek to be beaten. The one who wins the most is the one who hates defeat the most. *On ne peut pas simplement vaincre l'autre équipe. On doit vaincre la défaite.*" One must not simply vanquish the other team, one must vanquish defeat.

The team listens attentively. The coach utters the words quietly, as is his way. But the quality that makes them follow his words so closely is his passion, a sense that he *knows*, that he has just imparted a rare and immutable truth. They have heard the idea expressed before but never quite in this way, with the eloquence of pure conviction. He keeps his remarks short and the silence that follows them is also eloquent.

"I felt excited after he said those words," recalls Brisebois later. "It was like I had learned something very important, but very pure and simple. *Paulin c'est un vainqueur.* Paulin is a winner. He doesn't like to lose. He knows."

Donald Audette, as their bus rolled through the suburb of St-Vincent-de-Paul towards the Centre Sportif and home, recalls being caught, held by the moment.

"Paulin has taken a commonplace and raised it to a revelation," he says, smiling to himself at the elegant simplicity of it all. And simple it is, *vaincre la défaite.* Let other teams do the losing because they hate losing less and, hating less, deserve it more.

Audette is first on the ice for the warm-up against the Granby Bisons three nights later and the crowd at the Centre Sportif greets him with a cheer.

"Ti' Wayne!" they cry. "Ti' Wayne! Ti' Wayne! Ti' Wayne!" He hears the words, rhythmic in the chaos of crowd noises, but although he allows himself an inward smile he does not acknowledge them. He knows that something has changed since the opening game in St-Jean-sur-Richelieu. What has changed is the feeling, the same mystery experienced by Tracey Katelnikoff and Rob Lelacheur. It is fully with him and he skates slowly, almost as if savouring it, his compact figure erect. He feels the power in his legs, the precise and elegant transmission of that power from his legs to his skates, the skates to the ice. He is aware of the muscles of his entire body, can almost appreciate their individual workings, a finely tuned marvel of living machinery; his to control totally, with absolute confidence. He looks into the stands and picks out his father, his brother, Rickie, uncle Gaetan. There must be twelve to fifteen of them here tonight, a good family turnout, as usual. A boy wearing a Pittsburgh Penguins' hat leans over the boards near the bench and calls to him.

"*La vedette*," says the boy. The star. As Audette skates by he notices his Penguins' jersey bears the number 66, the number of one of Laval's most famous sons, Mario Lemieux. He completes his circuit and as he comes past again Audette skates over and hands the kid his puck.

"*Merci*," says the boy. "Ti' Wayne." The boy takes the puck, his eyes widening with amazement. Suddenly there's a crowd of fans, boys mainly, but girls, too, thrusting programs and lineup sheets at him, odd bits of paper. "Donald Audette #28," he writes, over and over, smiling at the kids, chatting with them, enjoying the moment. Suddenly, the kid with number 66 reappears, shoving his way through the crowd, brandishing a program, presenting it with a flourish for signing. Audette takes it and smiles again at the boy. *Spécialement pour toi, Donald Audette*, he writes and hands it back. The boy thanks him again, beaming. This is his night for sure. The crowd continues to grow, pressing against the boards. Audette signs a few last autographs, then skates away, forcing himself to ignore their clamour of disappointment. It is always the way, he thinks, wishing he could accommodate them all, but knowing he'd never get his warm-up in if he tried. He skates a few more circuits, pushing the puck ahead of him, then catching up to it, pushing it ahead, catching up. The buzzer sounds and the players skate off, Audette and Brisebois the last to leave. He smiles at Brisebois as, almost as one, they step onto the rubber mat leading to the dressing-room.

"*C'est écoeurant!*" says Audette and Brisebois nods his head, agreeing, that yes, this feeling, the sum total of this partnership of unstoppable team and benevolent fans is indeed amazing. They both also know that the warm benevolence has been granted only on sufferance, for as long as they continue to win and not a moment longer. On the day they lose, the warmth will cool and die, metamorphosing into instant disdain, blasting them like the wind from a cold river.

"*Ce qui se passe, se passe,*" says Brisebois. What will pass, will pass. Audette in his turn nods, then smiles at his teammate. He has this feeling after all. And he knows, at least on this night, what will pass.

○ 2

The grind of going to school each day, attending practices, and playing a gruelling schedule of games begins to take its toll on the players as the season wears on. When the Petes' schedule brings them close to John Tanner's home in Cambridge, he gets a rare long weekend off, and he loves it. He tells his diary:

I'm in my own bed for the first time in a very, very long time and, geez, it's nice. My mom looks so tired but so happy to see me, even with an eight-stitch cut at the top of my forehead whose golf ball-like swelling draws attention to itself. Yes, we got killed, 8–0, as I predicted [in a game earlier in the evening with the Niagara Falls Thunder]. With all the rookies in the lineup and Ricci, [Corey] Foster, [Tie] Domi, [Steve] DeGurse and [Joe] Hawley out of it with one thing or another I figure the score was almost flattering. I left at the eight-minute mark of the third when a screened Jason Soules shot found its way to my head, sending litres of blood cascading down my semi-prone body. I was bitter. Very bitter. But it follows if you think you can get away with a half-assed effort, you will consequently be punished. My head bears proof of this. I knew we were in for a long one when Jamey Hicks cracked the funniest line I've heard in two years, truthful as it was. As the vets departed from the bus, yelling their pre-game warm-up encouragement [Steve DeGurse is the traditional leader of this ritual], I yelled mine.

"Let's get Mo[mentum] on our side!"

Hicks leans over and in a low voice says in my ear: "I'm afraid our Mo [Ricci] is elsewhere."

I couldn't help but laugh and gulp at the same time. I found it tremendously amusing that when I returned from the Thunder dressing-room with my stitches, there was a chorus of oohs and aahs for the blood-soaked goalie, who was trying to convince his half-amused coach to let him back in the game. I loved it. I loved having centre stage and I guess I always have. I like being singled out, being recognized, being made to feel important. Everyone likes to feel important and I guess I'm no different. . . .

I've been home three days and, as was the case last year, I find things much different from the time I once lived here. But I think the difference is more in me than in the rest of the family. They go about their everyday business as if I were not a "hockey star"; they treat me for who I am and not for the job I have and it's nice. The last few days at home, I have found when shopping or running errands that people I once knew treat me now as John Tanner the goalie rather than John. It's like there is a newfound respect for me that I believe is silly; why would things be different just because I play hockey? On the other hand, I don't mind it—it makes me feel a little important. However, I usually end up "playing the role" and I feel silly for doing it as I act in a very airy manner and make things appear important that aren't. "Playing the role" is a term applied to this act players put on in an attempt to appear more important than they would normally be credited with being. Players keep each other in check however, teasing and ridiculing those who try to be so phoney, particularly with women. . . .

Over the past few days, I've had a chance to dwell on the season so far and I have come to a conclusion. The 1988–89 Petes are a team which will either lose in the first round of play-offs or advance to the Memorial Cup in Saskatoon. We have showed flashes of team brilliance, yet wallowed in mediocrity at other times. I knew it would be this way back when we lost 7–3 to the Soo. We were absolutely and totally outplayed. Only my good play prevented it from being a blowout. I can't remember so many defensive lapses as a team in one game, in the last two years. And we've never lost quite like that again (excluding the other night to Niagara Falls), but our consistency has been erratic at best. People wonder each game if the "real" Petes are going to play or not. People like my landlady expect a trade to occur and I can honestly say that she has been implying that I might be the one to go. I can usually ignore her incessant babbling, but this really bothers me. She is trying to suggest that I'm an expendable commodity and I'm the lesser of the team's goalies. I don't think I am. I think my first half has been quite successful, as I have a very good record. I'm at the top in goals-against and save percentage and as Anton [Anton Thun, agent advisor for Tanner and Ricci] told me Sunday morning on the phone, I'm the number one goalie for the NHL draft from the OHL on Central Scouting's list. It's surprising how many friends you have when the list appears.

I feel my play has improved dramatically in all areas except puck-handling. I can't seem to get any coaching for the area of play I need to improve on, but all in all it's been a good year and I predict a shut-out for the New Year.

While I have played better, I have not enjoyed the year like last year. The team, maybe because it's older, does not seem to be able to share any enthusiasm or exuberance for the game. Players talk behind each other's backs and too many (at least two) players are feeling too pretty because of a pro contract they signed. Many guys, but particularly one, are looking for contracts by playing an individualistic game that doesn't include their teammates. I'm sure I'm not the only player who resents such selfishness. A pro contract can ruin under-age Juniors, fooling them into believing they have worked hard enough to get where they want to go. I want one, but I feel it will drive me forward, urge me to excel beyond Junior status. Just thinking about getting drafted makes me ride that extra mile on my training bike, knowing that every little extra bit will profit me in the long run. I hope it will profit me for the remainder of the season and I can help turn around our team's consistency with my own.

His three days at home come to an end and John returns to the team. He also returns to the sometimes agonizing tension that develops between him and the Petes' other goalie, Todd Bojcun. He also reveals some of his current attitude towards his parents and school, and talks about a grating relationship with the couple who billet him:

We just beat the Kingston Raiders, 3–2, and I don't feel disassociated from the team's victory, as I usually do when I don't play. I played well last week and the players know it, so unconsciously they include me in on "the feeling" that comes from winning. However, I feel neither elated nor disappointed at knowing I made no significant contribution (other than holding out water bottles). I feel anxious to play this weekend and I want to have a good practice tomorrow and show Dick and the scouts who the best is. When Todd [Bojcun] is in net, I don't want him to play poorly, but I don't want him to play too well. There are some times when I like to see the red light burn his neck, but only as long as we get more. I wish I could play every game because I know I would be the best if I was given consecutive chances. But it's a problem when you have two capable goalies, who do you sit? I get so mad when I hear about goalies who aren't half as good as either of us, playing virtually every game for their team, while we play 50–50 undeservedly. I wish I could take over, become the goalie for the team and control its destiny. With the team we have now, I wonder if I'm an asset or a commodity.

My parents again insisted I move from the home where I've been boarding and they have a point. I get no privacy and a plethora of pathetic opinions from people who take me because I'm a "Pete" rather than for the person I am. I think I'll talk to Dick about obliging their wishes. Ricci again was first star, and I was again envious. Not at his talent and success, particularly, but at the poise and humility with which he reacts to the attention given him. He's first class in my books.

John is capable of getting marks in the mid-80s at school and has managed it in the past, even with the heavy demands of hockey. But just now Grade 13 chemistry is a problem and he allows the spectre of Todd Bojcun to distract him in the classroom, too. He writes:

I am in my second and last class, the one I despise, chemistry. And again, against all I've ever been taught, I wonder what I am doing here. I know I can't get 80 in this course and the only thing that really bothers me is that it hurts my parents. Maybe I should worry only about what I feel, but I hate letting down my parents. Half the reason I play hockey is because it's something I can excel at and make them proud of me for it. I know I have ability for school, but I think school acts as a buffer for my problems and pressures; here I can just string out and relax. Unfortunately, nobody understands that. If I'm going to get 80 in a course, I will have to like it. Todd tries to compete with me here, too, I think. He's beating me, but it bothers me only slightly because I know, and he probably knows, that on normal terms he doesn't stand a chance. Maybe by concentrating so strongly on school, his hockey has suffered as a result.

He was never strong mentally, but seems particularly weak as of late. I pride myself on being cool—though it's often a misleading exterior—most of the time and I think I can stamp him out by year's end. I don't think that will happen completely, but to the point where Dick's confidence is in my direction, when or if we get to Saskatoon.

Hockey at this level is so cruel; only the strong survive and the others are left crushed of their dreams, hopeless for the future. It is sort of like The American Dream as illustrated by Arthur Miller in *Death of a Salesman*. How can everyone reach the top? It's impossible, and as in the case of Willy Loman, those left behind can't handle being a failure.

After practice today, Dick told me I'm playing and I feel it's a good chance to lower my average and impress scouts with my poise. . . .

Todd and I went to Mike's practice and I felt good when all the kids recognized us.

"You're John Tanner," they all yell, and against what I think I should feel, I experience a sensation of importance. Humility is gone and cockiness takes over. I talk like I make a million bucks rather than the eighteen [weekly expenses]. Already I feel the familiar light anxiety which accompanies the game that is to be played tomorrow. The anxiety will build until it reaches a crescendo during the playing of the National Anthem, until it fades to a blank feeling of confident relaxation after the first few minutes of play and the first save (I hope!). . . .

We just beat a Windsor team [Windsor Spitfires] with much less strength than it had last year, 4–1. I played strong and stopped 26 shots and even scammed a third star out of it. I know, though, that it was one of the easier games of the year and they weren't the team that beat us four straight last April. The only thing that leaves me the satisfaction I have now is the fact that I stoned Darrin Shannon on a one-timer at the side of the net late in the game.

I felt so confident in the way I reacted to shots and in the way I handled the puck, it feels so good. The best, though, is when your mother, who isn't supposed to be there, gives you a great big smile and raised

arms—you quickly remember why you play the game. I
wish I could play tomorrow, but that's Dick's way.

I feel bad that Todd reacts negatively, at least without any sign of recognition (I only take it negatively), to
my recent success. It is as if I have offended him. It's
too bad because when I warmed the pines last year, I
never downplayed his success. That's why I think in the
end I'll end up winning the battle; I've had it tough
before, sat in Junior C and D for two years before I got
my chance here. He waltzed through the minor system
to Peterborough and never had to confront such difficulties. I usually just say "That's tough," but it feels
awful when your best friend apparently resents you for
doing well.

Tracey Katelnikoff has remained injury-free during his junior
career, except for a groin pull in his second year. Although he
appreciates his good luck, he tries to think of it as little as
possible, keeping the knowledge locked firmly into a remote
recess of his mind. Certainly it is something he never talks
about, because like every other player, amateur or professional, the possibility of injury haunts him always. A hockey
player knows that no matter how talented he is, no matter
how brightly the future beckons, it can all come to nothing
because of an injury. A player never says, "I haven't been
injured," because to say that might break the charm that pro-
tects him. If someone else happens to comment on the
length of time since a player has been injured, the athlete
will knock on wood or cross himself or say a silent prayer;
anything to appease God or the Higher Power or the Forces
of Darkness, Whoever or Whatever it may be that is responsible for protection. It is no affectation; it is an almost viscer-
al fear that the dreams of a young lifetime are quite capable
of disappearing— and very often do disappear—in an instant.

The night is icy cold in Moose Jaw as an early blizzard
dumps ten centimetres of snow over parts of southern
Saskatchewan. Inside the Moose Jaw Civic Centre, however,
the temperature is somewhat higher, warmed by flaring tem-
pers, as the Blades are in the process of embarrassing the

Warriors before 1,744 hometown fans. Although there are not a lot of penalties, those there are indicate a high level of ill feeling by the Warriors, understandable because by the end of the second period, they are losing 8–3, and that will be the final score.

In the dying moments, T.K., who has not figured in the scoring but has nonetheless played his usual demanding game, is jammed into the boards as he fights for the puck in the near side corner. Somebody crashes into his elbow, slamming his left hand into the boards with a sound that reverberates in his mind like a rifle shot. Tracey feels a blinding pain and knows from long experience of lesser injuries that this one is bad. He skates off the ice holding the hand close to his body, the very weight of it already painful. Jeff Thomas looks at it, the area around the base of the thumb already reddened and swollen. He tries to move the thumb, ever so gently, but Tracey, although he braces for it, cannot avoid flinching away. He gasps to try and control the pain, mind over matter, but already, as excruciating as the pain is, what hurts more is the awful fear that this—he looks at the hand in anger—this goddamn hand, this instant in time, will stretch into weeks on the sidelines, will mean no 50 goals, will mean his last season will turn to shit, will mean the scouts will turn a blind eye to him because they don't care a good goddamn whether you're injured or not; they just care what your stats are, and if your stats aren't there, forget it. Will mean goodbye to his last shot in his final year, goodbye hockey career, goodbye to sweet, fucking everything he has worked for.

"Geez," he gasps as Thomas probes, partly to negate the pain, but mostly to negate what he's feeling. The Warriors' team doctor doesn't make him feel any better when he tells him he's not sure whether the thumb is broken or the ligament torn, but whatever it is he'll be out for eight weeks. The doctor gives him something for the pain and instructs him to get a cast on it tomorrow when he's back in Saskatoon and the swelling has gone down. He manages to work into his street clothes assisted by Thomas and afterwards, as the game ends, he stands outside the dressing-room. His team-mates file past, see him standing there, make inquiries or express sympathy, their eyes, their faces expressing their concern, their *feeling* for him. But Tracey, for all that, is alone, absolutely and totally alone, with his pain and his anger and his fear. He raises the hand to look at it and the hand, now an angrier, more sinister shade of red, trembles as his adrenaline level starts to drop.

"The doctor says eight weeks," he says, but he's already marshalling his forces and there's a new tone in his voice. The tone says that if faith can move mountains, then will-power can ignore an injured thumb. What the hell's an injured thumb? A thumb's—what?—one percent of your body? Less? Sure, it's less. He doesn't know what percent a thumb is and he doesn't really care. He knows what he knows. What he *knows* is that a sore thumb is not going to keep him from playing. He'll stop playing when he thinks he's ready. Not when his goddamn *thumb* thinks he's ready. You don't quit until your mind tells you to quit. You don't quit until the job is done.

Dr. Brian Scharfstein, the team physician, tells him that the ligament is torn and it should have surgery to repair the damage.

"The surgery will have to wait until the end of the season," says Katelnikoff.

"Well, I'll put a cast on it and we'll see," says Scharfstein. "But it's going to hurt and it's going to hurt a lot."

Let it hurt, thinks Tracey, as the cast is set. Thus fortified by this iron will, he sits out three games before starting to play with the cast. When he finds it cumbersome, interfering with his mobility, he perseveres for a week and a half, then makes another decision. He does not ask the doctor for an opinion, does not ask anyone; he simply acts. He removes the cast himself, gets Thomas to tape up the hand and learns to live with the pain.

"It hurts a lot," he says later. "But I can't play with a cast." He plays without it, plays so effectively that his points average, which has been hovering around two, begins to rise.

"I guess the injury jolted me," he says, triumphantly. "Sort of woke me up. I can live with the pain. I learned to live with it."

Although he doesn't know it at the time, Tracey Katelnikoff will learn a great deal more about living with pain. It will be his constant companion through every game for the rest of his Junior hockey career.

○ 3

On the same night that Tracey Katelnikoff suffers through the pain of an injured hand, Rob Lelacheur sits watching in the press box, suffering a pain almost as severe.

Comeau turns to Dave Struch and Lelacheur as the team bus pulls in to the Civic Centre in Moose Jaw after the trip from Brandon. "Struch and Lelacheur, you sit out tonight," he says. Although Comeau is at pains to use exactly the same matter-of-fact tone he always uses on such occasions, Lelacheur, along with everyone else who has ever heard the words directed at him, manages to detect a special significance, something written in invisible ink between the lines. Later, he sits in the press box, alternately fuming with anger, then laughing at himself for being so silly as to fume, then fuming for laughing at himself. . . .

In fact, Lelacheur sees significance in everything. Significance in the choice of words. Struch and Lelacheur, not Lelacheur and Struch. Significance in the fact that Strudal (Dave Struch's nickname) has suffered a slight charley horse. They both know the injury isn't enough to warrant sitting out, but at least it offers the semblance of an excuse. Struch doesn't use it himself, but it's there if he wants it. Lelacheur has no excuse, nothing. He isn't looking for one, wouldn't use it if he had it. But still it rankles that he doesn't have one. You sit out, says Comeau. And, perfectly able-bodied, Lelacheur sits out. He knows he is sitting out thanks really to Darwin McPherson, who has arrived in a trade from New Westminster. The trade for another experienced defenceman pushes Lelacheur that much further down the pecking order. Bomber, as McPherson is called, is in his final year as a Junior and has been drafted by the Boston Bruins. He's twenty pounds heavier than Lelacheur and three inches taller. As Lelacheur sits watching, it seems the Blades are doing quite nicely without him, handling the Warriors. McPherson gets an assist on the Blades' first goal, a fast wrist-shot by Kevin Kaminski. The Bomber is having his usual good night. So is the Killer. So is KoKo and so is Bates—Kory Kocur and Darin Bader. Shit. Everybody is having a good night; Sutts and Gumby and Smurf and DooBee. Scizzo—Scott Scissons—is making like Mark Messier. Loyner's looking sharp, pure perogy power. Koonee's in goal, playing as if he's inspired by Grant Fuhr or Def Leppard or, Christ, maybe all the lasagna his mother keeps sending him. But he's playing, whatever it is. They're all playing, except me and the Strudal. The score mounts, 8–0 for the Blades by the end of the second, practically everybody making a hero of himself while he sits in the press box. You sit out, says Comeau. And what is written in invisible ink between the lines are words that Rob can see as if they were etched in fire: You aren't good enough. You can't do it. The words do not say: you will *never be* good enough. You will *never* be able to do it. Rob knows as surely as the first two statements are true, so are the last. And in a compartment of his mind, locked securely away against such assaults on his ego, Rob knows that in fact success will come. Given a year, it will be he who's out on the ice, helping the team, while some other rookie, angry and bewildered, fumes alone. But that doesn't matter here. It is the now that matters. The game plays out and he sizzles with frustration. To hell with fairness or logic or common sense. He's mad anyway. He feels like driving his fist through the glass of the press box, then realizes there is no glass and that strikes him as the most frustrating thing of all. Rob, knowing that he should feel ashamed, instead takes a kind of sour satisfaction from the fact that the Warriors score three in the third, and the game ends, 8–3.

John Tanner's season is actually developing quite well, although you'd never get that impression from the rumblings and grumblings of his diary:

> Maybe this is not going to be my year. Tonight was certainly no indication of good things to come. I was pulled after one, allowing three goals that included a [Bryan] Marchment blast from centre ice. [Tanner is referring to a 6–2 defeat by the Belleville Bulls.] Needless to say, I should've stopped it. The only thing that pissed me off is that whether or not Todd [Bojcun] is playing poorly, I seem to be the only one to get pulled. It hardly seems fair. I believe, however, that Dick [coach Todd] realizes that I'm tougher mentally and that I'm better able to accept the bad with the good. Nevertheless, I'm not too happy about tonight and am going to have to bounce back from it with hard work this week. I have resolved to have a good if not excellent season, so that I can be drafted high.

Tanner's pleasure at being chosen to start against Oshawa turns to dismay as the Petes lose 3–1 to the Generals. As he describes events afterwards, it was a very long game at the end of a very long day:

> We again were unusually lacklustre, unable to mount a spirited attack. Instead, we played with the intensity of a shinny game, just going through the motions and "playing the role" on the ice. I personally played with a great desire to win, but alas, the layoff hath affected my game. Instead of playing the stand-up, challenging style of goal that I vowed I would play, I played more like Flipper as I sprawled helplessly on several occasions. After the game, Dad said he noticed that—I was glad. He has learned through experience how to criticize me, by suggesting rather than attacking. He knows little of the goaltender technically, but

he can observe the more general things such as this. Tonight he came with Dennis Smedley, who has come with Dad to many games recently and is a *devout* Petes fan as of late. Dad took us out for a burger and we talked. But I think I act like an idiot after every game I don't excel in. I don't mean to, but I'm hardly pleasant after an unpleasant game. I should learn to separate the on-ice from the off-ice, but to me they're so very connected because hockey is my life.

My mom thinks that is so shallow and unrewarding and maybe it is. But at this point, I don't know any better.

That night, back in Peterborough following the loss to the Generals, Mike Ricci starts playing parts of previous seasons over in his mind. November 8 in Oshawa, his rookie year, just turned sixteen, the high and the low. He had already scored both goals to give the Petes a 2–1 victory. Late in the game, he is moving in on the goalie, roaring in at high speed, concentrating on the deke—when all hell breaks loose. He doesn't know yet quite what happened in the last split second before he crashed into the boards. Maybe the goalie stick-checked him and caught his skate, or maybe he reached back over the goal line, trying to score as he passed behind the net. Whatever happened, he is off-balance and vulnerable as he hits and he can hear his collarbone snap, the pain of it zapping down his arm and up into his neck with the sickening impact of a high-voltage charge. He lies there stunned, the pain hammering him, afraid to move because when he does it'll get worse and he has to work up to it, steel his nerve for what's going to come. The crowd hushes the way they do sometimes at the prospect of somebody being painfully or even mortally injured. It's all the same to them, part of the price of admission. He finally lets Jeff Twohey get on with it, slipping the stretcher under him and carting him off. He notices through the haze that the Oshawa fans give him a thin round of applause, passing acknowledgement that they share his hurt, they're feeling it right along with him: what a brave lad; good boy; now let's get on with the game.

This year he celebrates his seventeenth birthday by starting a scoring streak, which runs through 19 games. The previous record of 18 consecutive games was held by Brian Dobbin of the London Knights. By one of those far-fetched coincidences, Ricci ties the record in London, an easy but thrilling goal into an empty net with three seconds remaining to give the Petes a win. He makes up for it the next night when he ends the streak, scoring on a breakaway, two Windsor Spitfires buzzing behind him. The fans are going nuts as the shot hits the goalie's shinpads and then goes in. God, the crowd can get you going. Even when it's not a home crowd and they're more against you than for you, they can get the adrenaline going. Still, when the streak ends at 19, Ricci is kind of glad.

I want to score, he thinks, but if I don't, well, it's nice to get the streak out of the way, too. The thing with a streak is that at first you really don't notice it. But then slowly, even though you try to ignore it, you become more and more aware that it's there. You know you're going to miss a game sooner or later and when it finally comes it's too bad, but it doesn't shake me up that much.

Just before these reflections lull him to sleep, he has one last thought. Maybe tomorrow's the time to start another streak, he thinks. He smiles at that and goes to sleep.

Speaking of streaks. The Titans take the advice of their coach to heart. Let other teams do the losing, Bordeleau tells them. If they hate losing less they'll deserve it more. Laval starts their streak with the home-opener against Granby Bisons, winning 7–5. The feeling grows, *vive la victoire*. They beat Drummondville, Victoriaville and Verdun, Trois-Rivières, Chicoutimi, Longueuil, Chicoutimi and Drummondville again, then Hull. *La gloire, c'est fonne, c'est incroyable*. They are drunk on it, drunk with pleasure and joy, and they can skate forever. The players, always close, grow closer. As the Titans prepare for a game on home ice, which will be the eleventh of their winning streak, Patrice writes in his diary about some of his teammates:

My best friend on the team is Christian Larivière, my partner on defence. We're very close, one to the other. Christian picks me up for practices and games. I have the utmost confidence in Christian. He knows all about me—I tell him everything I'm doing. *Je suis ben fier de ce gars-là. Je sais que ce gars-là c'est un super bon gars.* I'm proud of this guy. I know this guy is a great guy.

He's not going to tell others what I've confided. I like the way he sees things. He knows about life and I need to confide in him.

There's also Denis Chalifoux. Denis. We were both sixteen when we began, so we're close. That's normal. *On a tout le temps d'excellents contacts, moi pis Denis.* We've always had a good relationship, Denis and me. We were both stars on the team. Denis is an excellent player and loved by Laval fans. More than just a friend, he's a super guy and super fun.

Also, Claude Lapointe. Claude is one of my favourites. He's a twenty-year-old player this year and it's not surprising he's our captain. He's already been captain before, so when I need advice, I go and see him, he's always there. *Quand t'as un ami comme ça qui ne refuse jamais de service. Mais j'pense que ça compte un de tes meilleurs amis.* He's never let me down when I've asked his help. When you have a friend like that who never refuses you, I think that counts him as one of your best friends. I like him a lot.

Also Donald. Donald is one of my best friends, too. Not that Donald and I don't care about the team, but we're, as it were, sort of in the same position. Donald is the best on the team. If you're the best, no one can tell you, don't do this, don't do that. If you're one of the best on the team, no one can reproach you. But that brings a responsibility. Donald and I are always the last two off the ice after practice. Donald and I have a certain very particular image of hockey, what it takes to succeed. *Il faut prendre les grands moyens.* You have to use all the means available to you. The more you play, the better you become.

Michel Gingras is nineteen years old this year. *C'est un de mes bons copains dans l'équipe.* He's one of my good buddies on the team. I also confide in him, because he's older and knows the world. Michel is a worker and we sometimes play defence together. If I'm not playing with Christian, I'm playing with Michel.

Patrice also reveals his feelings about the team's trainer, François Brûlé, feelings that contrast sharply to those expressed by Tracey Katelnikoff and John Tanner. Patrice's relationship with Brûlé appears to be all that other players hope their relationships will be with their trainers, who occupy a touchy and difficult position in the hierarchy of the team.

The trainers are close to management but not of it. They are close to the players but not players themselves. Management often uses them as a conduit for tapping in to players' attitudes. They provide a tacit liaison between the two and must always be careful of what they say in relaying information from one group to the other. Players want to feel confident that chance remarks are not passed on to be used against them and that real beefs are presented accurately and sympathetically. Management wants to feel they can trust what the trainer says. In short, both groups want to believe that the trainer is on their side, a difficult exercise in diplomacy. Thomas, of the Blades, is in his first year as trainer, and like any rookie has problems with his role. As time passes, he'll become better at his job, slowly gaining the trust of the team and losing the Casper image. Twohey, of the Petes, already has the trust of most players and John's unhappiness with him is temporary. In fact, it was Twohey who first scouted John, brought him to Dick Todd's attention and launched him on his career in Junior A. A trainer is much more than a trainer, as Patrice says of Brûlé:

Yes, he is very much more than a trainer. He's really well liked. I've known him for two years and I can talk to him. He's like a psychologist. If you have a problem, you can go and talk to him because he's gone through it—and he helps you. When you need to talk, you go to see him before you go to the coach. *Il faisait un job magnifique.* He did a great job. I haven't had a trainer like him before. *Il est number one.*

The Titans continue their roll for 11 games, the last another victory over Granby Bisons, 8–4. Donald Audette gets a goal and four assists, bringing his total for the streak to 15 goals and 16 assists for 31 points. He's had seven power-play goals and scored the winning goal five times. Patrice Brisebois has played seven of the 11 games and been forced to sit out four games after tearing a ligament in his right knee.

First I break my left thumb, he grumbles, now this, my right knee. *C'était super ben merveilleux.* I had a great beginning, marvellous. Everyone said I played well.

The knee injury will continue to trouble him throughout the season, but for now the prescribed knee therapy works and on this night he believes none of it matters. Oh, it's true that the hand still hurts, but that is a matter more cerebral than physical.

It hurts a lot and you don't play as well as you could, he thinks, but the scouts don't know you've got a broken thumb. And you don't want the other team to know it either, because they'll hit you harder if they do. It's harder to stickhandle and to shoot, but all that is behind him now.

He has worked his way through it all, regaining his finesse, working on his stick-handling and his strength. He has been so successful that he's had four goals and seven assists in the six games he has played. And on this night, his seventh, he scores once more.

J'suis pas arrêtable, thinks Patrice. There's no stopping me.

Two nights later the Titans lose 4–3 to the Shawinigan Cataractes, and they know they are dealing with more than

simply being away from home on hostile ice. The feeling has
turned hostile, too. It won't embrace them so warmly and
without reservation for the rest of the season. There will be
times, of course; they will have their one-night stands. They
will have their triumphs, shining strings of days. But never
again will they experience the certainty, the omniscient feeling that to win is theirs by right. They will pursue their
dreams still, but they will follow them in blood, sweat and
pain, not on magic wings.

o 4

It starts out as one of those crystal days you sometimes get in Calgary. As you drive across the Bow River you can see the snow-peaked Rockies glistening in the distance. But here, at Father David Bauer Arena, the air, four days before Christmas, seems heavier, containing, with the promise of snow, the promise of a dream realized.

That dream of being a member of Canada's national Junior team beats in the heart of every player between the ages of sixteen and twenty. It beats so fiercely in the heart of Donald Audette that he takes his failure to be invited to these tryouts for the Canadian national Junior team and shapes it into fuel to power his driving ambition. John Tanner, although he typically says little in public, does not hide his bitter amazement in private at having been passed over. He makes an angry entry in his diary the day he hears that Gus Morschauser, goalie for the Kitchener Rangers, has been invited to camp:

> I can't believe it. Gus Morschauser is trying out for the National Junior team because Rick (I Love Myself) Tabaracci [of the Cornwall Royals] has turned down the once-in-a-lifetime chance. I feel like I'm invisible to the people selecting these players. I may be young, but I'm relatively big [six foot three, 180 pounds], and I think under pressure. But he's in his final year and they're probably giving him his last shot.

Still, Tanner has utilized the anger well over the season. As of the halfway point December 14, he has played 800 minutes of hockey in 14 games, while sharing the goaltending duties with Bojcun. His goals-against average in these days just before Christmas is a satisfying 3.68.

Tracey Katelnikoff has long since been sent back from the Washington Capitals' training camp and is on pace to set a scoring record for the Saskatoon Blades in this his final season as a Junior. He does not speak of his disappointment, but the care with which he ignores the subject is a measure of how deeply he feels the loss of an opportunity which, because of his age, will never come again. Rob Lelacheur, as a rookie, never expected to be invited and he takes it best of all, if only because he knows he will have other chances in other years.

Mike Ricci is not only invited to camp; he's one of a handful of players considered a certainty to make Team Canada. However, although he has just turned seventeen, he has already learned that no matter how talented others may think you are, you must take nothing for granted. His landlord in Peterborough, Walter DiClemente, is reminded of this quality when he remarks about something Ricci must do "when you're in Anchorage."

Ricci looks at him, frowns and says, "I have to get there first. I haven't even made the team yet." Only when the final cuts are made does Ricci allow his feelings to show. "When I think that I'll be representing my country, I get a tear in my eye," he says. It seems like a fitting way to end the first half of the season. He has played in 32 of the Petes' 33 games, has 28 goals and 36 assists for 64 points. He has scored 10 power-play goals and 3 game-winners.

Patrice Brisebois, in his gallant style, glories in the fact that he is here to try and win a place on Team Canada, to be counted among the best Juniors in the world. He starts out having an impressive camp, although not without a fierce attack of stomach butterflies the night before it begins.

"I slept badly," he says. "I was nervous. I couldn't wait to get on the ice. We practised from 9:00 a.m. to 7:15 p.m., and after the two practices I was dead. I couldn't wait to get to bed."

The second day, he is excused from morning practice and in the evening, playing with Laval teammate Éric Dubois, who is later cut, scores a goal in an exhibition win over the University of Calgary Dinosaurs. His dream begins to shatter the next evening when he hurts his knee and the team physician, Dr Daniel Morasse, gives him a brace to wear. He misses the exhibition match against Sweden, where Canada loses 7–1, and he misses practice the next day.

"I can't play because of my knee," he says, and by his expression shows that he is trying to think it better, to force it by willpower alone to function. "It's very painful," he admits, finally. "*Ça fait mal.*"

The next morning he practises alone on the ice with Mike Murray, the Canadian Amateur Hockey Association's public-relations director, and finds the pain has disappeared. He leaves the ice beaming, but his pleasure is short-lived. He injures it again during the regular practice, and although he will not give in and continues to skate the pain is excruciating.

"The practice is very tough," he says simply and the next day, Team Canada coach Tom Webster cuts him. "Mr Webster came to tell me before we left for practice," he says, and although he is nearly weeping, he understands. "He told me that he couldn't take me to Anchorage because the team played seven games in ten days and he didn't want to take a chance with me."

Brisebois's dreams of playing for the nationals is over for the year, and he faces arthroscopic surgery when he returns to Montreal. Still, he consoles himself as best he can, thinking of the next year in Helsinki: "I'll be back next year," he vows, repeating the words like a mantra as he says goodbye individually to each of the twenty-three players still left in camp. "And next time I'll make the team."

The next day, the final three cuts are made: goalie Danny Lorenz, of the Western Hockey League's Seattle Thunderbirds, left-winger Scott Pearson of Niagara Falls

Thunder and Brian Collinson, a defenceman from ᴛ. Toronto Marlboros. Only two players will be back from last year's gold medal winners. Eric Desjardins, on loan from the Montreal Canadiens, is expected to anchor the defence, and high-scoring right-winger Sheldon Kennedy, from the Swift Current Broncos.

"As one player looking at another, you can't say, 'Well, they deserved to be cut,'" says Peterborough Petes' defenceman Corey Foster. "They are all great players. Sometimes it was injury, with some it was the numbers game or that the team needed more of one kind of player and less of another. Any one of them could have made the team."

Here's the 1989 edition of Canada's national Junior team (* denotes first-round NHL draft choices):

> Goal—Stephane Fiset, Victoriaville Tigers; Gus Morschauser, Kitchener Rangers.
>
> Defence—Eric Desjardins, Montreal Canadiens; *Corey Foster, Peterborough Petes; Danny Lambert, Swift Current Broncos; *Yves Racine, Victoriaville Tigers; Geoff Smith, North Dakota University; Steve Veilleux, Trois-Rivières Draveurs.
>
> Forwards—*Rob Brind'Amour, Michigan State Spartans; *Andrew Cassels, Ottawa 67s; *Rob Cimetta, Toronto Marlboros; *Martin Gelinas, Hull Olympiques; Sheldon Kennedy, Swift Current Broncos; Jamie Leach, Niagara Falls Thunder; D'Arcy Loewen, Spokane Chiefs; John McIntyre, Guelph Platers; Rob Murphy, Vancouver Canucks; Mike Ricci, Peterborough Petes; *Reginald Savage, Victoriaville Tigers; *Darrin Shannon, Windsor Spitfires.

On that last day in Calgary, Team Canada, comprised of twenty players who will go to Anchorage in quest of a gold medal, are in a reflective mood. Call it what you want: team spirit, unity of purpose, sense of family; but if that can translate into gold, then players like The Hawk and Pepe le Pew, Velluxy and The Count are already rich.

"It's a bit unusual to see such spirit among guys who have been together only a short while," says Sheldon Kennedy as he stands in his longjohns in the national Junior team's locker-room following practice. "But we have gotten to be close, and believe me that is essential if you are going to win in international competition. You've just got to think and work as a team, and that starts in the dressing-room."

Coach Tom Webster points out that the team that wins the World Junior Hockey Championship—scheduled to start the day after Christmas—will be the one that has the greatest abundance of the three elements he calls the Win Formula.

"The Win Formula is made up of, first, the ability to operate as a team, as a unit; second, it's made up of talent; and third, good general mental attitude," he says. "Talk to the players, talk to the team doctor, if you want to find out about their mental attitude, their feelings about themselves as a team, and then come back and we'll talk about talent and how I see it coming together as a coach."

In the locker-room, Kennedy is watching a video of his own performance during practice. For all his meagre nineteen years, "Teddy," as it says on his underwear, knows a little something about where gold is to be found, being one of the two players on the team with a previous gold medal to his credit. He and Desjardins helped Team Canada win the title at the previous year's Junior world championship in Moscow.

"It comes from down here," he says, as if imparting a huge confidence, tapping the area of his heart. His own nickname, he points out, comes not from the U.S. president and he flashes his mischievous smile as he explains. "The guys named me Teddy because I guess they think I'm kinda small and cuddly," he says. At five foot ten and 170 pounds he is small, but there is no hint of cuddliness when he goes into action on the ice. There he is an aggressive, whirling dynamo, a prolific scorer and a team leader. Around the room are some of the other players on whom Canada's medal hopes depend. There is Velluxy, Steve Veilleux, of the Trois-Rivières Draveurs, so dubbed because the

English-speaking players can't pronounce his name.

"Well, I don't mind a bit," says Veilleux. "The English-speaking guys have made us French guys feel right at home ever since we got here. We are friends on this team and you can win games for your friends."

Goalie Stephane Fiset of the Victoriaville Tigers neither speaks nor understands English. Tall and quick of movement, a goalie in the Ken Dryden mould, his eyes light up when he talks of the team. His nickname is The Whip and he is making it his business to get the English-speakers to say it in French.

"*Fouette*," they say, speaking carefully, and Fiset laughs as they labour to get it right.

"It is easy getting along with this team," he says. "They are great players. *Ils savent quoi faire*. They know what they're doing."

Pepe le Pew, known simply as Danny Lambert to his teammates on the Swift Current Broncos, is named after an amorous cartoon skunk, because "I smell so sweet after a workout," he says. The Count and The Hawk, Mike Ricci and Corey Foster of the Peterborough Petes, nod knowingly, wrinkling their noses.

"All these nicknames are just among the guys here, just for this team. And don't ask me how they got The Count," says Ricci, apparently oblivious to his royal-sized nose.

"The names give us more the feeling of a family," says Foster, a first-round pick of the New Jersey Devils, who will later be traded to the Edmonton Oilers. "They help maintain a winning attitude."

The Team Canada physician is Dr Daniel Morasse, from Mont St-Hilaire, Quebec. His eyes brighten with personal pride as he talks about the young men whose well-being is in his hands.

"Yes, I am proud of them, though that might seem silly to be proud because someone is healthy," says Morasse. "But these players are healthy physically, we have no injuries and their mental health, their mental attitude, is outstanding. When we first arrived at camp, we worried about how the French guys would get along, there might be a clique. But

that has never happened, not even at the very first. At the
team residence, they have been staying four to eight in a
room and we made a point of mixing French and English in
the same room. I think that has been a big help.

"They really pay attention to each other's moods, they're
really tuned in. For instance, one day they could see that
Scott Pearson [the Leafs' draft pick and Niagara Falls
winger who was cut] was sitting apart, not saying much,
kind of by himself. Well, the reason for that was it was his
birthday, his nineteenth on the nineteenth, so he was double lucky, and Scott thought we'd all forgotten. But these
guys, well they got him a cake, a big cake with one candle
on it, and when he saw it, his eyes lit up and he was smiling
from ear to ear. That's how this team is."

Morasse points out that the lads are healthy in other
respects, too.

"This is a great facility," he says, gesturing to encompass
the arena complex. "About the only thing they miss is their
girlfriends," he adds, deadpan. "They're on the phone to
them all the time, so they manage to cope. And when
they're not on the phone to their girlfriends, they talk about
sex. That's a favourite subject with them. They talk about
sex a lot."

Morasse believes this combination of locker-room cama-
raderie and mental edge translates into superior performance on the ice. "They need the skills, too, but I believe
they have those skills. The coaches can be more enlighten-
ing about that, but if you have the skills, then the psychological values can give the team an immense edge."

Coach Webster and his assistant, Alain Vigneault, not only
agree but point out that the psychological edge is one the
entire team hierarchy has been at great pains to foster.

"Everyone, from management to coaches to the support
staff, makes a point of being open, of realizing that every
one of us is here to do a certain job, that we are human
beings united for the purpose of bringing back a gold
medal," says Vigneault, whose regular job is coaching of the
Hull Olympiques.

Webster agrees. "We're going to Anchorage to win the

gold and we have the skills and desire to do that," he says, giving the usual coaches' line when asked whether their teams are going to win this or that. The question is rephrased: Do you think it is a reasonable probability that the Junior nats will retain their title as world champions?

"Yes. Definitely," he says, smiling. Then he looks serious. "This is a team of winners. They think in terms of winning. They'll meet other teams who can say that, too. But I believe the tougher it comes, the tougher this team can get. It's not a perfect team. We don't have as much offence as we'd like, but we'll have the offence we need. This team can pull together at every level. It has the elements for the Win Formula—skill, heart and mind."

Which on this day in Calgary seems to manifest itself in terms of confidence with one another's skills, confidence that can withstand the test of humour.

"Well, brother, how y'all doin'?" says Kennedy to Reggie Savage, after executing a prancy ballet turn by way of demonstrating his skating ability. The teammates, French and English, look each other over, taking their time.

"I think," says Le Tigre, careful with the English words, "you learn your hockey from your little sister."

They glower at each other, Teddy and the Tiger, enjoying the insult, barely able to contain their laughter. Webster blows his whistle to signal the start of practice and they skate away together.

The Petes are beginning to struggle without Ricci and Foster, and John Tanner is still smouldering like a banked fire. The problems are compounded by the absence of two other mainstays, left-winger Steve DeGurse and right-winger Tie Domi, both with injuries. Tanner stops 24 shots in a 5–3 win over the Toronto Marlboros, taking satisfaction from having robbed Shawn Costello and Jason Winch of what looked like sure goals. He contains his fury at members of the defence and the Petes' fourth line, accusing them of relaxing when the game is still close.

"The Marlies scored on a careless giveaway before we woke up and won the game," he fumes. This anger has been building ever since the news of Gus Morschauser. It still rankles that the Kitchener Rangers' goalie will end up going to Anchorage, while Tanner with a superior goals-against average isn't even invited to try out. Now the sloppy play against the Marlies causes the frustration to boil over, and it spills over in unexpected directions. He watches as the Petes are demolished by the Thunder 9–3, with Todd Bojcun in the net. Then he berates a rookie who takes a spearing penalty when the game is 5–3.

"That stupid penalty cost us our chance at winning the game," he grumbles. "We didn't deserve to win anyway. Our goals were fluky and theirs were good. Todd, in my opinion, had very little chance."

Then, later that night, he reveals his deep rage in the pages of his diary, directing it at the team trainer, Jeff Twohey:

> It's funny, but I think our trainer takes a loss more seriously than any player and acts as if it were a personal offence against him. No one really knows for sure, but all suspect he's one of the most influential members of the organization in that he's the eyes and ears of the coach. He can make you or break you—if he likes you, that's fine. If he doesn't, watch out. You'll have constant hassles over equipment, receive the silent treatment, and be reprimanded or "counselled" by the coach about things you have said or done. Silly little things, that for the most part went off with a laugh or unnoticed. With the trainer, one must say the right things at the right times, whether one is being honest or lying through his crooked teeth. Most players resent other players when this is pointed out, but they're hypocrites and don't know it (they can't spell it!).
>
> There is a bigger game off the ice than on, and some have mastered the skills to Gretzky-like perfection. I, on the other hand, despise such trivial games. I talk a lot, sure, but I prefer to do my talk in the form of my play, rather than in the crock that players feed our hungry trainer. Players who were wetting their pants out

there tonight were the ones who appeared so angry when either Dick [coach Todd] or Jeff appeared around the corner. That's called "playing the role", and they should be ashamed of themselves.

Donald Audette has quickly put his disappointment behind him, and instead takes immense pride in the fact that while he was passed over for the world Juniors, he has been invited to play at The Forum de Montréal on January 24 in the annual Quebec-Ontario Junior all-star game.

"I don't want to miss it for anything in the world," he says. "To play in The Forum is a dream I've had since childhood. *J'suis pas arrêtable.* There's no stopping me. Now it will happen."

The all-star game preoccupies Audette for another reason, too. The coach of the team that leads at the halfway point of the regular schedule, 35 games, is given the honour of coaching the all-stars in The Forum. The Titans play their thirty-fifth game on December 14, leading the league with 23 wins, 11 losses and one tie for 47 points. Audette has done more than his share to see that Bordeleau is honoured as the all-star coach, with 41 goals and 47 assists for 88 points in the 35 games. He's had 19 power-play goals, scored 7 game-winners, and has an average of 2.30 points per game, leading the league.

However, the Victoriaville Tigers won't play their thirty-fifth game until December 29 and there's an outside chance that the Tigers can squeak by to earn the all-star coaching honour for their coach, Gilbert Perrault. Increasing the suspense for Audette is the fact that chasing him as top scorer is Victoriaville's Stephane Morin. The Tigers edge closer to the Titans as Christmas passes.

"*Ils avaient le narf,*" says Audette, describing his team's feelings. "They were nervous, jumpy, and they got worse as each day passed."

Then, with their thirty-fifth game, the worst happens for the Titans, as Victoriaville wins. This gives the Tigers a record of 23–10–2, for 48 points. Bordeleau sends a telegram of congratulations to Perrault, but it is still a bitter disappointment because the Titans have led since the beginning of the season with 11 straight wins. Adding to the injury for Audette, Morin finishes with 43 goals and 56 assists, for 99 points.

"*C'est crissant*," is how Audette sums up his feelings. "It's a pain in the ass."

Patrice Brisebois, the happy warrior, is never one to weep about what is past, so he puts his disappointment about the Junior camp behind him almost from the moment he gets on the plane for home. He thoroughly enjoys his enforced layoff as he awaits surgery on January 3.

He spends the days before Christmas with Michèle and his brother Jean-Pierre in Montreal. He has missed a chance to play in the world championship and he may miss the all-star game as well. But he has also played in 30 of 35 games, has 11 goals and 27 assists, for 38 points. In the meantime he plays cards and generally carries on his love affair with life. He worries a bit about the state of his knee, but *c'est la vie; je m'en crisse*. Such is life; I don't give a damn.

Tracey Katelnikoff scarcely thinks about what's happening in Alaska. He has never been invited to try out for Team Canada, and, knowing the oversight would rankle if he let it, he typically shuts it out of his mind. He has more important things to concern himself with, anyway. As they hit the mid-point of the season, the Blades are in second place with 22 wins and 14 losses for 44 points. The Swift Current Broncos are in first with 54 points, having had things very much their own way since winning their initial 12 games to start the season. But the Prince Albert Raiders are only a point behind the Blades and that situation touches a point of pride with Katelnikoff. As captain, he wants to see his team if not in first place by the end of the season, a task he recognizes as difficult, at least maintaining second place. Part of the reason for this desire is personal; part of it concerns the entire team. The team aspect relates to the Memorial Cup. As host team, the Blades will automatically participate, even if they finish last in the standings. All the other teams must win their league championships in order to take part, so the Blades see a stigma attached to their free ride and every player wants to minimize it. The personal aspect is that Katelnikoff must have a banner year if he is to get a second shot at the NHL. Consequently, he is fiercely resolved that if the Blades don't go to the Memorial Cup as league champions, at least they must finish no lower than second. And he wants to surpass 50 goals for the first time in his career. At this point, having played 31 of the first 36 games, that milestone seems at least just possible. He has had 19 goals and 19 assists and he can still hit 50 if he can avoid injuries. That's a worrisome *if*. Since he tore the ligaments in his thumb during a game in Moose Jaw on November 26—his first injury in more than a year—the pain still nags him frequently. With determination he continues to exorcise his doubts from his mind. The glory of the World Junior Championship as Christmas approaches is far removed from the heart of Tracey Katelnikoff. His future, in almost a literal sense, is here and now.

Just before Christmas, Rob Lelacheur stops in St Albert and visits briefly with the Amigos, Chris Larkin and Kevin Lovig. Then he picks up his sister, Christine, who's been staying with their grandmother, and heads for California. Their parents have taken a house for the month at Rancho Mirage, near Palm Desert. Brother and sister are eager to get there.

Once on the plane, the four-hour flight is uneventful, although getting on proved to be a problem. They are stopped by immigration officials in Edmonton who don't like the idea of a seventeen-year-old crossing the border with his eight-year-old sister. No one has thought to give written authorization to the siblings and the official is adamant.

"Your sister must have authorization to cross the border," Rob is told, and for a moment he's at a loss. Fortunately, his grandmother has just left them, so he rushes back through the gate and catches her before she leaves the airport. She writes out an authorization, and the crisis is averted. They fly to LAX, where his family meets them for the drive to Rancho Mirage. Although Rob looks forward to the visit, he begrudges having to part from his friends. Still, all considered, he shouldn't grumble. His rookie year has gone well, so far. He's had good ice time, playing in 35 of 36 games, with one goal and seven assists. Comeau told him he's been playing well and when he steps into the California sunshine, feels it warm on his skin, Rob smiles. He recalls hearing on the morning weather report that the temperature in Anchorage, Alaska, is minus 18 Celsius.

○ 5

The DC8 tunnels across the Gulf of Alaska through the opaque Arctic night, a tiny pinpoint of light fleeing through the frigid sky. The Chugach Mountains slide unseen beneath the aircraft and minutes later the pilot announces the beginning of the descent to Anchorage International. The airport at 8 p.m. on December 23 is all but invisible under a coat of icefog so thick it looks like the tops of clouds. There are lights from the airport buildings, the first since Vancouver, but the runway-hugging cloud tops make the passengers nervous, wondering if technology can really substitute for the power of the naked eye. Perhaps it can, for the craft lands smoothly without a bump, and the players exchange smiles, quips and perhaps some silent sighs of relief. Anchorage is the largest city in the forty-ninth state, but it seems small as they drive into the city core. That's because the core, what until 1975 was the City of Anchorage, containing about 80,000 people, was merged with several surrounding communities to form what is now officially Anchorage Municipality. The city core plus the surrounding communities contains 230,000 people. Like the Chugach Mountains at night, many of these people are not visible.

Their first impression, as Team Canada players move from their bus to the lobby of the Anchorage Sheraton, is of vapour and hoarfrost and breathtaking cold. The door of the bus opens and the warmer air immediately freezes into icefog as it hits the cold air outside. Vapour from the bus exhaust billows into the light from the lobby door. Breath freezes and drifts into your eyes so that you squint into your own frozen mist. Frost starts to form on your eyelashes. Your nose runs. But the air is fresh and clear, like a jolt of pure oxygen. You are suddenly wide awake after four and a half hours on the plane, then a half-hour's doze on a hot bus. The players mill about the huge lobby, which rises six storeys high. They note the flags of Canada, the U.S.A., Sweden, the U.S.S.R., Czechoslovakia, Finland, Norway, West Germany, and a silence falls over them. Their eyes move from the flags of the participating nations to the signs saying, "Welcome to the IIHF XIII Annual World Junior Ice Hockey Championships." As they look from one to the other, the flags to the signs, you can almost see it click: We are here. This is special. My God, this is the big leagues.

"Okay, so where are the scouts?" asks Sheldon Kennedy, while Ricci and Foster and Danny Lambert smile in appreciation. As Kennedy speaks, a trim man with silver-grey hair walks out of the Calista Café and heads for the elevators. He stops, recognizing Dave Draper, Team Canada's director of operations, and they shake hands. They chat a bit and then the trim man walks away. Draper approaches a group of the players.

"That's Eric Taylor," says Draper.

"Who's Eric Taylor?" says Kennedy.

"Eric Taylor's a scout for the Montreal Canadiens," says Draper. The players look at one another and at the flags and you can almost see the thoughts flashing through their minds.

There's a mystique about the Soviet team, the elements of a riddle. Partly it is something they set out to establish with their implacable manner and their purposeful isolation, partly it is a byproduct of the vast barrier of language. If you say hello to a Soviet player on the street or in the Anchorage Sheraton where all teams stay, he will look at you with a sort of embarrassed suspicion or, what's more likely, ignore you completely. There is no sense of there being anything hostile about this. It is just their way and their way is incomprehensible to outsiders, and thus mysterious.

The way the Soviets tell it, you could almost make a case

for Canada handing over the gold medal right now and spending the next ten days seeing the sights. Certainly there is something about them, the mystique again, that makes them the big attraction here, a sense that they're always up to something, and that that something will spell disaster for the opposition.

"We have been practising hard and we believe we have the best team," says Soviet coach Robert Cherenkov, in a rare communication. "The opposition will find us somewhat more difficult to subdue than they did last year," he adds portentously. He declines to elaborate. Last year Canada won the gold at the previous World Championship in Moscow, while Russia placed second.

However, Draper, who is also the Canadian Amateur Hockey Association's director of scouting, has an idea of what might constitute that "somewhat more difficult" task.

"They gave a hint in their exhibition game with the U.S. on Friday that they are a much more physical team than we have seen in the past," said Draper. "Their skill level is very high. They are fast and they are big."

The Soviets return nine players from last year's squad, including their two leading scorers, Alexandr Mogilny and Sergei Fedorov, who'll be teamed with Pavel Bure to form an explosive line. The Soviets have won the tournament seven times, more than any other nation, and they also won three non-International Ice Hockey Federation world Junior tournaments, in 1974, 1975 and 1976. Canada has won three times: 1989, 1985 and 1982. Czechoslovakia has one of the most consistent teams, and although it has never won there is talk it could be strong after winning the European Junior tournament in the spring.

On Christmas Eve Mike Ricci is heard telling a reporter he wants to wish Merry Christmas to his parents, family and friends. He has just finished conveying those exact sentiments on the phone but he figures they'll look even better in print.

"Oh yes, I want my front tooth, too," he adds as an afterthought. He lost a tooth when he had a stick shoved in

his face during a shoving match behind the net earlier in the
season.

On Christmas Eve Tracey Katelnikoff sits in his mother's living-room in Calgary waiting for Dickens' *A Christmas Carol*
to start on TV, a family tradition for years, along with *The
Grinch Who Stole Christmas*. The traditional pictures of
Frosty the Snowman and Santa Claus are in their places on
the wall, and the time-honoured stuffed Grinch is on the
tree. Tricia is in and out of the room with her mother. Trevor
is somewhere about. Tracey nibbles at a home-made chocolate and idly tries to crack a nut between his thumb and fore-
finger, but eventually gives it up and uses the nutcracker.
The room exudes warmth, made up of the smells of cooking
and waiting delicacies, of friendship and love and belonging.
Even the lights in the room seem mellow, perhaps modified
by the glow of the Christmas tree, and Tracey leans back
with a feeling of contentment.

He thinks of Christmases past; the year his dad and
mother gave the boys a goalie net and they played with it
constantly, until the string was worn away, leaving only a
few strands hanging from the metal frame. The year he got
a toy pinball machine and drove them crazy with the noise
it made. His dad seemed relieved when it finally broke,
mercifully early in the New Year. He thinks of his father,
but the sense of loss, though still sharp and painful, is
something he has come to live with and to a degree understand.

It's not like the sun doesn't come up in the morning, he
thinks. It's not that I don't miss him, but there's nothing I can
do about it and that's a fact.

Still, he misses the sound of his father's voice and if he
holds his breath, he can still hear it.

A dream is for the person who's dreaming it, Tracey
thinks, suddenly, realizing this is something his father has
told him. You do not share your dreams, spend all your time
talking about them. The dream is for you and it's up to you to
make it come true. It depends on you.

He thinks of the few times in his career he has felt like

quitting and how his dad's firm resolve always gave him the heart to go on.

He always taught me not to quit, and he never quit himself. That is probably our common denominator. He always taught me not to quit. Whenever he did something, he tried to extract the fullest potential from it. You don't put a half-assed effort into something worthwhile. A dream requires the fullest effort, and that's what I've been trying to do. A lot of people say it and don't do it, but there's a difference between saying and doing that some people never seem to realize.

He thinks of the year and the uncertainties that face him and even as he thinks of the difficulties ahead, his determination freshens.

When I quit playing and decide I've had enough hockey, that's when I'll be through, he thinks. You are not through with a dream until you quit. You are not through with a dream until you stop dreaming it.

On Christmas Eve, as is the Tanner custom, they had opened their gifts; John and Mary and their parents. Then they went to visit uncle Otto, John's mother's brother. The gathering with the Tamboer relatives was crowded. There must have been sixteen people there and they returned home late and full of food. But before John falls asleep, he recounts the celebration:

> We opened our presents and I was really happy with the tackle and clothes I received. I was happier, though, at the enthusiastic response my dad gave to the top-of-the-line fishing rod and reel that I spent a small fortune on. I was happy as well with the response Mary and Mom gave to the gifts I gave them. I've always tried to please my parents, particularly my father, with my hockey. It's probably the biggest reason I play. Sure, I like the game, but I know how proud my dad is when I do well and give it everything I have. Half my motivation at least would disappear if he weren't around to witness my final conquest—my first NHL game. When

it seems I haven't got enough, and all motivational factors have been exhausted, his pride is what spurs me on.

I saw Patrick Swayze crying on a Barbara Walters special because his father couldn't see him hit the big time. The reason he said he was in the showbiz game was to make his father proud. I found his response 100 percent genuine and was able to relate to his sadness. He seemed to be a very empty man. I've been waiting a long time for these holidays, and now I can understand my anxious anticipation.

The house in Rancho Mirage is owned by two people from Los Angeles, people in the entertainment business, so naturally it has plenty of showbiz California excess about it. Rob likes it in an unsettled sort of way.

It's big, which is O.K., and it's got a swimming pool, which is O.K., too, he thinks. But it has this immense ostentatious stereo system that plays outdoors just in case people for miles around want to listen to whatever music you're playing. And the showbiz types are into off-white. Off-white walls and ceilings and bathrooms and furniture, even off-white tiles on some of the floors. They've got an off-white tree ten feet tall in one of the rooms. In fact, they've got these big artificial trees everywhere, an artificial forest, although thank God they're not all off-white.

However, any reservations are put aside when Rob sees the Christmas tree and sees what his mother and Grandma Greenwald have done to give it the touch of home. His mom has brought the family ornaments for the tree, and when he first spies them he feels a lump rising in his throat and he hugs his mother. The tree displays ornaments he and Christine have made: a Santa Rob made in Grade One out of wool and beads, some macaroni angels by Christine. There are the glass bulbs the children are given each Christmas, collected over the years, dozens of them now. There's the ornament they bought the year Rob got his driver's license, Santa in a car.

Rob examines the ornaments, the tree, and looks out at the golf course across the swimming pool behind the house. IIis mother comes out of the pool, then his dad, his grandma and grandpa Greenwald, then Christine, chattering behind them. He grins at them all, a large happy smile, and if he doesn't hit the swimming pool fast he's going to break out crying. It's a day before Christmas, his family's here, and because of them he's home.

○ 6

Christmas morning dawns bright and clear and you realize for the first time how spectacular this scenery is in Anchorage. The sun rises about ten o'clock and sets around three and on other days it has been obscured by cloud. But today it shines off the inch-thick hoarfrost that laces the trees and lends delicacy even to the hydro lines along the streets. You can see the Aleutian Range across Cook Inlet. You can see the Chugach Mountains. More than a hundred miles to the north, you can—unless the natives are teasing—see Mount McKinley, 20,320 feet high. It is the highest peak in North America and it glistens in the sun, awesome even at that distance.

Over coffee break in the Calista Café, the players reminisce about the 1983 championship in Leningrad, when another talented Canadian team was expected to win a gold but came away with a bronze. It's not clear whether the memory exercise is also a not-so-subtle prediction of what could befall this year's team, but it's interesting anyway. The top forwards were Steve Yzerman, Dave Andreychuk, and a future NHL scoring champ named Mario Lemieux. The defencemen were the likes of James Patrick and Gary Leeman. The goaltender was Mike Vernon. Future NHLers all, yet this talented team could manage only a bronze medal. Canada saved its best for last, outshooting Norway 66–6, and winning 13–0 in a desperate attempt to beat the Norwegians by 16 goals and wrest the silver medal away from the Czechs. The Soviets, meanwhile, had clinched the gold. Andreychuk was Canada's top scorer in the tourney with 11 points, followed by Lemieux with 10. Since the world Junior tournament began with an experimental series in 1974, Canada has won it just three times and finished second four times. The Soviets have won 10 times. Only Sweden, in 1981, and Finland, in 1987, have managed to break the stranglehold of the hockey superpowers.

Team Canada has drawn names so that each player buys another a gift. Mike Ricci opens his, from Sheldon Kennedy. He smiles as he sees what it is and pushes the baseball-style camouflage hat he perpetually wears back on his head. His present is a toy taxi, "Ricci's Cab" printed on the sides.

"Vroom!" he says. "Now I won't have to ride the bus!"

"That's for when you miss the bus, Count," says Kennedy, as the teammates laugh.

All things considered, thinks Ricci, I've done pretty well in the wheel department this Christmas: just before leaving for training camp in Calgary, he has heard that his mother and dad will get him a shiny black Jeep YJ.

The team has its meal, nothing special despite the fact that it's Christmas Day. As usual, Ricci has pasta—spaghetti with a meat and tomato sauce. The main strong point is that there's a lot of it. The food here generally, for the hockey players as for everyone else, is not so hot. In the case of the pasta, that is literally true, and Ricci speculates that they must have put it outside to cool. The turkey, say those who have eaten it, is cold, too, but it's also undercooked, so there's a certain balance. The cheese is pretty well picked over and looks like they might have set it out the week before. While Ricci's dark thoughts about the food are understandable, he might possibly modify them slightly if he heard the other side of the story.

"Yes, I know they've got complaints," says the hotel's director of catering, a slim, harried man named William McBroom. "If it's not the Canadians complaining, it's the Czechs. If it's not the Czechs, it's the Russians. My God, those Russians!

"They don't like sauces. I think the Russian coaches would be happiest if we boiled everything. The Soviet players like boiled potatoes before a game—in fact they like boiled potatoes all the time. Canadian and U.S. players go in for mounds of pasta. The Soviets hate pasta, won't eat it."

Other foods the Soviets don't like are soups with seasoning, spaghetti and meatballs—they're too heavy; pastries for breakfast—too starchy; any kind of fried foods—too much polyunsaturated fat. Danish pastries are ignored by everyone.

"We put them out and they just sit there," says McBroom. "Same thing with seafood. Once we put out salmon as an extra treat and nobody ate it, none of the teams."

The Canadian and American teams love things like hamburgers, fries and wings, something the European players seldom eat. The Russians are fascinated by bananas, something they don't see much at home, and the West Germans love pecans, probably for the same reason. Everyone loves orange juice, with cranberry juice close behind.

"I don't think most of them had ever tasted cranberry juice before, but they love it. We went through twenty-four cases in the first three days." And the teams keep changing their minds about what they want.

"The menus were supposed to be set at the beginning, but today I'm looking at twenty-five pages of changes." McBroom points out that breakfast generally isn't a popular meal: "When you come right down to it, I think they'd rather sleep in."

The players absorb this information, lookly vastly unimpressed. Still, this being Christmas, food's a very popular topic, and the range of local idiosyncrasies is broad. Someone points out that the first surprise comes at breakfast, when, if you like your bacon and eggs, forget it. Standard breakfast at the Calista Café is eggs and hash browns for $4.75, with any kind of meat $3.50 extra. Reindeer sausage are okay, sort of, but they take a lot of chewing. Heads nod understandingly as someone relates a waiter's response when asked how a sausage could be hard to chew.

"Well, that's because they're a very muscular animal," explains the waiter. "They run a lot, they're very fast and hard to catch, so that makes them a little—don't tell the manager I said this—tough." And coffee, well so much for America's pride. Coffee, at least in the Calista Café, is a prop for conversation, used to keep the mouth moist. It's widely believed they water it down, the way they used to do whisky in these parts during the gold rush days. The best is machine coffee, each cup individually brewed, for 25 cents. American machine coffee is much superior to Canadian machine coffee, which costs twice the price. It has already been discovered that the best place to eat is the Sullivan Arena, where mothers of the Alaska All-Star Squirt B Hockey League sell sandwiches ($3), chili ($2), beer ($1) and soft drinks (75 cents).

"It's like if you were at home with your own refrigerator, and your own mother to make the sandwich for you," says Mike Murray, the CAHA's public relations man. Again, everyone nods. A favourite culinary experience is the Squirt B baloney, cheese and lettuce sandwich, with a dollop of French mustard and barbecue chips on the side.

"Geez," says Ricci, as the conversation goes on. He has just been talking to his mother on the phone and he starts to regale his ill-fed teammates with his mother's holiday menu.

Shrimp. Lobster. Turkey. Each word is punctuated by groans. Frittelle, Italian doughnuts—cries of aaah. L'anguilla, eel in tomato sauce—gagging sounds from those whose tastebuds have fossilized at Burger King. Baccala, salted cod, marinated in oil for twenty-four hours, then broiled with garlic; panettone, cake-like bread with raisins and candied fruit—cries of ecstasy. Almond cookies, cheesecake—groans and sighs.

"Quit it," someone pleads. "I'm gonna die."

But Ricci is merciless, adding this is merely the menu for Christmas Eve. "Christmas Day, that's when we *really* eat," he says. Stracciatella, homemade soup; pasta—lasagna is his favourite; veal cutlet, roast lamb; more desserts, so many he can't remember; torrone, white chocolate with almonds.

"And of course, homemade wine," he cries, holding up his glass of cranberry juice. "My dad starts it in September and it's always ready for Christmas." Ricci takes a sip of the cranberry juice and looks at the remains of the spaghetti.

"Geez," he says.

Meanwhile, no sugar-coated visions dance in Soviet heads while the decadent westerners, in their various ways, celebrate Christmas. They spend the day with a lengthy practise session, then do a little sightseeing.

"There was no lack of people who wanted to feed them a little Christmas cake and Christmas cheer," says the public relations director of the organizing committee, Fred Summerfelt. "But the word came back that this wasn't a holiday for them and they wanted no part of the celebration."

John Tanner spends Christmas at the apple farm near Chatham and he enjoys the respite from hockey. The tree sits in the corner of the dining-room, never having looked more splendid. There is so much of everything; his mother always sees to that. He smells the turkey roasting, and the ham. He checks out the carrot pudding, his favourite Christmas dessert, for the umpteenth time, eats his umpteenth handful of grapes. Relatives start arriving for dinner, ten or twelve of them before they're done, everyone talking at once, everyone making a fuss over John, their hockey player. John laughs and smiles, trying to be modest but loving the compliments, being the centre of attention, he has to admit. Later, stuffed happily with turkey, ham, potatoes, dressing and, of course, carrot pudding, he drifts off to his room. He lies on his bed in a food-induced haze and feels pure bliss.

Anchorage is a small, cold city with a big warm heart. Each team participating in the World Junior Championships has a "sponsor," a local resident to take the team under their wing during their stay here in the Last Frontier. The Team Canada host is Bill Collins and when he invited everyone out for a bite to eat on Christmas Eve, there was much speculation in the team about where he'd find room for twenty hockey players, plus officials.

"They could have put three hockey teams in that house," says team physician Dr Daniel Morasse, as the main thrust of the earlier food discussion diminishes. "I never saw so much food or so much space!" Speculation then swung around to what Mr Collins might do for a living to afford such a large house.

"Maybe he's into snow removal," quips a player. Actually, Collins is an accountant, while his wife, Nancy, works for the Anchorage School Board.

In keeping with the Christmas spirit, the Anchorage police decided to forgive the Great Shoplifting Caper, but it'll be some time before it is forgotten.

"Nyet! Nyet!" grates Soviet coach Robert Cherenkov, when it is revealed that eighteen-year-old forward Sergei Gomoliako is detained after trying to leave JCPenney with a pair of unpurchased gloves.

"Can't you see this is very upsetting?" asks an interpreter walking beside the coach. "There will be no questions." The pair walk quickly away.

Police Lieut. Pat Donahue says other suspicious packages were found outside the store when the players were caught. The bags contained cosmetics, women's gloves and other items from another store. There were no sales receipts for any of them.

"I think they just got overcome by all those consumer goods and wanted to make a big impression on their girl-friends when they get back home," says Donahue. "Nah, there aren't going to be any charges. After all, this is Christmas Day, so what the heck. We want to warn them, though, that they're not going to get away with the gold medal. You Canadian guys, and our own boys, too, are going to make sure of that."

After Gomoliako and two other players are stopped by a security guard as they leave the store, police and JCPenney officials spend a nerve-wracking hour trying to communicate.

"We couldn't seem to get the spirit of glasnost going," says Donahue. "To give you some idea, we had five people speaking Russian, plus two police officers, a security guard and some other guy all speaking English. Finally we found a store employee who spoke some Russian and she got them calmed down a bit when she told them their coach was on the way."

Donahue said the thing that disturbed the players most was the pack of aggressive journalists intent on photographing them.

"They wanted us to stop the journalists, so we had to explain to them that the press is free in this country and we had no control over what they took pictures of. They were absolutely scared to death of the media."

When a coach and an interpreter arrive, the players become very subdued. Gomoliako offers to pay for the gloves but doesn't admit to shoplifting them.

There's a notion that talent will out, meaning if you've got the talent they can't keep you down. It's like believing the good guys always win, but Team Canada is relying on that idea as it faces the first game of the tournament.

"It was bad news when we found out that Jimmy Waite wouldn't be back as goaltender, but I think we can rise to the occasion," says Webster, referring to the next day's game with Norway in the Fire Lake Recreation Centre at Eagle River. He is referring to the fact that Waite, voted most valuable goaltender at last year's tournament in Moscow, and who was playing regularly with the NHL's Chicago Black Hawks, suffered a broken collarbone on December 10 in a game against the Philadelphia Flyers.

"I've told the players you can't dwell on it," says Webster. "It opens up the way for a couple of other guys to be national heroes."

Both Webster and his players believe Canada has the potential to overcome the loss of Waite, including five skaters who have played in the NHL at least briefly.

"It was an unfortunate thing to have happen two days before camp, but we have some good players who can step in," says the Peterborough Petes' defenceman, Corey Foster, who saw action briefly with the New Jersey Devils. Canada has two strong goalies, Stephane Fiset, who had a 3.25 goals-against average last year with the Victoriaville Tigers, and Gus Morschauser, who had a 4.60 average with Kitchener Rangers. Danny Lorenz, who was cut on the final day of training camp in Calgary, has returned to the Seattle Thunderbirds, but will remain on standby in case of injury.

"I am quite comfortable with the goaltending we have. It would be nice to have Waite, but we don't, so we go on from here."

Webster insists that Canada has the size, speed and skill to repeat as world champions. Forwards like Darrin Shannon, Martin Gelinas, Scott Pearson and Rob Brind'Amour are top notch with or without the puck. Others, such as Reggie Savage, Sheldon Kennedy and Mike Ricci, have a sure scoring touch.

"This team is certainly capable of capitalizing on offensive opportunities, but we are also working very hard at the defensive game. We've got a lot of good goal-scorers and guys who grind up and down their wings," said Foster, who has a powerful shot. "It's a good mix."

In fact, Canada has plenty of centres and Webster has converted some of them into wingers, including Brind'Amour, who is having a great year with the Michigan State Spartans, and Ricci, who leads the OHL in goals. Foster skates on a defensive unit that includes Eric Desjardins, who plays with the Montreal Canadiens. Webster particularly loves Ricci's style on the ice.

"He's very smooth," he says. "I think if he were available in the draft this year, he'd go first overall."

There is frost on the grass at Rancho Mirage, but it evaporates immediately as the sun rises over the desert country. Rob conducts the maiden test of his Christmas golf clubs at Laquinta with his dad, then the family lazes in the swimming pool while Grandpa Greenwald cooks the turkey for dinner. Rob eats everything in sight, then tops up with liberal helpings of chocolate log, his favourite dessert, made of chocolate slabs and whipped cream. Afterwards, he steps back into himself and watches, taking them all in, realizing, though it comes as no surprise, that he loves them very much. He sees his dad give his mom a little hug and his heart surges. He feels happiness out of all proportion to the gesture itself because it reminds him suddenly of a time when such a gesture would not have been commonplace. His parents had once separated when his mother became fed up with his dad's continual absences because of his business demands. Those were the most desolate days of his life. He admires his father's success. His father's word means everything to him and here on Christmas Day, he confides his feelings to his diary. Referring to the homesickness he had felt earlier in the season, he writes:

I told Dad that on the phone. He talked to me the way he does and said he thought it was too soon. He even got guys he played with on the Wheat Kings to call and talk to me. He did everything he could to help me through it. It turned out for the better because now I'm more mature and I'm proud about that. My dad helped me get there. It was very tough on Mom, too, when I left. For eight years, until Christine came along, I was her only child. Mom gets very emotional, very excited about some things, but that's just the way she is and I know it was hard for her when I left.

Dad, well Dad always knows what's going on because he played junior hockey and he knows how it feels. Still, he didn't have the experience of moving away from home at 16 because he came from Edmonton, and that's where he played. But I admire people for their guts and he taught me that. The person I most admire is Dad, no problem there. The only thing I don't like about him is the amount of travel he does and the amount of time he spends away from the family. It's all right with me, now. I'm basically grown up and moved away. But my little sister, Christine, he's going to miss her growing up, and I don't think that's fair. I think he should take a break. You can't let business get in the way of the family. That's what I think, anyway.

His friend Chris Larkin later relates an incident that vividly illustrates Rob's feelings for his father.

"Rob met a girl at a dance and for the next year, the year before he went up to the Blades, he went with her everywhere. He spent every minute of spare time with her. He left Kevin and I out in the cold and it was difficult for us to see that happening. He was infatuated with her."

The infatuation continued until the summer, when Chris tried to raise the idea that perhaps the relationship had become excessive.

"He just told me I didn't understand, I'd never felt that way about a girl," says Chris. "Then at a party, Trish came to me and said she wanted to talk, so we went up to a bedroom and she said, 'It's all too much. I want to break up with him, but I don't know how. I don't want to hurt his feelings.' As we were talking, Rob knocked on the door, and when he came in and sat down I said to her, 'Tell him.' She started crying and saying she loved him, but she wanted to be friends, all that stuff. She'd just told me a hundred times she wanted to break up, but when it came to telling him, it got watered down quite a bit. She didn't tell him what she told me.

"Anyway, we were sitting there after she left and although he was upset about the girl, he wasn't *that* upset. So I said, 'There's something else bugging you, isn't there?' That was the kicker. He broke down and cried like a little kid. I went over to him and we hugged each other.

"'Yeah,' he said. 'It's my dad.' He was upset that his dad wasn't spending more time with the family. Even when he was breaking up with his girl, the person he cared about most was his dad."

Now, on this Christmas Day at Rancho Mirage, Rob Lelacheur pauses in his writing. He can pick out each voice; his dad, his mom, Christine, his grandpa Greenwald, his grandma. He listens for a moment and then he makes a last entry for this day.

"I love them a lot," he writes.

o 7

It's the day after Christmas. The tournament begins, and both the Russians and Canadians have a light skate prior to their opening matches. Canada plays Norway at Fire Lake in the afternoon, the Soviets play West Germany in the evening before the big crowd at Sullivan Arena.

After the morning skate, the ever-prying media asks the Soviet coach, Robert Cherenkov, what lessons were learned as a result of the Soviets being forced to settle for the silver during last year's championship on their home ice in Moscow. This question is like waving the proverbial red flag at a bull, which of course is the idea. Cherenkov, who does not appear to fully appreciate the friendly give-and-take of this western innovation, the press conference, looks at the questioner accusingly.

"We enjoy finishing second the same as your Canadians enjoy finishing second," he snaps. "We don't enjoy it at all. Obvious. Nobody enjoys finishing anywhere but first. We finished second on home ice in Moscow. So. We finish first on visitors' ice in Anchorage. We even the score.

"No one can be satisfied with any position other than the position of first place. That's something you always try to achieve . . . but I think we're going to have quite a fight on our hands."

However steamed Cherenkov gets about media questions, The Moscow Express, in the person of Soviet forward Alexandr Mogilny, is steaming for more productive reasons.

The nineteen-year-old from the town of Khbarovsk has

impressively demonstrated during the exhibition against Team U.S.A. and in practice why he was named the most valuable forward at the world championships the previous year in Moscow.

"I feel very good, very strong. Like I could fly," he says, all smiles following the workout. During the Moscow tourney Mogilny had 18 points on nine goals and nine assists, leading all the scorers. That's one more point than Wayne Gretzky got when he led the scorers in 1978, when the championship was held in Hull, Quebec. Today Mogilny is on the ice early and leaves late.

"The work I do now will pay off later," he says. On one play during Friday's exhibition against the Americans, the nineteen-year-old zips around a surprised Adam Burt, then shoots the puck behind the U.S. net-minder, Mark Richards.

"He's got incredible speed," the chagrined Burt observes afterwards. "I just got taken to the cleaners."

But Mogilny sees this sort of performance as commonplace.

"I just try to motivate my teammates and show them that if they work hard, they can score goals too," he says.

When you start with low expectations, you are seldom disappointed. Team Norway proves this in the opening match, which takes place before 370 people, a capacity crowd, at the Fire Lake arena in the small town of Eagle River.

Mike Ricci stands as "O Canada" is played and feels a lightness spread from his stomach to his legs, as if water were being pumped into the veins. He has to take deep breaths, willing the feeling to go away. The puck drops and he begins to feel easier, but it takes a while for his muscles to relax entirely. Here they are in this tiny arena, in this tiny town in one of the remotest places on earth. Only 300-odd people are actually watching at this moment, but what happens in the next two hours will be known within minutes to millions not only in Canada, but in seven other nations as well. He scores at 11:03 on a power play, and the water turns back into blood again, a miracle of psychology.

The American crowd cheers every move Norway makes,

and although the players try to tune them out the noise grates on the ears, rankles the mind. They love underdogs in the U.S., particularly in this part of it, where a distrust of outsiders, including fellow Americans from what they call The Forty-Eight, is ingrained. This is a land of underdogs, who often feel themselves neglected and exploited even—or particularly—by Washington, D.C., and their hearts go out to their fellow-underdogs from Norway.

Still, they spare a few cheers when the Canadians score and even shout Ricci's name, getting it wrong. "Ree-kee, Ree-kee," some chant. "Riss-see, Riss-see," say others.

Into Ricci's mind as he skates to the bench flashes a picture of him conducting the crowd like an orchestra, leading them in a chant to get his name right. "Ree-chee, Ree-chee," he tells them, waving his arms. And they reply, "Ree-kee, Ree-kee" anyway, unimpressed. Oh well, they had trouble with Gretzky's name and Lemieux's, too, he thinks, as the image fades.

Canada wins this first game 7–1, and the Norwegians give thanks.

"To tell the truth, we had visions of Canada really embarrassing us, but that didn't happen," says their coach, Jon Haukeland. "Not when you consider that last year we were the 'B' group and after we won that in Moscow, were allowed to move up.

"It's much better to be playing in the 'A' group, but we aren't unrealistic about it. I tell my boys that if we can finish seventh this year, then improve a bit at a time from year to year, then that's what we expect to do."

Haukeland adds that only this year has more money started to become available for development programs in Norway.

"That started with our success in the 'B' group and now we must go on building from there."

Although the Canadians have it pretty much their own way throughout, the Norwegians are game.

"I think our boys may have given the Canadian Team a bit of a surprise," says Haukeland. "We lost and we lost by a big score, but we are here, playing with the best in the world and we are able to give them a game."

After the game there's uneasiness among the Canadians that they didn't win by a wider margin. This was supposed to be one of those games where the novice, Norway, comes to learn at the feet of the masters; but when it is over it isn't certain who's learned from whom. Events can be rationalized, put down to a combination of opening-night jitters and fine goaltending from Norway, but the players do not kid themselves.

"We learned that Norway has excellent goaltending and we must learn to take fuller advantage of our scoring opportunities," says Webster tactfully, when the game is over. "We had excellent offence, but we've got to work harder at controlling the puck in our own end."

All things considered, not a very impressive start to the series.

In the other afternoon game, Sweden beats Czechoslovakia, 5–3. Then, in the evening, the U.S.S.R. trounces West Germany, 15–0, and the feeling of vague anxiety increases a notch for the Canadians. It will be their turn to meet West Germany tomorrow and it is now no longer just a question of winning. It's a question of winning and by how much.

Tracey Katelnikoff is fed up. This is the last straw. He's waiting in the trainer's room for Jeff Thomas, but he can't find him. Casper's done his disappearing act again. Tracey's resentment has been simmering all during the Saskatchewan Cup tournament, which has been taking place in Saskatoon at the same time that the world Junior tourney is taking place in Anchorage. Teams from Russia and Czechoslovakia are playing Team Canada at SaskPlace, home of the Blades. Thomas has been helping the various trainers, although he has no connection with the teams, and this has caused friction among his own players.

Collin Bauer had already snarled at Thomas earlier in the week. "You suck around Team Canada, the Russians and the

Czechs," he complains. "You do Team Canada's laundry and ours is still wet."

Earlier, Thomas taped the wrist Tracey injured in Moose Jaw, but he has taped it too tight, cutting off the circulation, making the hand ache as if it were going to explode. You ask him to fix it and he gets it too loose, grumbles Tracey to himself. It's either one thing or the other, too tight or too loose. There was the time he'd asked before a game to have a rivet repaired in a shoulder pad. When he went to put the pads on just before game time, he found they were still not repaired. Thomas had returned them to their peg without repairing them. Tracey had been forced to use an old pair of shoulder pads during the game. Then there'd been the incident of the hockey sticks. Canadiens is the brand preferred by most of the left-handed shooters on the team, Tracey among them. In fact, only three guys on the team shoot right. Just before Christmas, they'd begun to run short of Canadiens and when players inquired, Thomas said he had no more. Ill feelings reached a boil when players discovered a bundle stashed in one of the arena offices.

Tracey starts retaping himself, resenting as he does so that he often ends up taping his own wrist. He knows that things like this, small upsets, should not be happening on the day of a game. Two hours from now the Blades meet the Spokane Chiefs in their first post-holiday game and now, when he should be deep into the pre-game rhythm, he is having trouble focusing. His feelings about Thomas are part of the reason, but there's more to it than that, and he can't put his finger on what it is. All he knows is that he does not have the feeling. The Blades manage a win, 9–8, but the game is sloppy and disjointed and Tracey's play matches that of his fellows.

But in Anchorage Mike Ricci feels right. Minutes before game time, at Sullivan Arena, he chews his jersey front as they play the anthems of Canada and the U.S. Then he taps his stick on the dot at centre ice, skates back to the bench and sits down in front of Tom Webster as the puck is dropped. The third game of the world Junior championships is under way. Earlier in the day the Soviets have beaten the Swedes 9–3, and the Czechs will beat West Germany 9–1. The Canadians beat the Germans 7–4, so now, with their third game, a win over the U.S. means that only they and the Russians will have preserved their perfect records.

Team U.S.A. loses the opening face-off, but to hear the crowd they might have won not only the face-off but the game and the world championship beside. Each time an American player touches the puck the fans go wild, the sound at ice level battering the players' ears. There are 6,200 on hand, a full house. Still, overpowering as they are, their commotion is merely sound and fury, nothing more. Ricci knows this and feels it from the moment he enters the arena.

"I feel good," he says. "I feel really good." So do his team-mates, dominating play from the start. At ice level, the sounds of cheering partisans buffets the Canadians, but the faces of the players are calm. Their looks say they're in con-trol. On this night, there is a feeling of rightness and you can see it pass among them, rippling outwards to encompass them all.

The feeling is a private thing, something not apparent to outsiders, and thus deceptive. The fans, even the American team, are taken in. From the stands, it looks as if the Canadians are hanging on, flirting with disaster, that the Americans are dominating the game. Stephane Fiset stops shot after shot and it seems only a matter of time before the first puck will end up behind him. But at ice level the Canadian calmness, the sense of control, prevails. It is not that Fiset has easy shots to stop; in fact he is spectacular in frustrating the Americans. But he has something else going for him and although every player on the ice, of either team, would recognize it, tonight it is his secret, his and his team-mates'.

"*J'ai le feeling*," he says and on this night, that says every-thing, despite what *appears* to be happening on the ice. Later, not wishing to speak of something so nebulous as feel-ings, Webster chooses to talk about what meets the eye, rather than what meets the heart.

"This is more like it," says Webster. "In the earlier two

games, I wanted them to concentrate on their offence and the defence suffered. You can see the benefits now, so I think it paid off. I wouldn't be talking this way, maybe, if we hadn't had some great goaltending. Stephane is hot tonight."

This obfuscation of Webster's is understandable, for what seems to be happening and what is happening are two different things. What seems to be the case is that Canada is lucky not to come out of the first period behind, 4–2, instead of leading, 2–0. Fiset makes 13 saves to five for the U.S. It looks as if the predictions of a chippy game are going to come true 30 seconds into the first period when U.S. forward Bill Guerin draws two minutes for high-sticking after ramming Kennedy into the boards. The power play sees Ricci come close, but before Team Canada has a chance to really organize itself Lambert is sent off for tripping. Canada's first goal comes at 5:56 after Foster's shot was first deflected by the U.S. goalie, Jason Glickman. But Reggie Savage came up with the rebound, scoring his second of the series, to go with three assists.

At 13:48 of the first period the Peterborough connection clicks, with Ricci taking a short pass from Foster, sneaking behind the net and stuffing it in under Glickman's stick. After the first two games Team Canada has seen nine of the twelve forwards score. The so-called first line of Cassels-Gelinas-Kennedy have not scored a goal among them. Team Canada scorers are Savage, with two; Ricci, who as in each previous game scores the winning goal; Sheldon Kennedy and Rob Cimetta. The U.S. scorer is Jeremy Roenick.

The second period starts with the U.S. holding much of the play in the Canadian end and again Fiset's fast glove saves them, particularly on a sizzling slapshot from Guerin. Canada is derailed momentarily on a nice pass from Darrin Shannon in the corner, which Andrew Cassels almost puts in the net. But time and time again Fiset comes up with big saves as the entire team seems to come unglued in front of him. It takes Savage, with his second of the game on a short pass from Cimetta, to slow the Americans. Kennedy follows up in the dying minutes of the period, with Eric Desjardins and Savage getting the assists.

In the third, Roenick, the Maryland native who plays for the Hull Olympiques, scores the Americans' only goal. He is assisted by Mike Modano, of Westland, Michigan, who plays for the Prince Albert Raiders of the WHL. The year before, Modano has become the first U.S. native ever to be picked first overall, by the Minnesota North Stars, in the NHL Entry Draft. Canada completes the scoring with a goal by Cimetta.

Throughout, the crowd has been delirious, cheering and cheering, but even their noisy efforts are not enough to please everyone. In one section, a man in a coonskin hat exhorts the crowd, getting angrier and angrier as the Canadians keep building the score.

"I fought in Viet Nam!" he screams. "I'm not afraid to cheer for America! I'm pr-o-o-u-u-d to be an American! What's the matter with you people? Cheer, dammit, CHEER!" The hoarse fans nearby fall silent, intimidated it seems as much by his headgear as by his incessant nagging. The hat is fashioned from an entire pelt and it looks like the raccoon is poised on his head, ready to attack. The fans look at the hat, look at the angry man, a small oasis of silence in the desert of chaos.

The score is 5–1 as the Canadians file off to the dressing-room, and Mike Ricci makes the observation that must be in all their minds.

"It may have *looked* like they outplayed us," he says. "But look at the score. It didn't *feel* like it."

8

This is not a happy New Year's Eve for Team Canada. The players file into the lobby of the Sheraton, heading silently to the elevator and entering it silently. As it takes them to their rooms on the fifth floor, they stare straight ahead, looking at the neck of the player in front, looking at the door. They are angry and disillusioned, having just been exposed to what amounts to a law at international hockey tournaments; they have been done in not by a team but by a Russian referee. The feeling of invincibility that they experienced in their victory over the U.S. has fled their psyches. Bad experiences with European officials are nothing new for Canadian teams and each seems to have its own story. In this one, Soviet referee Viktor Gubernatorov robs Rob Brind'Amour of a goal at the seven-minute mark of their game against Sweden.

The referee's ruling, that Brind'Amour put the puck in the net with his glove, especially rankles in light of how the game was played. Canada actually dominated the play and led for most of the game. Sweden finally tied it with a goal by Markus Akerblom at 16:59 of the third. Then Akerblom did it again with 27 seconds remaining and the Swedes won, 5–4.

"That was a goal," says Webster, his voice still strangling an hour after the game. Then, to allay any doubt that he means it, he says it again, biting off each word: "That. Was. A. Goal.

"The referee cost us at least a tie and probably the win. When the goal was called back, our team lost concentration and Markus got his second goal. Why they would have a Russian referee for a critical game that will eventually affect the Russians, I just can't understand. We are going to take

this up at the directors' meeting because we don't want that
referee again."

Gubernatorov claims the goal went into Brind'Amour's
glove, that Brind'Amour closed his glove around it and then
threw it into the net. But both the official game video and a
CBC tape show none of this happened. The puck went in off
Brind'Amour's stick and should have been a goal. Adding to
the anger and frustration is the knowledge that none of this
means anything in international competition, where no game
result has ever been changed, no matter how blatant has
been the official malfeasance. The disallowance of obvious
goals is a common practice among East Bloc referees.

Ricci is not comforted by the fact that he scored on a power play in the second period, and assisted on Cimetta's in the
third.

"It is bad enough when you lose in the normal way," he
says and then stops because he can't really find words to
reveal his feeling. "It's unfair, isn't it?" he finally says. "The
referee, right now, he knows himself it's unfair. I guess that
has to be enough."

It has to be enough, but it isn't.

Don Meehan sits in the Calista Café earlier in the day and
allows that, generally speaking, he is not inordinately concerned with what people say about him. He makes the
observation in the knowledge that, no matter how much
some say about him, it isn't enough. And alternatively, there
are others, who, no matter how little they say, say too much.

But whatever they say or don't say, the man they're talking
about is fast becoming the leading agent in hockey and even
now the dominant representative of Junior players.
Supporters, who tend to be his clients, say he's a friend, con-
fidant, big brother. He's the man with the golden pen.

His critics, who tend to be other agents, acknowledge that
in just six and a half years he's grown to be one of the biggest
of the big-time player agents, but as for the golden pen, let's
see now. Shark with the golden teeth might be closer to the
truth. Critics of Meehan don't say that, exactly. Ask why they

criticize Meehan and they tend to become tongue-tied. Sorting through how Meehan is regarded by his peers becomes a problem of sorting through what they don't say more than what they do say. You end up with the impression that if his success were smaller, his fan club would be bigger.

"I don't think I like that, being thought of as a shark," says Meehan, which reveals an interesting facet both of human nature and the writer's search for metaphor. Alan Eagleson, at one time the biggest fish in the agents' sea, gloried in being known as The Eagle, one of the largest predators in the air. Nobody, it seems, minds being regarded as an eagle.

But look in the sea for the biggest predator and you come up with the shark, a metaphorical pariah. Nonetheless, Meehan's agency, as the world championship is played, represents 10 of the top 21 Juniors listed in Central Scouting's mid-season report. Among them is Patrice Brisebois. Eight of those ten are expected to go in the first round of the Entry Draft on June 17. He is representing 40 Juniors altogether, although not all will end up being drafted. By comparison, the biggest player agency overall is Rick Curran's Branada Sports Group, which represents about 70 NHL players.

Curran is here in Anchorage, as is a smaller competitor from Winnipeg, Don Baizley. Baizley's most famous client is Edmonton's Jari Kurri and he specializes in European players, including all of the Finns. Anton Thun, the Toronto lawyer who represents the families of John Tanner and Mike Ricci, is not here and neither is the host of other agents who guard the business interests of big-time hockey players or those who are soon to be so. Meehan is the man when it comes to Junior hockey. While most agents start with lots of friends and little else, they do not generally start with enemies. Those come later. Don Meehan, perhaps typically, is somewhat different. His first client was the New York Islanders' star Pat Lafontaine, who has since become Meehan's very dear friend. But the signing of Lafontaine, his first coup, earned Meehan his first enemy of sorts; the former king of the agents, Bill Watters, who recently sold out to Curran. To this day, Watters appears to believe that the less said about Meehan, the better.

"Don Meehan has the right to earn a living," says Watters, biting off the words. He once said the only reason Meehan was able to sign Lafontaine was by agreeing to work for nothing.

"It hurt then and it hurts now," says Meehan, although, if you visit his office, you can see the hurt must be diminished somewhat every time he looks at the framed gallery of auto-graphed photos that cover most of an entire wall. "Besides, it wasn't true."

Watters backs away very slightly now from that old accusa-tion. "I wish I hadn't said that." He pointedly still does not retract it. "I didn't need the hassle."

Ron Salcer of Los Angeles, for instance, sounds like he's bitten into a Florida orange, but he manages a few words: "He is aggressive . . . and he works hard." Salcer makes a choking sound as if he might have a pip in his windpipe. In terms of number of clients, Salcer is small fry.

Another critic of Don Meehan is Edmonton agent Rick Winter, who, with Salcer and former National Football League Players' Association president Ed Garvey, has been intent on discrediting Eagleson as president of the NHL Player's Association.

"I think what they really want is to pick up a few clients along the way," says Meehan, such waspishness strengthened by a letter he will eventually receive from Winter. In it Winter chides Meehan for being one of a "limited number" of agents not on record as supporting the bid to unseat Eagleson. Winter says if he does not get Meehan's support, his name will be published in a newsletter and circulated to NHL players.

"That kind of ultimatum went out with the McCarthy Era," says Meehan testily. "I don't support them against Eagleson and they can say I'm a 'communist' all they want. That doesn't make me a communist."

This infighting among agents is not unusual. Now, as the world championship continues, Watters may hesitate to let Meehan's name pass his lips, but he does put the infighting into perspective. He points out that he got out of the field partly because of the lengths other agents will go to in winkling away hard-won clients.

"There is no honour among thieves," he says, being careful to mention no names and, interestingly, giving the impression that he does not include Meehan. "But sign a player in Toronto; then, when he moves to, say, L.A., someone will be rapping on his door. And that someone will keep rapping until he convinces the player he can't be represented in L.A. by an agent in Toronto. If a player moves to Chicago, it'll be someone in Chicago doing the rapping. Or Edmonton. Or Vancouver."

Players may occasionally turn snake in the grass, biting the hands that loan them money, by switching agents before their loans are paid back. Watters refers to this as the "generic example," indicating that it happens so often that the example is easily recognized. Meehan admits this sort of thing has also happened to him, although infrequently.

"Mainly, people repay fair treatment with fairness," he says, but still. . . . In a world populated by eagles, sharks and snakes in the grass, it's a wonder Meehan has become so successful. He became interested in agenting while articling at a law firm where Eagleson was a partner. Two years after Eagleson left to head the NHLPA, Meehan, along with Bob Watson and Jerry Ublansky, set up the player agency, Newport, and the law firm of Watson, Ublansky and Meehan. The two firms, Newport and Watson Ublansky, now have twenty-two people on staff.

Meehan, though exceedingly busy with the affairs of the stars of today and tomorrow, claims he's not rich. He warns that if one goes to the trouble of multiplying his number of NHLers, 55, by the average NHL salary, $180,000, and then taking his normal flat fee of five percent, one would get the wrong answer. Many of his clients are starting their careers and thus make less than the average. The salaries of players like Gretzky inflate the average, anyway. A Junior in the top 21 gets an average $100,000 signing bonus, but that doesn't help much, either, in figuring out what a top player agent makes in relation to the players. Whatever that is, Meehan does point out that his firm was untainted by profit for the first five years of its existence.

"And I don't have much money now," he says. He has the air when discussing money of one who doesn't have anything against it, exactly, but what he's in business for is the business itself. And the business itself boils down to his relationship with his clients. "They are great people," he says. "I have developed some fine relationships over the years."

His friendship with Lafontaine says a lot about him.

"Donny was an usher at my wedding," says Lafontaine. "When we chose him as my agent when I was seventeen it was one of the best decisions of my career. But before being a great agent, he is a greater friend. I am very biased on the subject of Donny Meehan."

There is a buzz around the Calista Café as agents and scouts, coaches and players replay the previous day's 3–2 victory by the Soviets over the Swedes. In fact, heads actually began shaking soon after Soviet forward Sergei Fedorov scored what turned out to be the winning goal. That accomplishment was complicated by the fact that when Federov scored, there were two pucks on the ice. The second puck appeared mysteriously in front of the Soviet net as if out of nowhere.

One puck was the focal point of a scramble in one of the Soviet corners, and as it was cleared out of the corner, puck number two simultaneously went into the net, apparently tying the score 3–3.

"We will launch a protest," says Swedish coach Claes-Goran Wallin, calm, despite the frustrating experience of the previous evening. "But I want it clear that we are not protesting to get two points. We are protesting to make sure that the game was won in the right way."

Soviet coach Robert Cherenkov is as always obscure as to the Soviet attitude. "I think we put the pressure on and caused confusion," he says, meaning no one knows exactly what.

Since no IIHF officials are taking a coffee break, Team U.S.A. public relations man Mike Schroeder is pressed into service as sort of an unofficial spokesman. "It was not readily apparent looking at the video where the second puck came from," he admits. "But one thing's certain, the IIHF will have to make a ruling quickly."

While we await this enlightenment, there are three schools of thought about the extra puck: It came out of the Soviet goalie's glove; a fan threw it on the ice; or a Swedish player had it in his glove.

The reason no IIHF officials are in the coffee shop is that they are upstairs in a penthouse meeting-room. There, they decide that no disciplinary action will be taken in the case of the magical extra puck. Present at the lengthy meeting are representatives from each competing country, plus the IIHF tournament director, Gyorgy Pasztor.

"The game results will stand," Pasztor says, giving some further explication of events in the third period when Sweden's Patrick Erickson scored what looked like the tying goal. "There will be no punishment of any team or player if one particular player placed the puck on the ice."

The Swedes have the right to protest to the IIHF disciplinary committee, and when the news filters downstairs coach Wallin says they will.

"The second puck came from someplace," says Wallin. "This does not seem to answer where the puck came from or whether the puck with which the disallowed goal was scored was the game puck. If we lost the game, that's fine. But we want to be sure we lost fairly."

The red light came on and then a second puck appeared in the corner. Referee Steve Piotrowski waved off the Erickson goal. Swedish assistant coach Lars Oberg says the Swedish players on the ice saw the extra puck come from the glove of the Soviet goalie, Aleksei Ivashkin.

"If it was a Soviet transgression, the goal should count," he admonishes his listeners. The Russians, who overcame a 2–1 third-period deficit, don't agree. Ivashkin says he was watching his defencemen skate with the original puck.

"All of a sudden, the other puck was inside the net," he says. "Maybe someone from the Swedish team threw it there."

Schroeder says a videotape of the game was inconclusive, but it seemed the second puck came into play after Soviet defenceman Alexandr Godynuk went down in the slot. When told of a theory that Godynuk may have dropped the puck to force a stoppage in play, Wallin said that was his idea all along.

Later, the subject revives when Frank Nosek, president of the Anchorage Organizing Committee, who has participated in the official meeting, offers a further insight.

"We have determined that the puck came from one of the players on the ice," he says. "But all we have power to do is discipline the player responsible. However, since we don't know who did it, our hands are tied."

He also points out that although Sweden is entitled to protest, the protest must first be made through the Swedish Hockey Federation, who can protest to the IIHF, who in the fullness of time can rule on the result.

"By then, we'll all be old and grey," he says.

The Soviets take themselves very seriously, not given much to smiling, but goalie Aleksei Ivashkin does try. He was in goal for the infamous two-puck game.

Ivashkin is backup the next night for a 10–0 win against Norway, and he takes time to do some souvenir-hunting between the first and second periods. When he indicates to linesman John Malinosky that he wants a puck to take home, John fixes him with a severe look and hands one over.

"Just be sure you don't drop this one on the ice," he says, poker-faced. Then, when Ivashkin isn't sure whether to take him seriously, Malinosky smiles. Ivashkin thinks about it for a moment, then hesitantly returns the smile.

The night before all of this activity in Alaska, the Blades visit the Swift Current Broncos. It is the last time they will visit Swift Current this season. It turns out to be a crucial game for the Blades, even though they lose it 7–5. Tracey has a goal, but what makes the game important to the team is the performance of goalie Mike Greenlay in his first appearance with the team. He stops forty-three shots on the night and would have won the game if the Blades had given him better support.

"He reminds me of what Sugar Ray Leonard once said," says Marcel Comeau. "If you want to see a great fighter, look at how he is when he's getting whipped. Greenlay looked good tonight when he was getting whipped."

Greenlay's ability to remain undaunted by the formidable scoring power of the Broncos will prove to be crucially important to the Blades by season's end.

This night, December 30, is also the second anniversary of a tragedy on the Swift Current team, the night four Broncos died in a highway accident just outside of town. Rob knew some of them personally, Tracey all of them. Players from both teams call up their memories as two minutes' silence is observed. A glass case in the lobby of the Civic Centre displays their sweaters and pictures: number 9, Scott Kruger, nineteen, Swift Current; number 22, Chris Mantyka, nineteen, Saskatoon; number 8, Trent Kresse, twenty, Kindersley; number 11, Brent Ruff, sixteen, Warburg, Alberta.

"This is the last picture of us all together," says Scott Kruger's mother, Louise, sitting in her living-room. She gazes at the picture for a moment, then stifles a sob and turns her head away. "He was such a beauty," she whispers. "Such a beauty."

She speaks lovingly then of a boy with an indomitable love of hockey and a clear mission in his life: "I've seen him sneak out of the house when he was very small and we'd find him playing hockey in the yard in his pyjamas. He was just so much fun."

The twins, Trevor and Darren, twenty, younger brothers of Scott and also Bronco teammates, are relaxing at home before their game with the Blades. Trevor is a goalie; Darren is a defenceman. The eldest son, Shayne, twenty-four, still plays hockey, although he has never played at the Junior A level.

"I'm a heck of a golfer though," he says. His father, Walter, who prefers his nickname, Scoof, looks at him incredulously.

"Your handicap must have dropped when I wasn't looking," he says.

"Don't worry about my handicap," says Shayne. "You just worry about your own, come to handicaps."

They laugh again, joking easily and often with each other.

"If it wasn't for my friends, getting together to shoot pool or have a beer or just talk, I don't know what I would have done," Scoof says later in his quiet way, referring to the dark days following Scott's death. "You learn how important your friends are when a thing like that happens."

Later, in the arena as the Blades and Broncos warm up, Louise remembers other details of those days.

"I worked like crazy after it happened," she says. "Lots of working and lots of praying. I just couldn't believe it. Waking up in the morning and he isn't there. I could never get used to that. So I worked and I worked and I prayed and after a while I knew it had happened and I knew he wasn't there. For me, working is like peace. . . ."

In the Broncos' locker-room, an hour before game time, the twins remember, too.

"It lets you know that it can happen to you," says Darren, as Trevor nods. "That's something you don't think about much when you're young. But when a thing like this happens, then you think about it. And it changes you."

Anger. Frustration. Helplessness. These sometimes seem to be the stock-in-trade of the dreamer. Mike Ricci feels all of these emotions on the first day of the New Year, as Team Canada struggles with Czechoslovakia.

There are now just two matches left to play for Canada, against Finland, which should be a pushover, and the grand finale against the Soviets, which most certainly will not. Canada is still a contender for all the medals, but at this moment Ricci does not think so far ahead. He is preoccupied solely with the here and now. We can either *win* this game or *lose* this game, he thinks, the italics taking form in his mind. He does not think in terms of tying. Tying is a possibility but it is really the absence of something rather than the presence of it. It is the failure to win, not the success of avoiding a loss. It's like not kissing your girlfriend goodnight. It's always possible that you won't but not because you don't intend to. If you don't kiss your girlfriend goodnight it's because you've failed, somehow, not because you've succeeded.

As the game grinds on, Ricci senses failure, and although he has been seventeen for a matter of two months he's still old enough in the ways of his chosen path to recognize the sour and bitter feeling in his gut. In fact, he personally has no reason to expect failure at all. He has had a fine series and will end up with five goals and two assists, twenty-eighth out of 164 in points ranking. But Ricci, young as he is, takes responsibility not just for himself, but for the entire team. His unselfishness and his superior abilities act as catalysts on his teammates. Even tonight, when Team Canada seems distracted and overwhelmed by the Czechs, Ricci several times succeeds in providing a focal point around which the team rallies. But the rallies spark, then fizzle, and Ricci regards their failure as the result of a personal weakness. I can't seem to do the right thing, he thinks. I can't seem to get it going.

Team Canada tries everything before the meagre crowd of 2,150, including the risky move of challenging the legality of a Czech stick in the dying minutes, but all that comes of that is a two-minute delay-of-game penalty. The Czechs are all over the Canadians, trigger-happy, shooting and shooting.

As the game begins, it looks like Canada has the momentum. Ricci out-manoeuvres several Czechs to dig the puck out of the corner in a display of sheer determination and dazzling stickwork. But around the two-minute mark the Czechs start to box the Canadians in their own zone. Robert Holik finally opens the scoring for Czechoslovakia at 5:20 and from then on, although Team Canada has individual players making spectacular moves, their efforts come to little.

Cimetta finally evens Canada's score at 4:02 of the second, but the team simply can't launch an attack after that. Holik scores his second to put the Czechs ahead, 2–1 at 15:32 and

that's how matters stand until Cimetta's second goal with just
32 seconds left in the game. Canada has a tie and that tie has
cost them the gold medal. They are still in contention for the
silver and bronze, but the loss of a chance at the gold hurts.

As the teams file off the ice after the game, Ricci is acutely
aware that just two people, Holik and Cimetta, are responsible for all of the scoring. The players undress, shower, dress
again, talk, do the dozens of things they routinely do after
every game. And although Ricci takes part, he is also replaying the game in his mind. He is displeased with his own performance, unable to forget that one goal from him would
have meant a win instead of a tie. Although there are five
other potential scorers on the ice at any given time, twenty
potential scorers in all, Ricci does not believe that this
relieves him of responsibility. He goes over the game in his
mind not, once the initial disappointment subsides, to blame
himself. He is ruthlessly assessing his own performance so it
will be better the next time, so he won't make the same mistake twice. "If I had scored just one goal, we could still have
a shot at the gold." The thought keeps coming into his mind.
He cannot avoid it. The fact that any other member of the
team could have scored a goal, too, doesn't even occur to
him.

Tanner's frustration deepens as he recounts the events of the
last few days. The team misses Ricci and seems convinced
that it can't win without him. But the dark thread that runs
through John's thoughts is his growing sense of alienation
from his teammates. There can be no emotion stronger or
hurt more painful for a young hockey player. He depends on
his teammates for so much: for friendship, laughter, fun,
strength—in short for virtually all of his emotional needs. He
alternately pretends that he doesn't care, or that it isn't happening, or that other things are more important. John carries
the burden of genius, and the dark side of genius is melan-
choly. He writes:

> It's both a letdown and a blessing now that I'm back in
> Peterborough. At the same time that I like to live at

home with my family, I couldn't wait to return to the ice. I want to make the second half of the season twice as good as the first. And I think I gave Dick that message today in practice. I was stopping everything and he gave me tomorrow night's big game against Oshawa. We need to beat them, if not for first place, then for desperately needed confidence. I could sense the familiar feeling in the room today. The guys don't believe we can win without Ricci or Foster, or Tie Domi [injured], so it'll be two tough games we have to play in one. My mother was very sad to see me leave this time, particularly because I was returning to Lorna [billet], who gets to see me more than she does. She doesn't believe that it's fair; she wishes I had never left home and just gone to school. In one way, I wish I could've stayed home, too. But then again, destiny calls.

9

Mike Ricci's parents tell him he began to talk at nine months, the same age he learned to walk. Shortly after this milestone, he began to wear skates around the house. A coach had seen him playing with a hockey stick at an arena, while one of his older brothers, Maurice or Bruno, finished a game. The coach went to Mario Ricci, told him his son showed great talent and suggested the boy wear skates around the house, to strengthen his ankles and improve his balance. Little Mike took to the idea and from then on it was hard to get him to take the skates off. As a result, the first time he actually stepped on the ice, at about two, he was able to skate.

"I don't remember Michael being much of a baby," Anna Ricci says. "He knew what he wanted from the moment he was born."

These snippets flash through Ricci's mind even as the anthems are being played for this final game of the world Junior championship against the Soviet Union. He doesn't know whether he was born knowing what he wanted, but he knows what he wants now. It has been drummed into the team's players, by the media and again by team officials, that Canada can still win a silver medal if it beats the Soviets. The Canadians can win a bronze, they are told, even if they lose. They don't want to accept a bronze; they want to win the silver. The fact they can't get the gold makes beating the Soviets, the gold medallists, that much more important.

The silver dream glimmers throughout the first period,

162

although there is the hint of nightmare lurking. The Red Machine swarms over the underdog Canadians from the opening face-off, but these jitters are brought under control after a player—it sounds like Sheldon Kennedy, who helped beat the Russians the previous year—makes a caustic observation.

"Geez, ladies, get a grip on your purses," he says. "This is being televised back home, ya know, so let's pull ourselves together. Let's start the show!"

They like that, the idea of getting the show on the road, showtime, the big leagues. Ricci knows this is a very difficult game, mentally and physically. The Soviets are one of those teams who are beatable only if you are exactly on, if both aspects are precisely right. They have a high skill level. They have big players. They are strong and fast. Some of them are real bruisers, too, which is tough. Sergei Gomolaiko, for instance, star of the Great Shoplifting Caper, is 223 pounds, six foot four or something, a real ox. Running into him would be like running into a tank.

Team Canada is a bit disorganized, taking risks on the attack but staying out of trouble. Then, suddenly, Ricci can feel his team sag, ever so slightly. Dimitry Kristich grabs the puck from the neutral zone, moves across the blue line and scores from the point. It is one goal, just one goal, nothing to panic over. The period is less than half over, so there is lots of time. But Ricci senses there is a panic there, too, just waiting, lurking. It is born of a combination of several things; the Soviets have a better record in the series. They are the favourites. And looming over all is what amounts to almost an unspoken conviction that the boys from Moscow are somehow like bogeymen and that they'll get you, one way or another, no matter what.

Yet the Canadians are still part of the game, still dangerous themselves. They prove this, striking for the tying goal when Andrew Cassels scores at 18:30. As the first period ends, Mike smiles grimly.

We can get the silver, he thinks. It's there for us. It's there if we want it. Do we want it enough? For a hockey player, the answer is always the same. Do you want to win? Then win. That's your proof. Lose, and it's your own fault. You didn't want to win enough.

Mike Ricci knows his own answer. But he does not know the answer in the heart of his teammates. So he worries, as the first period ends, 1–1.

Tracey Katelnikoff and Rob Lelacheur begin watching the game in a mood of detached excitement, but the detachment changes fairly quickly. Katelnikoff watches part of the first period, then into about eight minutes of the second when he can't stand it anymore, turns off the TV and heads out on the town. This is one of those rare nights when there's no game and no curfew, and the team members, in various ways, make the most of it. Tracey has an early dinner at the home of his girlfriend, Deanna Darling, something they don't normally have time to do. After they watch a bit of the match, Deanna wants to study and Tracey has arranged to meet some of the guys at The Pat, a bar at the Patricia Hotel in Saskatoon. Some of them look like they might have been to Esmeralda's first, sampling the $1 tequila specials. They all eat too much, but for the most part they drink sparingly. A chance to unwind, a change of pace. To take it too far would undo it. There is no shortage of girls at the bar, but unless they're buying they don't get far with the handsome players.

It's not that the lads are woman-proof, because many of them will bemoan their lost opportunities for weeks to come. The fact is they have no money. Rookies get $120 a month plus room and board, second-year players, $160; third year, $200. The over-age players, of whom there can never be more than three, usually two in Quebec and Ontario, get a whopping $600. But even with that kind of money, there's no time.

"If you're going to play hockey, that's the price," says Katelnikoff. Someone at the bar, impressed by the feminine talent, has just asked him if he never feels like going AWOL to take advantage of what's on offer. Tracey looks at the barfly almost pityingly, knowing that to an outsider the truth sounds patronizing. He knows that few people ever learn to delay gratification in pursuit of the larger goal.

Down the bar, Rob Lelacheur demonstrates the lengths to which players will go in self-denial, in delaying gratification, if it compromises the larger goal in even a minor way. Dave Struch, with whom Rob is having a beer, suddenly decides he wants a dish of ice cream.

"Hey, that sounds great," says Rob. Then his face falls as he remembers that he can't have any himself because he already had his quota earlier in the day. Rob finds himself telling about a trip he and his peewee team made to L.A.

"I don't remember a whole lot about the hockey," he says. "We stayed up all night and swam all day. I think the hockey was an afterthought. In fact I played house league that year, because if I'd played rep it would have meant missing the trip."

The teammates listen enthralled to these tales of a carefree childhood, memories of actually staying up all night and swimming all day. Rob remembers the motel at which he and his family stayed was reputed to be the same one where Chevy Chase made a movie.

"What movie?" asks a doubter, and of course suddenly he can't remember.

"Well, I told you I don't remember much about the trip," says Lelacheur. He does recall that besides St Albert, there were two California teams, one from Trois-Rivières, one from Utah.

"The one from Three Rivers won," says Lelacheur. "That's another thing I remember. They were the only team that came to play hockey. They even had a curfew."

It's the start of the second period in Anchorage. The Canadians keep on trying, never quitting for a minute, but even their eagerness works against them. They keep boring in, using their bodies against the Soviets. Foster lays out a Soviet player on the ice, but that draws a penalty, two minutes for slashing. Yves Racine, a minute later, gets two more minutes for interference. But that makes Canada two men short against the buzzing Soviets, an impossible handicap. Alexandr Mogilny scores again, four seconds before Foster's penalty expires and then Roman Oksuta, 11 seconds before Racine returns. Ricci scores at 18:30 to make it 6–2 to end a devastating second period.

A thoughtful Tom Webster indulges in a bit of group analysis in the dressing-room as the period ends.

"I think the defence let Fiset down," he says, referring to several unnecessary penalties, including two two-man advantages the Soviets enjoyed in the first period. He is forced to give the goalie a rest midway in the period, sending in Gus Morschauser, his first appearance since Canada beat West Germany 7–4 in the second game. "You can only ask a guy to kill so many penalties for you and he gets tired. There were times, after the first period, you let the Soviets skate over you. There can be no letup in a series like this. I think you've learned that and when you return to your teams, you'll be better players for it."

Then Webster pauses and smiles across the room at his players. "I may sound critical," he says. "But the fact is I'm very, very proud of you all."

As Mike Ricci tries to deal with the Soviets, John Tanner deals, in his diary, with feelings evoked by some of his school marks and other problems of life in Peterborough:

> I went to school, but again was lost to thoughts of hockey. I don't comprehend even a tidbit of chemistry, and I know I'll end up dropping it. It seems I just don't care too much about it. History, on the other hand, looks like it might be a high mark, as I believe I have over 80 percent in it and I generally do well on a final exam. I enjoy the course, not only because I like the facts of history, but also because of the opinions that the teacher allows us to express. Those kind of participatory teachers are a rarity among their well-paid (overpaid) profession.
>
> Had a mediocre practice today and won't start in tomorrow's game vs. the Toronto Marlboros, in Peterborough. That's some surprise, after Sunday's game, the loss to Belleville. I talked about moving with

Dick today and he's narrowed it down to two; the Perrys, where Jamie Pegg lives, and the Emerys, where Rob Wilson lives. I'd rather live in town with the Perrys but on the other hand, I hear Larry and Sherrin Emery are nice people, too, so it doesn't matter. Dick wanted me to move in with a complete loonie before—a guy known for his heavy use of pot and hash. No thanks, Dick.

I can't stand it when some players won't show any respect for the goalies in practice; I feel like Rodney Dangerfield sometimes. Today, Paul Mitton just missed my head twice from close-up range and Dan Brown, as per usual, hit it. It not only aggravates a goalie, but in practice, it impairs concentration. And like Dryden aptly stated: "I get scared out there." In a game, no such fear exists ever, but in the looser, less important confines of practice, such is not the case. One good (or bad, it depends how you look at it) hit could put me out for a long time. I guess I understand why we goalies are considered crazy and flaky, because I am.

In Anchorage, the Canadians trail 6–2 as the third period starts. Sergei Fedorov makes it 7–2 at 50 seconds of the third, the third power-play goal against Team Canada. From that point on, the U.S.S.R. plays it safe. Remote as the Canadians' chances of overcoming the 7–2 deficit are, the Soviets make them even more so. They stop trying to attack and simply concentrate on defence, dumping the puck back into the Canadian zone. The Canadians, tired and frustrated, launch attack after attack, but every one is thwarted. The score remains 7–2 as the game ends. Still, on the bench, the feeling of disappointment is tempered slightly by one thought: "At least we'll get a bronze."

The Canada-Soviet game is broadcast in Montreal starting at 11 p.m., and although it won't be over until about 2 a.m. Patrice Brisebois does not intend to miss a bit of it. The Titans have been doing well in his absence with the knee injury that cost him a berth in Anchorage. Patrice is the kind of person who takes as much satisfaction in the team's success without him as he would if he were playing. The day after New Year's, Claude LaPointe has turned in a dazzling effort in defeating St Jean 7–4.

"A whole game for Claude!" exults Patrice. "Five goals and one assist! He stole the star of the game!" Patrice's enthusiasm is too great for proper expression in English. It does not express the feeling. *Il était extraordinaire, de toute beauté*. He was extraordinary, a thing of beauty. "He gave them a piece of skating the Castor defence will long remember!"

However, his enforced holidays have held their share of worries. His knee will keep him out of action for another month. Although the doctors are reassuring, no athlete ever takes his body for granted, particularly where surgery is involved. There's a definite sense of relief when later he's able to tell his diary that the problem is not as serious as he had feared. Of the operation on his knee the previous day he writes:

It all went well. *Je suis très heureux*. I am very happy. I went to the hospital at 7:30 a.m. *J'étais très anxieux*. I didn't want to hear any bad news about my knee. The operation lasted an hour and while I was in the recovery room the doctor came and told Michèle that there was nothing seriously wrong. I'll explain what I had.

When I play hockey, I wear special knee braces. As I play, the brace rubs against my knee when I skate. Thus a cyst formed, putting pressure on the ligaments and surrounding tissue. The doctor removed the cyst. When I awoke and Michèle told me all that, I was very happy because there was no damage to the ligaments or tissue. I left the hospital at 7 in the evening and took a taxi home. It cost $32. *Très cher*!

Patrice and Michèle watch their TV screen as Team Canada files off the ice, heads down, shoulders hunched,

faces grim. The announcer has just finished explaining
something the team itself does not yet know. Upset as they
are at the beating the Soviets have given them, they
nonetheless believe they have won the bronze. Instead,
Czechoslovakia has beaten Finland, also by a score of 7–2,
unexpectedly high. This means their goals for/against ratio is
higher than that of the Canadians. The Czechs win the
bronze; the Canadians win nothing.

"*C'est crissant, c'est dommage*," says Patrice. It's a pain in
the ass, it's a shame. "I wouldn't want to be in Anchorage
tonight."

Neither would Donald Audette, who more than any of the
others has the capacity not only to endure but to triumph.
His triumphs, as on this night, are often celebrated in the
privacy of his mind, the same arena where, equally privately,
he endures adversity. He uses the word *adversity* because
he is never defeated. Defeat is a state of mind; adversity is a
condition. When he is told, over and over during his career,
that he is too small, he endures, he overcomes. "You're too
small to play Midget"; but he plays. "You won't make
Junior"; but he does. "You'll never score goals"; but he leads
the team and at this moment is second in the league. "You'll
never play in the NHL." Well, we'll see. Tonight, he remembers without any rancour, simply as a fact, that he was not
even invited to the national Junior camp and how much it
hurt him at the time. Hurt him then but no more. Tonight,
as Team Canada loses to Team Soviet, le Titan de Laval
beats le Collège Français de Longueuil, 5–3, with Donald
Audette scoring two goals and two assists. In the process he
has an experience that athletes treasure above all others. He
ascends into that quiet place where he surpasses his physical
self, where all things are possible, where he can skate forever and joy is unceasing. He achieves peace in the midst of
chaos. In that golden time he masters himself.

Ricci hears the news only after the game is over and they
are walking back to the dressing-room. The Czech-Finland

game ended just four minutes ago at Fire Lake. The Canadians have been beaten by something called goal differential.

"What's goal differential?" asks somebody, but for most of them, including Mike Ricci, the explanation doesn't matter. We beat ourselves, he thinks, restating his unbending creed. He can see by the faces of his teammates that they are all thinking the same thing. He takes no comfort from the fact that he has scored a goal in this game, that he has had five goals and two assists in the series. What matters is that at this moment, this fragment of history, he and this team did not hate defeat enough to win. This is the first time Canada has been shut out of the medals since 1984.

Ricci hurls his hockey stick at his locker in rage, but even his rage is calculated. What has he learned? How can defeat become adversity become triumph? How can the negative become positive?

○ Part 3

LIVE THE DREAM

o1

Memorial Cup Final, Blades vs. Broncos, May 13: The Warm-Up.

Tracey Katelnikoff hurts so much during the warm-up for the last game of the Memorial Cup that he has trouble skating. The torn ligament to his right thumb is still excruciating if it takes a sudden knock. And he separated his left shoulder on February 28 in Victoria. He stretches the ligaments of his right shoulder in the last game of the season, March 19 in Regina. He gets a hairline fracture to the left wrist while cross-checking Brian Sakic in the division final against Swift Current. (My stick was supposed to break, he thinks wryly. Instead it was my wrist.) In the game with Peterborough, the Blades' second of the Memorial Cup, he hits Corey Foster hard and Foster retaliates with a slash to his left ankle, giving him what he suspects is another hairline fracture. Which brings him here, to the most important game of his hockey career.

Both hands are throbbing with pain. Both shoulders hurt with every movement. One ankle has a hairline fracture. It is not only hard for him to skate, but he notices as he moves in on the net that he has difficulty handling the puck and it hurts to shoot. He compresses his lips in a grim line. His face is white with pain and concentration.

It is May 4, 1989, a sunny, warm Thursday in Saskatoon. There are white clouds in a blue sky, blossoms on the trees, leaves unfolding. The Laval Titans have been uneasily sharing the same aircraft with the Peterborough Petes.

173

"*Christ! Ils sont grands*," exclaims one of the Titans as the Petes self-consciously file on board.

"You could feel the tension on the plane, the intimidation," says Patrice Brisebois. "We sort of looked at each other, the two teams, out of the corner of our eyes. There was not really anything mean going on, but there was certainly intimidation."

Mike Ricci does nod to Donald Audette, whom he knows from the all-star challenge earlier in the season. Ricci starred for Ontario, Audette for Quebec. He says hello to Neil Carnes, who played for Team U.S.A. in Anchorage, before being sent to Laval later in the season in a trade from the Verdun Junior Canadiens. It's a day for a grand adventure and the excitement, which has been building in the hearts of the players during the flight, reaches a zenith as they file into the airport concourse in Saskatoon.

"I could hardly believe it," John Tanner says later. "The media! Cameras! Lights going off! People all over the place! Everybody wanting to talk to you!" Here are young men—boys, really—many of whom are making their first plane trip, and for virtually all of whom this is their first exposure to the full media glare. They are all used to the local media, but this is an exotic and overwhelming experience. Every major media outlet is here, a monolith that does not rouse easily, but once awakened, is insatiable.

"This is the big time," says John, and that's what it is. It is two days prior to the Memorial Cup, the Grail of Junior A hockey. It is for the right to be here, the chance to leave a special imprint on eternity, that the teams have fought all season in their respective leagues. The Titans are the champions from Quebec; the Petes are the champions from Ontario. The WHL champions are the Swift Current Broncos. The Saskatoon Blades, who finished in second place in the WHL during the regular season, are the fourth team, entitled to compete because they represent the host city, Saskatoon. Hockey players will tell you that the Memorial Cup is more difficult to win than even the Stanley Cup of the NHL. A Stanley Cup can be won at any time during a career, but a player has only three years, four in rare cases, to win the Memorial.

It is said that memories fade with time, but this is not true of the Memorial Cup. Among those who flared into brilliance as Most Valuable Players (MVPs) or stars in past Memorial Cups, many still play with distinction today. Others are farmers and coaches, businessmen, salesmen and skilled tradesmen. But whatever has happened to them since, they agree on one thing: Their lives were never the same after they'd played the Memorial Cup.

"It's something every Junior hockey player dreams of, and when the dream comes true you never forget even a bit of it," says Dennis Sobchuk, hockey's original "$1 million baby."

His hat trick for the Regina Pats in the last game of the 1974 Cup changed his life forever. Sobchuk had signed a ten-year, $1-million contract with the World Hockey Association's Cincinnati Stingers in August, 1973, for the 1974-75 season. Instead, he spent 1974-75 on loan to the Phoenix Roadrunners because the opening of the Stingers' new arena was delayed.

"The money was easy come, easy go," he says with a chuckle. "I liked to have fun, and maybe sometimes I had too much."

But he'd saved enough at twenty-two to buy a 320-acre wheat farm near his hometown of Lang, Saskatchewan, population 100, forty miles southeast of Regina.

"My life has come full circle," he says. "I was born in Lang and started my career playing for the Pats. Now I farm in Lang and I'm coaching for the Pats."

Ed Staniowski, named the CHL's player of the year in 1974-75, was in the net for Regina during that 1974 Cup, and he adds a footnote to the history of the hat trick: "We were down 2–1 at the end of the first period, and we all knew that Bob [Turner, the coach] was going to chew us out. You could see that he was fuming.

"But before he could say anything, Dennis stood up and said, 'Bob, I know you're angry. I know we're not playing the way we can. But don't worry, we'll play better.'

"Then, very quietly, he added, 'And I'm going to score three goals.'"

Joe Contini has never forgotten the excitement of his Memorial Cup. In 1976 he earned six points—three goals and three assists—in one game, a record that stands today, in leading the Hamilton Fincups to victory over the New Westminster Bruins. He also set the record for the fastest two goals in Memorial Cup history, eight seconds, and the fastest three goals, 1:12. The Fincups won, 8–4.

That quick, brilliant burst overshadowed the efforts of such distinguished teammates as Dale McCourt, Ric Seiling, Al Secord and Willie Huber, and carried him into three NHL seasons, with Colorado and Minnesota.

"I played in the NHL, and I played in the Memorial Cup," says Contini. "Looking back, I wasn't the best player in the world; I was a fringe player. But in terms of the world at large, I was pretty good."

After retiring from the American Hockey League's Hershey Bears in 1982, he coached the Guelph Platers until he was replaced by Jacques Martin in 1986.

"It would be nice to play hockey all your life," Contini says. "But that's not the way it is." He now helps operate Royal Cleaners in Guelph.

Bruce Boudreau has the record of five goals in one game, scored during the 1975 Memorial, when the Toronto Marlboros won the Cup.

"I remember like it was yesterday," says Boudreau. "Pucks were going in off skates and off posts, and I felt like all I had to do was get the puck and I could score. I think if I'd had the puck, I could have had four more goals. It was just that kind of day."

Boudreau spent part of a year in Minnesota and parts of five other years in Toronto. He spent the 1989-90 season with the Phoenix Roadrunners of the International Hockey League. The previous season, at age thirty-four, he was the oldest player in the AHL, playing 50 games for Springfield Indians and 20 for the Newmarket Saints. Still going strong, he had 35 goals and 52 assists, top scorer in the league.

Perhaps the essence of the Memorial Cup is best demonstrated by Richard Brodeur.

"That's where it all started for me," says Brodeur, named outstanding goalie in 1972, when the Cornwall Royals won. Now he's retired from the Hartford Whalers after a distinguished career.

"Big was in then," he says. "The Big Bad Bruins and the Broad Street Bullies, and everybody said I was too small for the NHL. That was my break, that Memorial Cup. It made me believe in myself."

Brodeur was a mere five foot seven and 160 pounds. But he dreamed himself big enough.

They come from the villages and towns and cities of a wide land, here to Saskatchewan Place for the Memorial Cup. They are the best and the brightest, the champions of champions, all here to follow their dreams.

This is the seventy-first Memorial Cup. The Petes meet the Broncos in the first game on Saturday, May 6, and the tournament ends on Saturday, May 13, when the champion will be declared. Some will go on to fame as players and stars and superstars in the NHL. More than 50 scouts will be here, representing every team in the hockey big leagues, and before it's over general managers from virtually all the NHL clubs will put in an appearance.

But whatever the players do tomorrow, they will never forget today. The Memorial Cup is made up of a thousand freeze-frames from the players' lives. One is the memory of Donald Audette of the Titans, eating a shrimp-and-pineapple pizza at Le Pot de Feu in Laval. Carefully, he eats off the topping, then slathers the crust with butter.

"I need the weight," he says and there is a glint of steely resolve behind his smile. Audette, who had 76 goals and 85 assists in the regular season, went 17–12–29 in the play-offs leading up to this Cup series. He is sensitive about his weight. He's small, five foot eight, and at times weighs only 177 pounds. He lathers on the butter, because little things add up to realizing his dream.

The Memorial Cup is John Tanner looking up into the stands and seeing his father there after the Petes win the league championship over the Niagara Falls Thunder. His mother doesn't come because she can't bear the suspense.

"It feels so good," says Tanner, named the OHL's leading goalie. He wipes a tear from his eye. "I'm so proud he was there to see me."

It is the way that Rob Lelacheur feels as he stands in the huge arena while crowds file in to watch a practice. He is a seventeen-year-old defenceman in his first year with the Blades. He thinks of his dad, Rick, who once played Junior A for the Oil Kings.

"Now it is my turn," he whispers. "I've played here all year, but this is something else. You can feel it in the air."

It is Tracey Katelnikoff's mother, Marcia, thinking of her son with misty eyes: "If Fred were here, he'd be so proud. But he's not, so I'll be proud for both of us.

Katelnikoff is the Blades' all-time career scorer with 156 goals, 41–38 on the season.

"I know my dad will be watching," he says. "It will be as great for him as it will be for me."

It's Mike Ricci one night in the regular season. He scores a hat trick, then admits, but only under duress, that he's had an O.K. game.

The Memorial Cup is Patrice Brisebois in Saskatoon, alight with the joy of all he sees around him. The flat prairies, the wide sky. The girls on the streets, the hotel, the food.

"*Super fonne,*" he says in amazement, as is his way. "*Ah, bon. Super! Super!*"

He enthusiastically tape-records his impressions almost as he receives them. A bus picks up the Titans at the airport and takes them directly to the arena, SaskPlace.

"*C'était de toute beauté, l'aréna là-bas,*" he says. It was really beautiful, that arena there. The bus stops at the entrance, the huge blue security door you can see from the air as the plane lands. Then, astonishingly, the bus actually rolls *into* the arena.

"That was new for us," says Patrice. "We went crazy. We got off the bus and went to look at the arena. Everyone went, 'Ahhh!' when they saw it. 'Wow! *Que c'est beau, quelle belle aréna!*'

"We're playing here, we really are," we said and the players would shake their heads in amazement. "We couldn't believe we were actually playing in the Memorial Cup."

After their first glimpse of SaskPlace, the Titans go on to their hotel and Patrice loves that, too.

"The Holiday Inn! *C'est un super bel hôtel-là.* The meals there were great. We really ate well and that's really important. When you have a competition like the Cup, you have to eat well. You have to sleep well, build yourself up for the games."

In the evening the Titans have their first practice at SaskPlace and the team is impressed anew.

"We looked up into the vast stands and I said, 'My God! When that's filled with people, it's going to be amazing!'"

John Tanner shares the general tension and elation, which remind him strongly of his feelings after Peterborough's final victory in Niagara Falls. That success earned them the right to come to Saskatoon. He captures some of that feeling in his diary:

> It's four in the morning and the boys are all up partying. Guess what? Peterborough Petes just won the OHL title. We just got back, we won 8–2. I stopped 42 shots out of 44. I got third star. It could have been second or first.
>
> I can't sleep. It's the most awesome feeling I've ever had. It really is no different from when I won my Midget title back when I was 13. I won a Major-Midget title, or our team did, and it was such a feeling, like I described before, the Ken Dryden feeling. The one that you want to just live forever with. And it more or less, how do you say it? It's something, you know, you

don't live for, but it's something that makes hockey worth playing.

It's such an accomplishment. You feel on top of the world, totally, because there's no one can beat you in your own league. It was unbelievable. I got interviewed by a couple of TV stations. I don't even know what I said. I was just floating on air. I've never been so happy in my life. It was just unbelievable. Tonight, we got back and had a couple of beers and all the guys got the bar. And this was my disappointment for the evening. The guy at the Carousel [a restaurant in Peterborough], Tommy, gave us the bar for the night and everybody got to drink whatever they wanted. The whole bar was theirs. But the guys were getting hammered and I just don't understand how that can be the case. I don't understand why you'd want to. Why not remain conscious of what you've done? And to me that's just the essence of playing.

The feeling's great. You look up in the stands and Dad was there, I held up the trophy and just looked at him. That's the culmination of everything I've ever done, winning that trophy. And he's a part of it, just because he was there. I couldn't have been more happy. My uncle was there, friends were there, but I didn't see anyone in the stands except him. I can't make any heart-touching stories about how I had tears in my eyes, but basically, well, it's so overwhelming. And holding the trophy, I felt I could have lifted a trophy ten times that size over my head, just for him. I've done everything, basically, to make my parents proud. My dad watches every game possible, but my mom can't stand the suspense. Sometimes she'll come, then go and pace up and down the corridor under the stands because she can't bear to watch. My dad will call her to tell her what happened tonight. Of course, I get self-satisfaction from something like this, but to make them proud is the greatest feeling and I think I've done that tonight.

In fact, the nerves and pressure are shared by all. The Blades, whose home is SaskPlace, are next to practice and Tracey Katelnikoff sits in the stands, watching the Titans work. The rest of the team is there, too, because there's a feeling that if they can't beat the Quebec team they have no chance at the Cup.

"They were exactly the same kind of team as the Broncos," says Tracey. "Small and fast. Attack, attack, attack. A very offensive team. We are a defensive team. We played a tough, grinding game. We could see these French guys were very good. They'd be the first team we'd meet and watching that practice, watching Audette and Carnes, and we'd heard of Brisebois, we knew they'd be tough. I was very apprehensive."

That night, before he goes to bed, Katelnikoff does something heroes often do in times of high stress, when the variables are too many to control. He says a prayer, appealing to a Higher Power. Nothing formal, just a request.

"Please, Lord," he says. "Help me do my best."

○ 2

The pain has faded only slightly, but Tracey Katelnikoff is skating more easily, his shots smoother and almost fluid, by the time the warm-up period ends. It still requires an immense effort of willpower on his part to keep from wincing with each step, though, and when Tracey enters the dressing-room both Dr Scharfstein and Jeff Thomas can see the strain in his face.

I will simply ignore it, thinks Tracey. I can do anything for sixty minutes and I will do this.

They give him an injection of painkiller and that helps smooth out the jagged edges, but long before the drug takes hold Tracey has begun to withdraw deep into his centre. He has trouble describing his feelings later, but the most overriding sense is one of peace. He can still feel the pain, somewhere on the edges of his mind, but it is under control. He feels a great excitement, nervousness even, but instead of inhibiting him the nervous energy fills him with a sense of power. He is in his quiet place, free of both desire and fear. Being free, he feels as if a burden lifts. He knows that whatever happens, he will be equal to it; nothing *can* happen to which he'll be unequal.

Dick Todd is in a reflective mood as the Peterborough Petes prepare to meet Swift Current Broncos to open the Memorial Cup tournament. It is hours before game time, and while the players rest he reminisces about their victory over the Niagara Falls Thunder to win the OHL championship.

"It is my habit, on such occasions, to smoke a cigar," says Todd, referring to the celebration as the Petes' bus headed home after that victory, 8–2, to win the final in six games. "Neither champagne nor beer was available to us, nor did we ask for it."

And that says a lot about the Petes. They are not flashy champagne types, but they're not ordinary beer types, either. Besides, they last won a Memorial Cup in 1979 when Todd was the trainer. There have been other good teams since then, but that was the only Cup. Now they are twenty-five men with a single mission. At stake is the Memorial Cup, and the Petes are well aware that three other teams will be on hand. None of them—the Laval Titans, the Swift Current Broncos or the Saskatoon Blades—intends to lose. But with the Petes, the concept of teamwork is on a higher level.

Opposition coaches, such as Tom Webster of the Windsor Spitfires, Bert Templeton of the North Bay Centennials or Wayne Maxner of the London Knights, will tell you roughly the same thing when you talk about playing the Petes.

If you can break them down as a team, you can beat them. If you can't, you can't. That's that, forget it. And it has become harder and harder to break them down as a team. The latest team to discover that was Niagara Falls, coached by Bill LaForge. After Niagara whipped the Petes 9–3 and 8–0 during the regular season, media and fans predicted dire results in the play-off final.

"Not many people thought we'd beat the Thunder," says Mike Ricci. "I think we were underdogs."

Ricci can understate the time of day. He scored 19 goals in the play-offs and admits that was pretty good.

"We knew we could take them," says John Tanner. "We were far superior as a team. It was definitely a team effort. There are individual components, but definitely a team effort."

It didn't hurt the team effort that Tanner had a 3.34 goals-against average on the regular season, tops in the league. It's 4.08 in the play-offs. Bojcun had a 3.59 GAA in the regular season, improving to a 3.23 in the play-offs.

"The only reason we lost two games is because they [the Thunder] used a lot of intimidation," adds Tanner. The intimidation backfired, with five Niagara players eventually being suspended. Bojcun mentions the goalie's friend, the defence, as another vital cog in the team mechanism.

"Outstanding," he says. "They only rarely make any mistake."

"Everyone plays his role on our team," says Ricci. "We don't split up as individuals."

In fact, it sometimes seems that the worse an opposition team treats the Petes, the harder they work.

"When we get behind, we don't give up," says Foster. "We have the capacity to play harder."

Instead of beer or champagne on the bus after the championship the team members buy a supply of stogies from a nearby store, enough for Todd, assistant coach Terry Bovair, trainer Jeff Twohey and twenty-five players. Despite anti-smoking bylaws, the air soon fills with the pungent aroma of twenty-eight White Owls. Everyone, from the youngest player, sixteen-year-old Jassen Cullimore, to the oldest, twenty-one-year-old Rob Wilson, takes at least one drag. Some gasp for air; some choke; some cough. Others puff with quiet assurance. But for all, the symbolism of the cigars is perfect. But it takes Templeton, an outsider, to come right out with it.

"Peterborough has this pride factor," he says. "They expect to win. All the time. And when young players come along, they catch it from the older players. It never stops. They think they should win all the time."

That's the kind of talk Todd likes to hear. Besides, if all this translates into winning something like the Memorial Cup, it would be worth another cigar. Maybe even a sip of champagne.

In private, John Tanner shows his insecurity during the hiatus following the play-off victory over Niagara. Once the immediate euphoria wears off, he is assailed by a flood of

conflicts. He begins to worry about everything from the attitude of his teammates to a growing conviction that coach
Dick Todd is turning against him. He steals private
moments to record his thoughts on a tape-recorder:

Personally, I feel it's just a waste out there at this point.
You know, there's nothing happening that's creating any
excitement in my end of the game. We're not doing
anything to work with the goalies. No extra time, nothing. We go on for an hour and that's it. A lot of the guys
right now, they seem to enjoy the looseness. I know I'm
not the most dedicated player in the entire world, but I
think I work harder than 95 percent of them. I think
that's going to carry me through to the NHL. They've
got to show some more desire in the practices. They
seem to have forgotten that we've got some big games
coming up. It seems to me we just don't have that
focus.

It's like in the play-offs, before we met Cornwall.
Then, guys were going out late. Drinking. You know, I
don't mind the odd drink myself but to go out on a continual basis and enjoy alcoholic beverages . . . getting
hammered. Picking up chicks. And what goes along
with that, well, that's just not conducive I don't think to
what our final goal should be. Hopefully, we can
resolve that through hard work and practice. I haven't
lost sight of what we're trying to make happen. Right
now, we don't seem to have any intensity. I've never
been Dick's favourite, so I sort of think Todd will get it,
the start in our first game, so I don't know.

Basically, looking back, I just seemed to be getting
more lost and more lost as the play-offs went on. It's
really tough to keep your feeling of involvement. I was
drafted to win this Memorial Cup. But it's almost as if
they've forgotten me. I hate that feeling. That's why I
play goal, for that feeling of being able to control the
destiny of the team, being such a part of it. You know,
as a goalie, you're such an integral part of it, the most
important cog in the machine. But, what the heck, it's

going to happen sooner or later, and better sooner than later. If for some reason they don't want me to play, I can accept it. If I can accept it then the scouts will see that I can accept it and when I come in and I have to do my job, then they'll have that much more respect for me. I've got to maintain my confidence, I know that. I've got to maintain my confidence and my focus during this series. I've got to get that eye of the tiger back. I want to play, I want to win. We know what it takes to win. This is a tough building. Todd just doesn't have the mental toughness, as far as I'm concerned. Of course, I'm always going to be critical of my goaltending partners because they're my competition. But I think I'd be better for this building.

Round Robin, Game One, Petes vs. Broncos, May 6. Although the boys from Peterborough come close to beating the Broncos, in the end they just run out of time. The Petes lose the first game of their round robin 6–4 to Swift Current before a crowd of 9,001. So close is the match that it isn't until Sheldon Kennedy scores into an empty net with 35 seconds left that it's beyond reach.

The Peterborough scorers are Tie Domi with two, Mark Myles and Jamey Hicks. For the Broncos, they are Tim Tisdale, Kimbi Daniels, Brian Sakic, Kevin Knopp and Kennedy.

"I think if the team plays just a little better, we can win this Cup," says Tanner, who is given the start despite his earlier doubts. He's named the game's third star. "We were both a bit nervous, and maybe they recovered faster than we did. They're not that good."

Both coaches agreed with at least parts of that assessment.

"Peterborough is a very tough team, very hard for us to deal with," said the coach of the Broncos, Graham James. "But it also shows we can win against their kind of precision play."

Todd says the Petes aren't as sharp as they can be. "I think we can do better, I know it. Now the players know it, too."

It turns out that many key Peterborough players are suffering through various stages of illness. Ricci has chickenpox but insists he'll keep on playing.

"It'll leave scars all over my face, and I've got spots all over my stomach, but I'll keep it up as long as I can," he says.

The Petes are also plagued by the flu. Tie Domi is ill and Tanner feels the first symptoms. Defenceman Corey Foster, who played well in the opener with two assists, spent most of the night before the game in the bathroom.

It is thirty minutes after the tough loss, but John Tanner wants to talk about fishing.

"As soon as the Memorial Cup is over, that's where I'll be," he says. At six foot three, Tanner is seen by scouts as a goalie in the Ken Dryden tradition and his ambition is not only to duplicate Dryden's success as a goalie but as a writer as well.

"If I wasn't a goalie, then I'd like to be a writer," he says. But back to fishing. Although he is clearly upset by the loss, mention of his next favourite sport brings a smile.

"My dad, Gord, took me out for the first time when I was about four," Tanner recalls. "He took me to a trout farm and I got a very small trout, but I guess you could say I was hooked."

His biggest catch was a thirty-pound salmon, taken from Lake Ontario in Oakville last year.

And finally, Tanner tapes his analysis of the loss to Swift Current:

> I played a pretty decent game. I won the third star, but I didn't stand up like I should have. I could have played a lot better, I think. A lot of people told me I played well, but personally, although it's hard to say when you get a third star, I just didn't seem to play my game. I didn't seem to stand up and challenge like I should have. Even though I did make a few good saves here and there, it was disappointing the team didn't play

really well. I think we were distracted. . . . Guys weren't playing their game. Mike Ricci's really sick. It looks like he's got the chicken-pox. It doesn't *look*, we know he does. He's all over red spots. Tie and Foster are quite sick, it seems. Particularly Foss; Tie's not bad. But Foss has been puking and he's had this cold sweat going. It's tough to play your best when that happens.

Ahhh, we just were sloppy in our own end. We gave up a lot of pucks. We didn't take the body to them. We're not as quick as them, so we've got to hit them, but we didn't. We took a lot of stupid penalties. We knew their power play is supposed to be phenomenal. It wasn't overwhelming, but it wasn't shabby either. They got two in the first period. One thing for sure, we've got to win our next games if we want to stay in the tournament.

Oh God, Sheldon Kennedy is just incredible. He got two goals, one to win the game and one as an empty-netter, which I didn't have too much chance on. But he's just so fast. He's got a great shot. He's smart. He'll play in the NHL for sure. Detroit got a good pick on him.

I think Swift Current are a good team, but I don't think they're *that* good. No reason we can't beat them. If we can beat Niagara Falls, we can beat this team. They thought we checked them really well. Well, surprise, surprise, if we ever check them like we can, they'll really get a shock, won't they?

John doesn't know it, but this will prove to be his last game of the series. As the days pass, he tries to put the best face on it, but his bitterness over not playing eats away at his earlier joy and pride.

Tanner has already had one experience of being sat out for a long period of time. He was sidelined from February 12 to March 2, a stretch of six games, and the ignominy he felt will probably haunt him forever. He tape-records his version of those events.

It's about one in the morning and I'm at home in Cambridge and today we just beat the Knights, 4–2. I sat for the third game in a row and I'm not too happy about that, but that's the way it goes. Yesterday's game was fairly close, but we were better. We won, 4–2, but you could see we were better than 4–2. Peter Ing [London Knights' goalie] played well and Todd [Bojcun] played quite well, so the game was relatively close. When goaltenders play well, the games are always close. They're the most important players on the team.

It was a good game. Mike Ricci scored, which was nothing new. He'll be scoring goals for quite a long time.

At this point, I feel pretty detached from the game again. This is my third in a row. Maybe I should get used to it. I had my three games in a row [when Bojcun sat out] a few times earlier in the season and maybe it's his turn. We'll see how it goes when I get back. I'll just have to work hard and hopefully I'll be back in the line-up and playing soon.

Today's Tuesday, February 21st, and it's been a rather boring last two days. I came home [to Peterborough] to the same old Larry and Sherrin [with whom John lives]. Not much going on. I guess Rob [Wilson] went home and had a good time, if you know what I mean. The last two days we've practiced relatively hard because we got a tough weekend coming up against Ottawa, Belleville and Oshawa and we want to get the six points out of that, want to keep our streak going. Right now, it's at three games. The team is really starting to come alive and for the first time since maybe the beginning of the season, I feel that maybe the team is coming together, it's jelling, and that perhaps we will be Memorial Cup-bound.

I hope so. I just hope I get to play and be a part of it. That's my only concern at this point. Anyway, I went out with a Minor Atom team tonight and really enjoyed that. The kids seemed to enjoy it, so as long as they enjoy it, I enjoy it because basically I remember when I was a kid, I could have used some Junior A players or even Junior B players joining our practices just to show us what we have to aim for.

Tomorrow's practice, I want to have a good one. It's two hours, power play and all that, but if I have a good one perhaps I'll play against Ottawa Thursday night. Or maybe Belleville, Saturday. I'm sure I'll get a game this weekend. I'll be very disappointed if I don't. I think I deserve it, I've played well enough this season that I deserve one. I don't think Bojcun is that good that he should get more than what I've had so far, especially since I'm rated high. I think I deserve the chance to show off my wares like he did last year. Anyway, it's late and I better get some sleep. G'night.

It's Wednesday, February 22nd, and I had a good practice today. Really good. Stopped everything. But again I won't be playing tomorrow against Ottawa. Todd will. I don't know why, but it just seems I can't get a start now.

School today. Starting to scare me. I know exams are coming up. I hate that, I hate exams. But the teacher knows I won't be taking the chemistry exam. I think my history I should do quite well on. I got 82 percent right now, so hopefully I can get up to at least an 85 after the exam. I want to have at least some good mark. If I'm going to play Junior hockey I might as well get something out of it, besides, hopefully, a good draft. I might as well get an education. This [hockey] isn't going to last me forever. I should be writing in my diary, actually, but I'm too lazy tonight. Might as well say what I've got to say.

Talked to Dick today and he suggested maybe I wasn't as concerned about the team as I should be, and we sort of got into a bit of an argument. I think I got it across to him that I want to play and I think maybe I'll get a start. We'll see.

It's Thursday, February 23rd. The game with Ottawa is over and it looks like I'll be sitting on the bench again. Dick said after the game whoever wins is going to keep playing. Like he's said the last few games. It's funny how he's started that up now that Todd's in net. It's good that the team's winning and it'll probably help me in the long run, but I think I deserve a start pretty soon.

One good thing out of tonight. Mom and Dad came down. We went out to Field's, had a pizza and talked for a while. They knew I was disappointed, but this time I didn't show it and get mad at them. Dad was pretty concerned. He's probably even more concerned than I am about me not playing. I enjoyed going out with them afterwards, but underneath it all I have a really burning feeling that I want to get in that net, I want to prove I can still play. And it almost feels like I'll never get the chance. I hope I will.

It's Friday, February 24th, 1989, and I'm back again speaking in my low voice. Sorry, Bob, I'm talking so low, but if Larry or Sherrin or especially Rob found out I was sitting in my room talking to myself, they might think I'm a little flakier than I really am, and I am pretty flaky and crazy, but this might just send them over the edge.

Basically, I had a pretty good practice today, but again, I'm not playing tomorrow. It really hurts, because, like, today I remember walking down the hallways of the school and people coming up and especially a couple of teachers saying "Oh, you're not playing. How come?" I just say, "Oh, he's pretty hot," I don't know.

I couldn't give them an answer. I'm pretty sensitive to that type of thing. I have a lot of pride and you know, I sometimes talk a lot about pride, but this is a more personal thing with me. Whenever I'm not playing it really hurts. Especially when people ask me why I'm not and I can't give them an explanation. Because I know I'm good. I wouldn't be here if I wasn't good and I wouldn't be rated higher because I'm not good. I can do the job. I'm just not getting the opportunity, right now. I remember the other day I was telling Mr Armstrong—he's my old English teacher—that I'd probably start Saturday. Then I go to practice today, play superior to Todd in every way, yet Dick still names him as the starter. It's really becoming perplexing. Will I get a start again? Am I going to play? What's going to happen? Obviously, I will eventually, but I just wonder when it's going to be.

I called my parents and I talked to them and they're disappointed. We didn't really get in an argument, but I think they don't know how to handle my not playing any better than I do. It's hard to say. I don't know. I know they really get distressed when I call home with my problems. I've done that the last two years and I think I deserve someone to talk to. I really need some-one to talk to. It's nice talking to this tape-recorder or writing in my diary, but to tell you the truth, I really like talking to my parents and I think I need them. I don't like getting them upset, but it's really tough when I can't play the game I really want to play. . . . Oh well. Talk to you tomorrow night when we beat Belleville.

All right. It's Saturday, February 25th, 1989, but you already know that. The Petes are playing superlative hockey as we defeated Belleville, in their own rink, 6–1. Todd played well again, but on the other hand he was assisted by our very experienced defence. We com-pletely dominated the game. Belleville didn't even see a minute. Now it seems like we're on the right track. It seems like we're Memorial Cup-bound. I don't think there's a team in our league that can compare to us as far as our defence or all-around play. I think we've got the goaltending, defence and forwards to be the best team, at least in Ontario if not Canada. But we'll see that in the long run, won't we?

Still. I sat on the bench and I could barely even cheer for the team. I like to think I'm a character player, but maybe I've got to show a little more and maybe give a little more to the team. I really tried at times, but it's so disappointing when I know I could be in there doing the exact same job. But I'm sitting on the bench, you know, with Jeff Twohey. Handing out water bottles. They might as well put "Trainer" on my arm, instead of one, my number. It's really disappointing, almost crushing. My parents couldn't make this one because Belleville's a long way. But Dad said on Friday he'll probably be in Oshawa, and I think Anton Thun, my agent, is going to be there. Anyway, talk to you tomorrow night.

Sunday, February 26th, and we just won tonight in Oshawa, 5–2. A far cry from losing, 5–2, two weeks earlier. We played a hell of a game again. I didn't play again, but I feel 100 percent better. Rob's just in the other room, so I've got to keep it down again. . . . Previous to the game, I had another argument with Dick. He asked me why I wouldn't even go out and celebrate the victory with the team and I said, "What victory? I wasn't part of the team." I said I was handing out water bottles and he responded negatively to that. He wondered if I thought I had to play every game. I said, "No, Dick, I just have to play one." He didn't really know what to say to that so he said, "Well, maybe you should learn." I said, "Well, maybe it would be easy for you, but I'll tell you, for me it isn't very easy."

But you know, during the game, after that talk, I said, "What the heck. Goalies in the NHL go through this. I guess I can go through this." So I cheered the team and I got involved in the game and I felt I even made a contribution as far as cheering the team and assisting wherever I could. Helping with the equipment, just something to keep the positive atmosphere up, and I think I did everything possible to do so.

And after the game I talked with Anton, who I think knew of, I guess you'd say, my emotional state and he told me that he had tickets for Minneapolis for the draft and he was going to be flying me out. Basically, I think he was just trying to build up my kind of down-trodden attitude. . . . He made me feel, you know, sort of important again. I needed that, because at this point I haven't been feeling too important to anybody. I haven't been playing and nobody's given me any attention. I've just been the practice goalie, basically. It was my pride that really hurt, but to feel this change is so good and to see Dad tonight. I think I'll be playing soon. If I don't, it's Dick's loss, not mine.

It's February 28th, 1989. Nothing much happened except I went to a movie and saw *The Burbs* with Pegger [Jamie Pegg] and Todd, who appears to be treating me much better now that he's getting the ice time. To me, that doesn't reflect a true friendship. At this point I'm being selfish. I'm taking what I can get. If I can get a ride, get to see a movie, that's great. Then I get to see the movie. I wouldn't say that's a healthy attitude, but basically I'm not here to make friends; I'm here to play hockey. I've played well in practice, I worked hard the last few weeks. The first few games that I didn't start I kind of sat in practice and looked bad on purpose just to . . . I don't know what I was trying to do. Maybe punish Dick. But in the end I realized I was punishing myself. I worked hard on standing up and challenging and I think when I get back to my first game or two, that will prove I've been working on my game. I hope so, anyway.

All right. It's March 2nd. We just won 6–4 over Kingston and guess what? I played. No, I can't believe it, either. I played quite well. Stopped 37 out of 41 shots. I made several good saves, quite a few glove saves. They scored with approximately 26 seconds left to make it 6–4, otherwise I would have a three-goal game. In any case, I was quite pleased. My dad was there, my mom was there, and they were really happy to see me play. So was I, so we went out to Field's Pizza, got a great big one. Hot peppers, everything. I'm still breathing fire right now.

All right. It's 3 a.m., and I almost forgot to talk to my tape-recorder like us flakes usually do. But I couldn't sleep because tonight I got the second shut-out of my OHL career! Five–nothing over the Kingston Raiders. I stopped 27 shots, not all of them very hard. But I played a very good stand-up style. Very solid. I stopped a lot of pucks really well, I was really happy about it.

Ricci got two goals tonight. God, he's really playing well.

When I skated off the ice, I looked at Dick and although I actually smiled at him, I was laughing in my own mind. He sat me all that time, but in a way I kind of showed him. And I showed myself. That was more important to me than anything. I showed myself I could still play the game.

That shut-out, equivalent to a no-hit game in baseball, puts Tanner back at the top of his game and increases the Petes' momentum on the road to Saskatoon. John, as he says, is breathing fire.

○ **3**

Memorial Cup Final, Blades vs. Broncos, May 13:
First Period.

Tracey Katelnikoff stands by the face-off dot on the left side, eyes glued to the very top of the flag. The national anthem plays and with every beat, as if activated by a metronome, thoughts and questions start ticking through his mind. What makes a champion? The thought pops into his head and he doesn't really know, doesn't even know why he's thinking about it at this particular time. A champion comes from a lot of places, he thinks, and immediately images start ticking through his mind.

Summertime. A hill in the centre of the park in his home-town of Blackie. Hosing down one side for a mudslide, then sliding down it, risking life and limb, small boys bursting with life. Parents finding out and putting a stop to it. Tick. A seven-room tree house, twenty-five feet up an old beech tree near his house. Tick. Football in the park. Tick. Street hockey with tennis balls, should be the name of a painting. Tick. A girl who tries to pick him up as the team files off the bus outside a Burger King in Prince Albert. It is after a game and she is one of those girls in the hockey towns who seem to know where the players eat after a game and when they'll be there, to the minute. She is cheap and cheerful in her dad's pickup truck, offering him a ride as his teammates nod and laugh and he can only smile and keep on walking. But he thinks of her for half the trip back to Saskatoon. Then he forgets her until now. Tick. Back in Blackie, swimming in the High River pool. Tick. Calgary, his best friend Lee Davidson, the two of them on a team of fifteen-year-olds on a trip to Vancouver. Tick. A hockey tourney in West Germany. Skiing in the Alps near Lake Constance on the Swiss border. Two duffers, the friendly girls helping them up when they fall. He and Mark Reimer, now with Adirondack, laughing and laughing as the girls giggle. Tick. Short-sheeting Collin Bauer after he puts mustard on Tracey's shoe during a road trip. Shoe polish on the telephone receiver.

The pictures tick through, part of his mind registering them, another part noting the fact that the anthem is winding down. He does not know how you make a champion, exactly, but he does know that the ice is crowded with them now. Right here and now, the ice is crowded with champions. And in the next sixty minutes of play, the most important sixty minutes of any of their lives, Tracey Katelnikoff thinks he may find his answer.

Round Robin, Game Two, Titans vs. Blades, May 6. Swift Current's victory over Peterborough in the afternoon opener is, by a mysterious process of second-guessing, considered a good omen in the dressing-room of the Laval Titans. This assurance is based on the shakiest of foundations. The reasoning is based on the fact that the Titans, an offensive team like the Broncos, are about to meet the Saskatoon Blades, a defensive team like the Petes. If the Broncos' offence can triumph over the Petes' defence, the Titans' offence can beat the Blades.

But as the evening game gets under way, the theory seems to suffer during the translation into practice.

The Blades' goals are scored by Tracey Katelnikoff and Brian Gerrits, each with two, and Kory Kocur. Patrice Brisebois, Donald Audette and Michel Gingras score for the Titans. They are even lucky to survive the period down by a mere 2–0. The first Blades' goal, by Katelnikoff, comes on a five-on-two situation—the third one of the period—with Laval penalized for too many men on the ice and delay of game.

To give an idea of how intensely the game was played, Kevin Kaminski is helped off the ice in the second period, when he was knocked out cold after being slammed into the boards. He came back for the third period.

The Titans continue to have trouble coming to a satisfying understanding with the Blades. And not just the Blades, either. The 9,200 partisan fans, plus three not exactly unbiased officials, also seem to have trouble speaking the kind of language the Titans want to hear. The result is a bitter battle, ending in a 5–3 defeat for Laval. And the fact that the loss is to the Blades, who earned their berth in the tournament as Memorial Cup hosts, not as league champs, makes it no easier to accept.

Donald Audette sits in the dressing-room afterwards and he feels an ache in his throat as he surveys the gloomy faces. The ache comes not so much from the loss itself, but from what he fears the team will take from it. He knows that the Titans have it in their power to win it all. They are good enough to beat the Blades, and that's the lesson he hopes his mates will learn. They can beat the Blades or the Broncos or the Petes, and to his mind the nature of their loss to the Blades proves it. When he hears others, like Patrice, talk about how awesome everything is, he's of two minds. He's as impressed as everyone else. With the arena —*C'est pas disable*! It's unbelievable—the hotel, the way everything is laid on and organized for the players, the big-time way in which everyone is treated.

But winning the Memorial Cup, ah, that is special and it'll take special efforts. *Ça te prend tout ton petit change*. It'll take everything you've got. It'll take all your small change. You will have nothing left when it is over, nothing left to give anyone or anything. But you will have the Cup, the first Quebec team ever to win. This team, these Titan de Laval, are big enough to do it, win it all, confound *ces anglais*, take it from them for the first time, ever, *toute la cabane*. Take it all, the whole house.

Donald thinks, as Tracey does, about what it is to be

champions. Like Tracey, he thinks it is the sum of many things, some of them seemingly disparate, but in reality all parts of a single harmony. He knows from experience that winning, excelling, is more than a question of physical prowess. Winning is a question of completeness. It is *lâchez pas*, hanging in, never giving up, but it is more than even that. It is finding peace. It is beauty. The way your girl-friend's hair curls against her face, sunlight shines through leaves, a breeze touches your brow on a hot summer's day. Success is something, if you know it well enough, if you work hard enough, if your faith is strong enough, if, if, if, but truly if . . . it will come to you.

This is one of those times. Success wants us; success seeks us; we are worthy of it. If we lose faith, it will know and it will flee us. And it's that thought, of the flightiness of success, that freezes Donald's heart as he sits in the Titans' dressing-room after losing to the Saskatoon Blades.

If we lose faith now, we'll blow it. If we keep the faith, it's ours. So easy, but so hard.

Paulin Bordeleau looks relaxed following the game but you realize that perhaps appearances are misleading when he says he'd rather not talk about it. He runs a hand over several days' growth of beard and that helps move the conversation off in another direction.

"I started the beard during the Granby series and it stays until Sunday," he says, then smiles. "That will be the day after we win the Cup."

Bordeleau, the QMJHL's rookie coach of the year, is no newcomer to the Memorial Cup battles, so maybe he knows something. He played his first Cup at sixteen, when the Montreal Junior Canadiens won the second of back-to-back titles in 1970. He played on his second Cup winner when the Toronto Marlies won in 1973.

That year, he distinguished himself in game seven of the OHA final against the Peterborough Petes. With the Marlies trailing by a goal, Bordeleau scored on a penalty shot with 54 seconds remaining and the Marlies went on to win in overtime. Dick Todd was then the Peterborough trainer so an old score remains to be settled when the Petes meet Laval.

Bordeleau lived in France for eight years after his playing career ended with the Quebec Nordiques of the WHA and the Vancouver Canucks of the NHL. A wine connoisseur, his cellar contains 700 bottles of prize vintage.

"The trouble is, it's still in France," he says gloomily. "I'm going to have to get back there and drink an awful lot, or figure out a way to bring it here."

Folks would be disappointed to have a tournament without at least one lost luggage story. In that sense, the Petes are not disappointed. Ten players learn that their luggage is missing, including right-winger Tie Domi, who is left without a change of clothes. Cooper, the sporting goods manufacturer, donates a track suit to Domi, which brings a sigh of relief from Todd.

"Everybody's going to be grateful for that by the time the series ends," he quips. It takes a couple of days, but eventually all the luggage turns up.

The team favoured to win the Memorial Cup before the tournament started was the Swift Current Broncos. Now that the Broncos have beaten the Petes in game one, and minutes after Laval has lost to Saskatoon in game two, that opinion has changed a bit. The Broncos are still favoured, but it's now admitted there are other teams in the tournament. Still, they are an exciting team. Whether they are the dominant team in Canada is still open to question.

"We'll know that by the end of the tournament," says coach Graham James, after watching the Saskatoon victory.

"The next step for us is to get past the Blades. They've beaten us three times this season, on their own ice. If even a few of the other teams had done as well against us, we wouldn't be here."

When they play the Blades, the Broncos will be putting a perfect record on the line. They haven't lost in fourteen play-off matches, even though the Petes pushed them to the brink in game one. But why they're still favoured is a story that goes back to the hockey philosophy of the coach and the tragedy of December 30, 1986. That's when the team bus, setting out for a game in Regina, skidded off the highway outside of Swift Current, killing four players.

"It's hard to see any good coming out of a thing like that," says James. "But what it did do was to unite the team, bring us very close together, give us a common sense of purpose. That's held over until today."

The other factor was the attitude of James himself, and that has hockey people talking.

"I don't know exactly what the coach's part in this is," says the New Jersey Devils executive vice-president Max McNab. "But what the Broncos have done is take Junior hockey to a different level in the west. They are the first team ever to combine the tradition of the hard-hitting physical style of the west with the fast-skating, high-scoring style of the teams from Quebec."

At the root of James' philosophy is the conviction that hockey should be fun, both to watch and to play. "I think players like Danny Lambert or Sheldon Kennedy or Tim Tisdale are fun to watch," says James. "Other teams have them, too. Donald Audette or Neil Carnes of Laval, Tracey Katelnikoff or Jason Christie of the Blades. And there should be a place in the NHL for them."

James believes that pro hockey is slowly moving towards acceptance of the fast, highly skilled player and away from the strictly physical aspects of the game.

"We have always been on the lookout for players with basic skills, who have the potential for development," says James. And because we play in the league we do, we have had to learn to deal with the physical.

"But they can't hurt you if they can't catch you, and we spend at least forty-five minutes every practice working on skating and skill hockey, working on ways to avoid being caught. I think there will always be guys who will go into corners and guard the front of the net and that's part of hockey," he says. "What's wrong and what hurts hockey are constant displays of violence."

Patrice Brisebois is determined that Laval's second game tomorrow against the favoured Broncos will not be a repeat of the first game.

"I think like I said before, maybe we still didn't realize that we are actually playing in the Memorial Cup," he says shortly after the loss to Saskatoon. "What we had to do to win today didn't sink in. Everyone was so impressed just to be playing here that it didn't sink in. We have to change that. We have to regain the feeling we had after we won the league cup in Laval . . . During the year, everyone said, 'Oh, Laval won't win. They're too small, they haven't the energy, they're not big enough. They'll choke.' Yes, that was something we heard very often. *Quelquefois, on en a plein le capot.* Sometimes, we got fed up. The *Journal de Montréal*, the biggest paper in Quebec, they always said we'd choke, they always had articles in the paper against us. *Les joueurs l'ont super bien pris—l'ont pris comme source de motivation.* The players took it really well. They turned it into a source of motivation. Well, that was great. We showed them."

Hours later, back at the hotel room in Saskatoon, Patrice leafs through his diary to the entry he made in those delirious hours following Laval's win over Victoriaville in the league final, when the Titan players first realized that yes, they would be playing in the Memorial Cup. Now, following the Laval loss to Saskatoon, it seems important to Patrice to relive the feeling of those hours and the succeeding days.

It's great, *magnifique*. When the reporters came into the room after we won, it was funny. We knew we could win all along, and we did. But the reporters knew they had made a mistake. They hadn't cheered for us, they had cheered against us.

I had told *ma blonde, mon amie Michèle*, to come onto the ice after we won. When I saw her come out of the crowd, I began to cry. I cried for joy and she did, too. Then, I was looking for my brother. My brother,

Jean-Pierre, and when I went back to the dressing-room, there he was. Oh, it was such a thing to see him. We grabbed each other and danced around like wild men. We even posed together with the Cup for the photographers. *Mon frère aussi était super, super content. Lui aussi avait le goût de pleurer.* My brother also was super, super happy. He also felt like crying.

All the emotions you feel winning a Cup like that, the Memorial or Stanley, those feelings will stay in my memory all my life. That's what playing at Laval did for me. I learned that not only do I not like to lose, I learned what it takes to win. A guy has to be ready to do anything to win a game. I don't like to fight, but I'll do it if I have to; whatever it takes.

Puisque gagner-là, c'est la seule affaire que j'ai dans ma tête, pis au monde. 'Cause winning is the only thing in my head, the only thing in the world for me. The dressing-room is crazy, total craziness. Everyone was crazy. I had shivers up and down my spine, *c'était incroyable.*

Reading the diary in Saskatoon, Patrice pauses, savouring again the dressing-room scene, recalling the story Paulin told at the start of the season about a bottle of Côtes du Rhône. The vintage wine spilled, turned to sugar, and was lost when it was decanted over a candle. But the dressing-room in Laval on the night they beat Victoriaville seems the perfect ending to the wine story. Lynne Bordeleau comes into the room with a bottle of wine and hands it to Paulin. It's another bottle of Côtes du Rhône, but this time Paulin takes no chances.

Patrice describes the event:

He uncorks the wine, then gives it to Lynne, who takes the first sip. Paulin takes the second, then passes it to me and I sip third. I pass it to Donald Audette and the bottle makes its way from hand to hand. Not a drop is spilled as everyone sips. The players crowd around Paulin, congratulating him, cheering him.

I was so happy for that, it was *super fonne*. I'm sure those moments will stay in Paulin's memory as well. During the year, when things weren't going so well, the owners, the Morissette brothers, were ready to toss Paulin out. But now it's, Oh, Paulin, *t'es le meilleur, t'es le meilleur*. You're the best, you're the best. And Paulin, when he had the Cup in his hands, he began to cry.

C'était de toute beauté de voir ça. It was a thing of beauty to see. I'll never forget it. After the team finishes partying in the dressing-room, they move on to the Morissette Hotel in Terrebonne, where the party continues. Each of us was given a room and Michèle and I were together. It was a fantastic night, but I was exhausted, dead, *vide*, emptied. I slept and then I'd think about the night and I'd get shivers up my spine and I'd feel like crying again.

I'll keep the memory all my life.

○ 4

Memorial Cup Final, Blades vs. Broncos, May 13:
First Period.

Rob Lelacheur, as he stands at the bench while the anthem plays, does not feel like a hero or a champion. A hero, as far as Rob is concerned, is someone you read about in books. And a champion is what he might be about sixty minutes from now, if the Blades win the Memorial Cup. Correction, *when* they win the Memorial Cup. Champions are appointed. Championships are official rewards.

Sixty minutes from now. He is awed, as who wouldn't be, with the thought that whatever he does, whatever his teammates do in that stretch of time, will be with him forever. He doesn't think about all of this consciously, but it's there just the same. He is, simply, more scared than he can remember being in his life. He is not, like Tracey Katelnikoff or Donald Audette, able to marshall his resources quietly within himself, at least not tonight. He meets his fear head-on, hopes that he is able to do his job as required and, Lord above all, don't let me make any mistakes.

The puck drops and the game begins to unfold, each side striving not to make a mistake. Still, there's nothing cautious about it and the game is played at high speed. Both the Broncos and the Blades are up, playing at the top of their form. The Broncos try to break away with their usual offensive style, but they're wary, respectful of the tougher but slower Blades, who beat them three times in the regular season and have given them their only defeat in this Cup series. The Blades are wary, too, but they're playing more of a waiting game, waiting for the hell-bent Broncos to make just one mistake. They sense that the loser tonight will be that team.

At 17:55 of the first period Kennedy takes a pass from Lambert, burns the Blades' Darwin McPherson in the slot and walks the puck in to score on Mike Greenlay. It happens so quickly that McPherson, a fine defenceman, shakes his head, unwilling to accept that he's been sucked in by the lightning-quick team of Kennedy and Lambert. As Kennedy scores, the roar of the crowd of 9,078 is deafening, but the tension is so high it's hard to tell whether the sound is one of dismay or joy. Maybe it's a bit of both, for there are home-town boys on both teams, and for the first time in history this is an all-western Memorial Cup final.

The period ends 1–0 for Swift Current and the teams skate from the ice as they've done so often, but this time something feels different. The atmosphere probably affects all the players, certainly Rob and Tracey, the eternal adventurers. They're in the middle of their dreams, where there's no turning back and no one can stop them and nothing, no matter what the outcome, will ever be quite the same again. They are alive, in touch with their higher selves, carrying the dream for all the dreamers on the ice that night. No matter what, they are almost champions.

Round Robin, Game Three, Petes vs. Blades, May 7. The Peterborough Petes have won twice on this second day of the Memorial Cup round robin. First, they beat a virus they can't see, then they beat the Blades, whom they see all too well. The virus—actually two of them, flu and chicken-pox—hit some of the Petes' key players. The Blades hit the rest of them while trying to stave off a 3–2 defeat. The game is chippy from the opening face-off, with 8,990 fans loving every minute, except maybe the final result. Peterborough comes out looking like a new team against Saskatoon. There is none of the uncertainty that marked their 6–4 loss to the Swift Current Broncos in their tournament debut. Ross Wilson opens the scoring with the Petes shorthanded at 5:11, then scores again to start the second period. Andy MacVicar gets the other Petes' goal. Ken Sutton and Jason Smart score for the Blades.

"Both teams played very hard," says Ricci, whose chicken-pox was diagnosed the previous day. "But I think our guys were a little better at concentrating on the defensive coverage. I think both Tie [Domi] and Corey [Foster] worked very hard for us."

Since Domi is recovering from the flu and Foster still has it, that is quite a compliment. The other flu casualty is goalie John Tanner, a standout in the Petes' first match. Ricci's face and body is a mass of sores; he's running a slight fever; he itches; he feels like grim death. Dick Todd, on simple humanitarian grounds, suggests he might be forgiven if he wants to sit out, but Ricci is adamant.

I knew on the plane I was getting something, he thinks. But I am going to play because I owe it to the team. I came here to play, and if I give in then I'll feel I let the team down. Besides, you don't get that many chances to play in a Memorial Cup, and I'm not about to give up any of mine.

He not only dresses for every game, he plays his full load of shifts. While he's on the ice, actually caught up in the game, he can almost but not quite forget the objections of his body. It's when he's on the bench that it's worst and the nausea threatens. Finally, late in the second period he comes off a shift and can't help it; he leans over the back of the bench and vomits. For a moment he feels that nothing in the world would please him more than to lie down somewhere and sleep. The vomiting makes him feel somewhat better, but only slightly.

You can sleep anytime, he thinks. But vomiting in front of 9,000 people at the Memorial Cup, that's got to be once in a lifetime.

Tanner's replacement, Todd Bojcun, turns in a strong effort and is selected as the game's first star. He robs the Blades on several power-play opportunities. On three occasions in the final period shots come rocketing out of scrambles at him, but each time he makes the save, robbing Scott Scissons twice, then Kevin Kaminski on a wrist-shot from the slot.

"Todd Bojcun made a couple of big saves, particularly on Dean Holoien," says Blades' coach Marcel Comeau after the game. "When teams are as similar in style as ours are, that's all it takes."

John Tanner feels his alienation from his teammates grow and when he hears the praise heaped on Bojcun, he compares it bitterly with the silence that greeted his own efforts after the loss to Swift Current. He knows his bitterness is destructive, but he can't totally shut it away. Alone in his room, he tape-records his reaction:

> All in all, the team's not playing as a team. We played all right against Saskatoon. We deserved to beat them, we're a far better team than they are. I don't think they're that good at all. They're tough and they work hard. They give it an effort, but they aren't up to our calibre of hockey. If we'd played really well, we would have killed them. Todd got first star—I don't really know how. The other guy [Mike Greenlay] played awesome. He got lucky sometimes, but so did Todd. I was really surprised because a lot of the shots were right at his pads. Todd really didn't make any tremendous saves but the sheer number of shots counted, I guess. I think he made 35 saves out of 37 shots. Maybe that was the overriding factor, considering there wasn't much scoring done. But I don't really care, I just want another start. I think I deserve it.

Although there has been nothing previously in the series that can be classified as fighting, Domi and Kaminski rectify that situation. An altercation starts when Kaminski—Killer—gives Domi a shot with his elbow late in the second. Kaminski survives the fight with merely a cut around his eye, which is the best that can usually be said about anyone who comes up against Domi. Both players draw five minutes for roughing.

More significant, at least to Tracey Katelnikoff, is a confrontation that goes unseen by the referee. Katelnikoff checks Foster, who retaliates with a sharp slash on the former's left ankle. Tracey has it X-rayed after the game when the pain worsens and although the doctors can't actually find anything, they suspect he has a hairline fracture. Tracey refuses to wear a cast, and through his pain he finds himself offering a weak smile as he totals up his injuries. Two dislocated shoulders, a torn thumb on one hand, a broken wrist on the other. Now a broken ankle. Can this be a Memorial Cup record?

It seems only fair to give credit for zeal to referee Dean Forbes, who assessed 22 penalties, for infractions real or imagined, by the end of the second period. On two occasions, there were as many as seven skaters crammed into the penalty boxes.

Lelacheur tapes after game three, Petes vs. Blades. He tapes these remarks after he had been used moderately in the game. He played well. He takes the loss almost as if he were personally responsible. He is angry with himself, with the team, with the world:

> I hate people who just whine about everything. They can't face up to reality, they just have to make excuses. Excuses are for losers—that's one thing I learned last year in Midget with my coach, Terry Masylyk. "Losers make excuses," he'd say. And eventually I learned just to listen to what he had to say. I'd take it in stride and I'd do what he said to me. I'd take the criticism. I wouldn't mouth off back to him. I think a good player listens to a coach, does what the coach wants. It will get you a lot of places, I feel. Maybe if we had all learned more about listening, we wouldn't have lost to the Petes.
>
> We came out strong that first game, beating Laval. That was pretty satisfying because Laval is a fast-skating, really finesse team, and although we're a good team we don't have quite the talent they had. But we banged them around and we beat them.
>
> The Peterborough game we should have won. We spent the second half of the game in their end. It's just that they have a very good goaltender.

I have been playing hard, the best I can. I was told, and I felt myself that I've had two good games. I didn't play a lot, but when I did I felt I'd played steady hockey out there, not making too many mistakes. I've been happy. Marse can look to me as a fifth or sixth defenceman, not one of his top stringers. I didn't mind sitting on the bench because I knew I wasn't one of the best. Oh, I minded, but . . . there's nothing I could do. I kind of wish he had given me a bit more ice time. . . .

Prior to game four, in which his Titans meet Swift Current, coach Paulin Bordeleau thinks he has his boys convinced the Broncos are ready to lose. They haven't lost in fourteen straight games, since April 15 to the Prince Albert Raiders, so it's about time. In addition, the Titans have a private streak going, but to understand the impact of it, you need to know a bit more of Bordeleau's family history.

Paulin, born in Noranda, Quebec, is the youngest of three brothers to play in the NHL. Chris, the oldest, played for eleven years in the big leagues; with Montreal, St. Louis and Chicago of the NHL and with Winnipeg and Quebec of the World Hockey Association. His brother, Jean-Pierre, spent nine years with Chicago. When Chris began his career he asked a priest for a prayer suitable for a hockey player. As his younger brothers broke into the NHL, he gave it to them, and the three brothers, through all the years of their careers, recited the prayer before each game.

"It worked pretty good over the years," says Paulin. During the play-off series against Granby Bisons, he does not shave one night and when the Titans win, he vows to keep the beard until they win the Memorial Cup. The same night, he gives his players the prayer that has protected the three Bordeleau brothers during their hockey careers. They have been saying the prayer ever since and they say it before they meet Swift Current.

> *Vous m'avez chargé de distraire ces gens . . .*
> *Vous m'avez donné le talent, le courage et la santé;*
> *Il faut travailler fort . . .*

Soutenez-moi, Seigneur, dans cette joie;
Rendez mon travail fructueux.
Merci, Seigneur, de vous servir de moi
Pour semer de la beauté dans le monde.

You have given me the task of entertaining these
    people . . .
You have given me the talent, courage and health;
I must work hard . . .
Sustain me, Lord, in this joy;
Make my work fruitful.
Thank you, Lord, for using me
To sow beauty in the world.

Round Robin, Game Four, Titans vs. Broncos, May 7. The
prayer doesn't hurt, but in the end heavenly blessings are
undermined by mortal failings. The Broncos manage to win
6–5, and Donald Audette raises another kind of prayer.

Tabernac! Tabernac! he says, muttering under the noise of
the dressing-room. Although it doesn't seem to have much
force to English ears, *tabernac* ranks with whatever is your
notion of the worst English swearword. Donald would repeat
it twice only in cases of severe frustration. *On aurait dû les
battre! On aurait dû les battre!* We almost beat them! We
should have beaten them! *L'affaire était ketchoppe!* It was in
the bag! Donald feels a great tiredness come over him,
something he does not often feel.

He wants to get back to his room where he will make two
phone calls. The first will be to his family in Ste-Rose, where
he knows his father, Claude, will be eager to rehash the
game with him, minute by minute. Often he finds these post
mortems beneficial, but tonight he does not want criticism,
however well-meant, even though it comes from his father.
He wants to hear the voice of his mother, Véronique. She
has always been able to calm her intense and driven son, and
he knows she will do it again tonight. He doesn't know how
she does it, for she only ever says very little to him, but her
voice is like a tranquillizer to him. He wants to hear the
voice of his brother, Rickie, with his quick words and his

sense of fun, talking him out of his bad moments when they come. And then he'll call Manon Lachance, his fiancée. Even over 2,000 miles, she will make him forget his disappointment. "Hang in, don't give up," she'll say. "*Lâchez pas.*" And tonight, for a little while, he wants to forget. But of course he will not give up.

What makes it so difficult for the Titans to accept their loss in game four is that they were able to put the Broncos' streak in jeopardy until a span of six seconds late in the third period. That's when the Broncos' Bob Wilkie ties the game, at 15:14, and Kimbi Daniels gets the winner at 15:20. Daniels and Danny Lambert each score two goals and Tim Tisdale and Wilkie add one each for Swift Current. Neil Carnes, with two; Claude Lapointe, Patrice Brisebois and Patrick Caron score for Laval.

The Daniels goal at 15:20, six seconds after Wilkie ties the game for Swift Current, will haunt Brisebois for some time to come. The goal comes on a giveaway by Brisebois, and although it's a mistake there was more to it than that. His giveaway can be traced back to the game against Saskatoon, when one of Laval's top defencemen, Eric Dubois, was sidelined with an injured shoulder. With Eric out, Laval was left with only four top defencemen, the situation becoming so acute that left-winger Michel Gingras was put on defence. When Gingras took a penalty for tripping, Brisebois was on the ice for four minutes straight and played nearly forty-five minutes of the game. Although he had an outstanding game, he was all in by the time Daniels took the puck from him at 15:20.

"I played literally all the game," he says, and although he is shattered by the defeat he has high praise both for his teammates and for Swift Current.

"*On a joué une partie de tout beauté,*" he says. We played a beautiful game. "We were ahead 5–4, then it was 5–5 because of Swift Current's power play. They have the best power play. Dan Lambert, Sheldon Kennedy, Tim Tisdale; they're just excellent hockey players."

Later Brisebois goes over the game in his mind, random thoughts crowding in. There were five minutes left and we thought the game was in our pockets. . . . When you play against a line like that [Lambert-Kennedy-Tisdale], they're not going to miss their shots. . . . Just before they got the goal that made it 5–5, Neil Carnes hit the post. That would have made it 6–4. . . . So close.

Still, the Titans make no attempt to disguise the fact that this was a game that was theirs to win. Paulin Bordeleau calls a meeting after they return to their hotel. They examine various reasons for the loss, none of them particularly convincing. Eventually it is admitted that all players seem to be intimidated by the crowds.

"I think the crowds are making all of us nervous," says Audette.

"Well, it's not the spectators who are playing the game," says Paulin, reasonably. "You guys have to make the effort. Just ignore the crowd. Relax. Play the way you played in Quebec. Forget about the crowd."

Assistant coach Jacques Cossette, also a former NHLer, seems to strike a chord when he talks to the players about toughness: "I've always said you have to be tough if you're going to win the Memorial Cup. You're going to have to be even tougher here than you were in Quebec. Tough mentally. Tough physically. There'll be a lot of intimidation here, and the crowd's part of it. You've got a day off tomorrow, and there's no reason to learn a new game. Just skate with the girl you came with," he says and the players like that.

"*Jusse patine avec ta partenaire,*" they say, repeating it one to another, laughter rippling around the room. Just skate with your partner.

○ **5**

Memorial Cup Final, Blades vs. Broncos, May 13:
Second Period.

Any marginal effect the painkillers ever had have worn off by the time the second period starts, and Tracey Katelnikoff is operating on pure reflexes and willpower. The fans, watching him as one skater among others, see nothing different about him this evening. The captain of the Blades performs as a leading player on the ice, just as he always does. Not even their teammates know at the time that both Katelnikoff and Darwin McPherson have had their ankles frozen with Novacain. But freezing in the ankle does nothing for Tracey's other injuries and it is only if you know what he is going through that you notice him flinch slightly the instant before making a check, see his face whiten when he makes a sudden move. The fact that he is able to play at all, let alone as one of the best on the ice, is incredible.

If this were a regular game, I wouldn't play, he acknowledges to himself. But this is the Memorial Cup and I'd rather die than not play. I can do this for sixty minutes, do anything for sixty minutes. He repeats it over and over to himself, a mantra from which he draws some comfort. When his shifts end, he sits hunched on the bench, his head down. At such times, his pain is so great that he must devote every fibre of his resolve to keep from crying out. And even then, no matter how hard he tries to suppress it, he cannot keep from groaning. His breath comes in sobs and there are times that the waves of pain are red in his eyes, wave upon wave of red and yellow lights so sharp and harsh and bright that he prays they will end, for he cannot face another. Yet even as he mouths his silent invocations, he knows they will not end, not the terrible lights or the hard, hot pain. He knows they will both go on forever and if they go on forever, then he will too. The only way this will end, thinks Tracey, is when the game is over and maybe not then, either. Maybe the pain will truly never end.

Swift Current's second goal comes on a turnover at the red line after they come in on a rush. It is a soft shot, nothing pretty, Blake Knox from Kyle Reeves and Lambert, at 5:24. Tracey watches from the Blades' bench as it catches the far corner and goes in. We can't afford any more of this, he thinks, a mixture of dismay and anger in the thought. He is angry at chance for staying Greenlay's glove, angry at Greenlay for letting chance fool him. Angry at the player— he doesn't see who it is—who allows the turnover, angry at the red line, for being there. Then, as he heads for the blue line, he feels a sudden bleak resolve and sees it mirrored on the faces of his linemates, the Special K line; Kocur, Kaminski and Katelnikoff. He smiles at that, the Special K, smiles to himself. The oneness it brings him melds with the resolve. The potent combination hits him like a jolt of adrenaline, and the pain is forced back into its cave, where it crouches in the dark, biding its time.

There are no games on Monday, May 8, so Mother Nature puts on a show of her own. The wind starts picking up in the forenoon, howling out of the northwest, and by noon there's a full-fledged dust storm blanketing Saskatoon. Skies that were clear and blue turn within minutes to a brownish yellow, then grey, then lowering black. Roads are closed. Visibility shrinks almost to zero at times. The wind is warm, moist, and the dust penetrates everywhere: eyes, mouth, nose. You can smell it in your hotel room, despite the labours of the air-conditioner. To the players in the Memorial Cup it's a dazzling piece of Canada they'll never forget, a prairie weather display with which to amaze the folks back home in Laval and Drummondville and St-Foy, Kitchener, Bobcaygeon and Brantford. All the teams have a day off, except for the awards banquet in the evening. The Petes, for instance, spend part of the day at the Greenbryre Golf and Country Club, determined not to let a mere dust-storm diminish a rare day of leisure.

John Tanner enjoys the golfing along with everyone else, but, in a tape where he records his thoughts on that day, his resentment at not playing keeps intruding.

> Went golfing today out at the beautiful country club with absolutely no trees and an 80 km/h windstorm, and I'm still picking sand out of my ears and teeth. Just a great experience, golfed with Mrs Todd and another couple and we had an absolutely wonderful time. It was hot out, and it was totally windy, I got filthy. We came back to the hotel and had a good swim, wrestled in the pool.
>
> But basically, I'm not enjoying myself here. It's a real great disappointment knowing I'm probably not—I won't—play again, you know, no matter what happens, unless he gets hurt. I've got to stay ready for that, but I know in myself I won't get a start with any intention on Dick's part. And it really bugs me, but . . . I'll try to refrain from laying it all on my parents.

John's resentment moves a notch higher the evening before the day off when Dick Todd announces that the team will not skate the next day. The fact they won't skate is a tip-off that there'll be no change in goalies.

That means my tournament's done, basically, thinks Tanner. I'm really bitter about that, because I deserve a start. It could hurt my draft, too, that I'm not playing. It's bad that a guy goes to the Memorial Cup and can't even play, except for one game. Dick says something about going out and golf on our day off. I hope we do something. I'm looking forward to it, but I'd rather be going on the ice and playing . . . I didn't play too shabby in the first game and I think I deserve another chance to get back. I phoned Mom and, well, they're a little depressed I'm not playing. I think they understand how I feel, but they're really upset that I feel upset and it bothers them a lot. I feel bad about laying my problems on them, but then again, who am I going to talk to?

When Dick is questioned, he says only that since Bojcun is playing well, it wouldn't be fair to the team to make a change. He knows John wants to play, but . . . he lets the thought remain unfinished. Not until nearly a year later, after Tanner is traded to the London Knights, does the coach admit there might have been more to it than that. He says there were two things, one an incident with Roger Neilson immediately after the Peterborough-Swift Current game. Todd had asked Neilson, who came to Saskatoon with the Petes, to give John some extra coaching on puck-handling and clearing the puck. Neilson, as a favour, devised some special drills and took Tanner out onto the ice. Tanner took exception to the drills, refused to do them and skated off the ice.

"I'd never seen a player do that in my life before," remarks a still-bemused Neilson months later. Still, says Dick Todd, his talented goalie might yet work himself back into the starting rotation.

"But the fact is he alienated himself from the other players, and that was the second thing. He'd stand out in the hall, not go in the dressing-room. It was as if he didn't want Todd to do well. He seemed to think it was his show and if he couldn't have it his way, he didn't care.

"John is a very talented goalie," concludes Dick Todd. "But sometimes he's his own worst enemy."

Tanner, when he gets a chance to cool down, will agree there are times when this is true.

By the time of the evening awards banquet, at which the most outstanding players of the season are honoured, the duststorm has receded into history. And as the awards are to show, this night belongs to a player whose team didn't make it to the Memorial Cup but who's had a remarkable year of his own.

Bryan Fogarty of the Niagara Falls Thunder wins all three of the Canadian Hockey League's top player awards: most valuable player, best defenceman and the plus-minus award.

"It really has been quite a year for me," he says after the ceremony. "It makes me very proud to know that these awards have been won by some very great players."

Among those players are Mario Lemieux of the Laval Voisins (predecessors of the Titans), 1984; Pat Lafontaine of the Verdun Junior Canadiens, 1983, and Dale Hawerchuk of the Cornwall Royals, 1981.

"But more than anything, this is a tribute to my team and to my coach, Bill LaForge. Mr LaForge has been like a father to me. I wouldn't be here to get these awards if it wasn't for them."

Fogarty, six foot one, 205 pounds, nineteen years old, is the first defenceman ever to win the OHL scoring title, with 47 goals and 108 assists in 60 games. That's 155 points, surpassing the record of 123 set by Denis Potvin of the Ottawa 67s in 1972-73. His goal total surpasses the record of 38 set by Bobby Orr of the Oshawa Generals in 1965-66 and tied by Al MacInnis of the Kitchener Rangers in 1982-83.

His 108 assists broke the record for assists in a season by a defenceman previously set at 96 by Doug Crossman of the 67s in 1979-80. Fogarty also broke the CHL record for points in a season by a defenceman, 140, set by Cam Plante of the Brandon Wheat Kings in 1983-84.

If he hadn't been suffering from sinusitis—he missed six games and saw limited ice time in others—his totals might have been even more impressive. Although he showed signs of brilliance in his first three seasons, he was generally mediocre with the Kingston Canadians. In his first season he was suspended several times for curfew violations and alcohol abuse. In his second season, his mother moved from Brantford to Kingston to provide him with support. Two years ago, he and several other players were sent home from a Junior Team Canada evaluation camp for drinking. But that changed when Fogarty was traded to the Niagara Falls

Thunder. He responded well to the trade and his relationship with his new coach, the controversial LaForge. Opposing coaches and players accused LaForge of ordering his players to fight, encouraging goon tactics on the ice. More than one coach still believes he shouldn't be allowed to coach. Whatever the case, LaForge proved the salvation of Fogarty in his final Junior year. The player insists that, proud as he is to have broken the records of Orr and Potvin, he doesn't think he should be compared to them.

"I still have a long way to go before I fully prove myself," says Fogarty, the first choice, ninth overall, of the Quebec Nordiques in the 1987 Draft. Fogarty has a plus-91 on the season.

The CHL coach of the year is twenty-eight-year-old Joe McDonnell, who led the Kitchener Rangers to first place overall in the OHL with a record of 41–19–6 and a win percentage of 66.7. It was the first time since 1983-84 that the Rangers led the league in the regular season. However, they lost their division quarter-final to the North Bay Centennials, four games to one.

"The thing to be said is that it takes an entire team and a great deal of hard work by all concerned to achieve that record," said McDonnell.

Stephane Fiset of the QMJHL's Victoriaville Tigers wins the Hap Emms Trophy as outstanding goaltender. The six foot one, 175-pound goalie finished the season with a goals against average of 3.45 and was picked second by Nordiques in the 1988 Entry Draft.

"It has been a very hard-fought year," says Fiset, who also was a key player in the world Junior championship at Anchorage. "But we had very good defence and scoring to help me as well."

Yanic Perrault of the Trois-Rivières Draveurs wins the rookie-of-the-year award with 108 points, including 53 goals in the regular season.

The Scholastic Award is won by Jeff Nelson of the Prince Albert Raiders. Sixteen years old and in his first year with the Raiders, he averaged 90.8% in Grade 11. He also had 87 points, including 30 goals.

Round Robin, Game Five, Titans vs. Petes, May 9. Paulin Bordeleau has said all season that his team would win the Memorial Cup but they pick a nerve-wracking way to start as a crowd of 8,517 watch them defeat the tired-looking Peterborough Petes 3–1.

Patrick Caron, Donald Audette and Neil Carnes score for the Titans. Jamey Hicks scores for the Petes and Patrice Brisebois rewards him with a punch in the mouth.

"Some people have pointed out that Quebec has never won a Memorial Cup," says Bordeleau, relishing the moment after the game. "Well, I've never lost one and this team has never lost one."

Bordeleau acknowledges that Peterborough is not playing at its best, but then he shrugs. "I don't think we should give it back. I know Peterborough can play better, but that does not take away from what my boys did. This is not the first time that Laval has been the underdog this season and then come out ahead. People have been telling us that all season."

Donald Audette looks almost as if he has been unjustly accused when someone mentions his spectacular play throughout the series. "We all do what we can," he says. "I have been lucky enough to score a few goals."

Later, in his diary, he does not dismiss it so lightly:

> I think luck has not much to do with success. Luck, really, is hard work by another name. Or so I think. Maybe there is a tiny bit of luck in what we do, but mostly it is sweat and blood and guts and faith. Faith is the greatest. You can push yourself to all the other things, the sweat and blood, but you must have faith or you won't do it.

Brisebois makes a joke when asked about his fight with Hicks.

"They always say I am an offensive defenceman," he says. "So today, I am very offensive." Then he turns more serious. "For us, we were being very careful, particularly in the third period. But it shows that Laval is not just a bunch of free-wheeling players. We have big teams in Quebec, after all."

Dick Todd, naturally enough, is not happy with the Petes' effort: "There were times when we were not sharp at all. We will have to make up for that on Thursday."

Goals by Caron and Audette in the opening five minutes give the Titans a 2–0 lead en route to their first win of the tournament. Hicks scores a power-play goal before the first period ends to make it 2–1, but that is the extent of offence for the Petes, who fail to capitalize on six other power-play opportunities.

Carnes scores the insurance goal at 7:04 of the second period. He is tied with Audette for the tournament lead in goals, each with three. The goals by Caron and Audette come in a span of less than a minute.

The Petes are outshot 27–16 through two periods, but come on strong in the third. Overall, the Ontario representatives are outshot only 31–30. As the round robin winds along, the Blades (1–1) next meet the Broncos (2–0). A Saskatoon win will create a four-way logjam at the conclusion of round-robin play. With a win, Saskatoon would get a bye to the final. Whatever the outcome of this game, there will be an extra play-off match when the regular round robin play ends. Laval's win was the first for a Quebec representative over an Ontario or Western League rival in fourteen straight Memorial Cups.

John Tanner has some comments for his tape-recorder following the Petes' loss to the Titans:

> It's Tuesday night, May 9th, mark it down. The worst thing that's ever happened—we just lost to Laval. The first time they've beaten either an Ontario or a western team in, I think, about three or four years and, well, Peterborough Petes are the first victim. They beat us 3–1, and don't ask me what happened. I can't even explain it. We couldn't score. The shots on net we got were terrible. Everything seemed to go against us. The big thing was that Ricci's really sick. He's got the

chicken-pox and I don't think they're helping him too much because he's not feeling too well. All in all, the team's not playing as a team. We played all right against Saskatoon, not great. If we'd played well, we would've killed them. But Laval, there's no reason we shouldn't have beaten them, but, heck, that's the way it goes. Todd got first star, I don't really know how.

Ask any hockey player at the Memorial Cup to name the opponent they think is the toughest to play against on the Swift Current team and right off the top they'll mention Sheldon Kennedy. Then they'll think for a moment, and add something like, "And, um, oh yes, that other guy, Lambert."

Danny Lambert, the tiny perfect defenceman from St Malo, Manitoba, laughs when he thinks of that.

"It's like they can't quite believe me," he says before a workout leading up to a do-or-die semi-final match to determine which team will meet the Blades in the Memorial Cup final.

"They've heard about the size of this defenceman with the Swift Current Broncos and then they look at me. I can almost hear them thinking, 'Nah, that guy can't be a defenceman. Give him a push and he'll fall over.'"

Since he's five foot seven and 175 pounds, one can understand the reaction. But it's a reaction that has led to grief for many an opposing team in the Western Hockey League, where the Broncos finished in first place, 25 points better than the competition.

Following the Broncos' 5–4 loss to the Blades, the one that robbed the favourites of a bye into the final, Lambert had contributed two goals and four assists, leaving him a point behind the scoring leader, Donald Audette of the Laval Titans.

"Danny Lambert has always been a mainstay of our team," says coach Graham James. "Yes, along with Sheldon Kennedy."

Kennedy, Detroit's fourth-round pick in 1988, seems always to get the attention on the Swift Current team. Lambert has not been selected by an NHL club, despite his universally acknowledged skill. At nineteen Lambert still has two years of Junior eligibility, so this Cup is not his last hurrah.

But you can't blame him for a touch of frustration and even impatience, the result of playing in Kennedy's shadow, coupled with the long, hard grind he's endured getting to where he is today. In fact, he's been practising his skating skills ever since his dad, Laurent, built a rink alongside the house when Danny was two.

"I even remember my first hockey game," he says. "We won, 9–1. I got seven goals and one assist and I thought, 'Gee, this is the game for me.'"

He thinks about that for a minute, about all the uncertainty over where it will finally lead, about all the years of effort.

"It still is," he says. And then he smiles again.

Round Robin, Game Six, Blades vs. Broncos, May 10. Rob Lelacheur agrees with Danny Lambert, at least about the beauty of his chosen game, as he skates from the ice. The Blades have beaten the mighty Broncos, 5–4, and although he has played only spot shifts, he shares the elation of the team. What this means is that the Blades, who are in the Memorial Cup only because they are host team, have finished the round robin portion of the tournament in first place, with more points than any other team. Laval must now play Peterborough to break their round robin tie. The winner of that game will meet Swift Current and the winner of that will meet Saskatoon. The Blades, the Cinderella team that no one wanted to be there, is in the finals. The championship teams are playing catch-up.

How sweet it is, thinks Rob. The victory has been an enormous boost to morale, but without Mike Greenlay in the net and Ken Sutton thinking he's Steve Yzerman, getting two goals and an assist, we would have been nowhere. The Broncos start with two quick goals, then another one, and they're 3–0 before we even get started. Holy shit, here we go again. Just like in the play-offs when they swept us

four straight. Then there's Loraas [Darren Loraas, the refer-
ee], who's not calling anything they do, calling everything
against us. So on top of everything else, they seem like
they're always on the power play. But then Dean Holoien
gets going, and Sutton, and we get a lead. One, two, three,
four, just like that. Lambert's everywhere, trying to buzz us,
and Kennedy ties it. But we're going and nothing's stopping
us, not today. And so we're in the driver's seat, we've got
them all waiting on us. And ain't it, oh my yes it sure is, life
is sweet.

It's the end of the round robin. The Blades are in first
place and have a bye into the final. The Broncos are in second. The Titans and the Petes must play a tie-breaker to
decide who plays the Broncos, earning the right to meet the
Blades in the Memorial Cup final.

o 6

Memorial Cup Final, Blades vs. Broncos, May 13:
Second Period.

The Blades are still trailing 2–0 a bit more than midway
through the second period, but there is more to it than that,
more to what's happening in the game than the score. Tracey
Katelnikoff can feel the energy of his team, his team's
rhythm, ticking over like an engine waiting for the merest
tap of a foot on the pedal, the smallest mist of high octane, to
burst into power. He knows his teammates, knows what's
there waiting for somebody, anybody—him, Marcel, KoKo,
Killer, Smartie, geez anybody—to just flick the switch and
turn it on. He knows what's there, knows. He knows from
thousands and thousands of miles on a bus every season,
across the cold plains and into the high mountains where a
prairie boy's soul feels nervous and alone. He knows from a
dozen shoe checks and short sheets and Red Rovers and
card games beyond counting or knowing, beyond all remembering. But he does remember what is worth remembering.
Remembers earlier in the season when he and KoKo were
suspended and fined $50 each for, of all things, breaking cur-
few. It's the kind of thing Tracey never does, break curfew,
but there it was, and even the memory is slightly embarrassing still.

It starts as a misunderstanding when Marse remarks, "No
curfew tonight, so you guys can howl." Everyone assumes
this means they can go out, renew acquaintances on the bar
scene. So that night he and Killer are on "Sportsnight" on
STV, when KoKo and Ken Sutton see them and decide on the

spur of the moment to meet them after the broadcast. They end up in a bar, Koko and Killer and Sutts and Tracey, having a great time, enjoying their night on the town.

They are still laughing the next day when Marcel calls Tracey and Kory into his office. He tells them a fan has turned them in and is it true, them in a bar? They both say, yes—never a word about the others, who escape unrecognized. Comeau puffs out his cheeks, expels his breath and tells them to go home; "Don't come to the game, don't come back until I think you deserve it." It was all kind of a farce because Tracey's hand is keeping him from playing, anyway. Marcel called him back the day he was ready to play so he didn't actually lose any time from the suspension. Later, he wins the team award for most dedicated player and the guys still kid him about it. The most dedicated player getting caught in a bar like a thirsty rook: "Geez, T.K., how could ya?" Then they laugh and carry on like fools, but that's how he knows.

So although it's a pleasure to see, it's not really a surprise when Sutton works the puck across the line. He gets poke-checked by somebody so he stops and Strudal grabs the puck and shoots from the top of the circle. Trevor Kruger, the Broncos' goaltender, sees it all the way and stops it, but the rebound gets away and Scott Scissons pounces on it, like a cat on a butterfly. Scizzo shoots from the opposite side around the blue-line dot. It comes in hard, hits Kruger's glove, bounces over and onto the shelf. Tracey, engaged in his between-shifts struggle with pain on the bench, smiles as he sees the twine move behind Kruger. It is 12:35 of the second period of the Memorial Cup final. Tracey Katelnikoff knows.

Something's about to happen. The Blades have the momentum.

When Dick Todd has a tough job to do during this Cup series, the player he calls on more and more is Jamey Hicks. With centre Mike Ricci in the lineup but still suffering the effects of chicken-pox, Hicks has been seeing even more ice time than usual.

He has had 28 points in 17 play-off games, a goal and an assist in the Memorial Cup, but the points tell only part of the story. The nineteen-year-old Hicks is a team leader, centring his regular line with Ross Wilson and Joe Hawley and working the power play with Ricci and Wilson.

"It works very well, but on our team that's the way things work," says Hicks, who comes from Kitchener. "If one of us is off our game for some reason, it's up to the rest of us to put in that much more effort. In the game we lost to Swift Current, we were down 3–1 before we knew what was happening." He scored a goal in the match. "But we could have won if we'd gotten into our game a little sooner. In fact, in any of these games the other side could have won, but that's the way play-offs always are."

There were only two fights so far in the first five games and Peterborough's Tie Domi is involved in both. Domi, five foot ten and 205 pounds, first takes on Saskatoon Blades' Kevin Kaminski, five foot ten and 175. It was no contest and Kaminski's ear was cut.

Then Domi takes on Titans' Gino Odjick, six foot two and 205. Odjick hits the ice, and Domi jumps on him.

"They keep getting in my way," observes the right-winger from Belle River, Ontario. However, Domi hasn't been fighting all the time. He also has two goals.

Tie-breaker, Titans vs. Petes, May 11. The Peterborough Petes have not been in a do-or-die situation this season until this tie-breaking game with the Laval Titans.

The experience seems to agree with them. The Ontario Hockey League champs eliminate the Titans from the Memorial Cup, with a 5–4 victory before 7,060 fans at SaskPlace.

The tie-breaker is forced when the two teams end the round robin with one win and two losses each. The victory last night gives the Petes the right to meet the Broncos in today's semi-final, the winner taking on the Blades in the final. The Petes' goals are scored by Mike Ricci, with two, Geoff Ingram, Jamey Hicks and Jamie Pegg.

Denis Chalifoux, Claude Lapointe, Donald Audette and Neil Carnes score for Laval. Although the Titans outshoot the Petes 41 shots to 32, the Petes carry the play by a wide margin in the first period and to a lesser degree in the third.

"This is the team we came through the season with," says Dick Todd after the game. "We came through a bad time in the round robin, but tonight shows that is behind us. The team played very well. Our defence were doing what they need to do and our offence was there. This team has the heart to overcome difficulties and they can be proud."

Todd is referring to the illnesses plaguing the Petes throughout the tournament.

"We are disappointed, but I'm proud of my boys," says Paulin Bordeleau, outside a sombre dressing-room. "Our team showed it can play with the best Juniors in Canada."

Inside the Titans' dressing-room, Donald Audette sits in front of his locker as the impact of the loss settles over his teammates like a sudden, devastating illness. He closes his eyes to shut out the sight of anguished faces, and makes a conscious effort to ignore the sounds of weeping. Players whose macho image of themselves would prohibit any flicker of emotion shown in public have no such restraint in the sanctity of their dressing-room among their friends. They stand, weeping in each other's arms. They sit alone and stare at the floor. Or, like Donald Audette, they close their eyes and remember something happier, something to tide them over these first couple of minutes of shock and loss. He thinks immediately of *le défi des étoiles*, the all-star challenge between the Quebec and Ontario leagues. Ricci was there for Ontario, and Foster, too, but the shoe was on a different foot that day and it was not they, *nos cousins à Ontario*, who were laughing then. The Quebec stars won 5–3 playing at The Forum, a dream come true in itself. Ricci gets a single assist, but he's still one of the few effective Ontario forwards and he's named the third star of the game. Stephane Morin of Chicoutimi has two unassisted goals and they give him first star, and Stephane Fiset, the all-star goalie from

Victoriaville Tigers, is the second star.

Although I was not in on the scoring, I played a good game and I have reason to be proud of myself, thinks Donald. My game resembles Ken Linseman of Boston, but in spite of the game I am still not on the NHL's Central Scouting list. *Je suis frustré*.

But he does not want to open up that old frustration just now, so quickly he casts about for something else. The image of his fiftieth goal of the season comes to mind, the fans going wild, *beaucoup de sensation*. Then getting the 300th point of his Junior career, his 152nd of the season just before the season ends. Seventy-six goals and 85 assists, third in the league. Again the fans applaud, for he is their favourite, the favourite son of Laval. "*J'avais beaucoup de frissons sur le corps, ça ma touché*. I felt shivers up my spine, it touched me so." The fans love him again as he wins the Guy Lafleur Trophy as MVP of the league play-offs.

Donald comes out of himself, back into the room with his team, his friends now and for always. He makes consoling noises as he goes from player to player, but in his heart, he is inconsolable. He makes the rounds, because he's one of the team leaders, but he thinks of something their coach Paulin always says:

"*Il ne faut pas simplement vaincre l'autre équipe. Il faut vaincre la défaite*. One must not simply vanquish the other team, one must vanquish defeat." Everyone desires victory, thinks Donald. *Tout le monde*.

Ricci, partially recovered from his chicken-pox, scores two goals and is the night's second star, behind Carnes. The Petes' goalie Todd Bojcun, who has played brilliantly throughout the series, wins the third star.

"I couldn't have done that without the defence," says Bojcun. "They played a very heads-up game and our offence was in much better shape as well."

But the benefits for the Petes of having Ricci even partially healthy weren't measured solely in goal production.

"Yes, he produces scoring power," agrees Todd. "But he also has the ability to lift the whole team."

Ricci says that although he had played in the previous games, it was extremely hard going and he hasn't helped the team as much as he would have wished.

"Not just that I didn't feel well, either," he says. "I think the knowing I wasn't playing up to my best and letting the team down in a way, that was the worst. I got the chicken-pox and it was something, well, I knew I had something wrong with me when I was on the plane. My body was really aching while I was sitting there. You start to play mind games with yourself and I thought I could shut it out of my mind. But when I had to step on the ice, even when we'd had a couple of days' rest at the start, I knew something was wrong. I'm not making an excuse; I thought I played all right for what I had. I just wish I'd had all I had to give on the ice. Personally, I could have helped the team out a lot more."

The Titans, who were game underdogs in the series, expect to fly back to Montreal today.

"It is hard to go home without going all the way to the final," says Patrice Brisebois, who put in a strong night for Laval. "I think that except for a break either way here and there, we could have done that."

In the ten minutes before they meet the press, the Titans share their misery and their pride and regain a semblance of composure. Patrice records his thoughts on tape an hour after the final scene in the dressing-room.

> *Alors là ça faisait mal au coeur, cette défaite-là.* It was sickening to lose. We were all confident. We should have won. We had played so well against Swift Current that I really thought we could beat them if we had got-ten to the finals.
>
> After the game, the guys—I never saw them so dis-couraged—everyone was crying. *L'on sait c'est quoi la défaite.* You know what defeat is. We didn't give as much as we had to give; that's why we lost. You try to cheat on what you give, you try to hold something back, and that's why you lose. Everyone was saying,

"Why didn't I do this, why didn't I do that?" But by this time of course it is too late. . . .

But, oh, what an experience, *c'est beau*. We are so happy to have played in SaskPlace, and don't forget: We were the best team in Quebec and we could have won the Memorial Cup. I don't think any Quebec team has won a game in the Memorial Cup in the last five years, but we won one and I think the people in Quebec will be happy for us.

Sometimes I ask myself why we're different from the other two leagues, we players from Quebec. Maybe it's a way of finding a niche, something special to us. We play offensively, go for broke. I do it myself. *Je suis pas arrêtable*. There's no stopping me. Sometimes we are so busy taking risks that we forget to defend ourselves. But maybe even taking risks is a way to protect ourselves. We say to the rest: Sometimes you can beat us, but we have the élan. We'll try for *la gloire*. But sometimes, like now, there's no glory and we're left with just being different. We shouldn't be different.

"*Ah, vous allez voir; l'année prochaine on va gagner la Coupe Memorial*," the players say. Ah, you'll see; next year we'll win the Cup. And maybe we will. We lost to the Petes by one point. We wouldn't have been eliminated otherwise. We were supposed to win. We thought only of winning. With a little more luck on our side, we would have won.

Ahhh, Paulin. After the game, Paulin comes into the dressing-room, tells us how proud he is of us. The room is absolutely silent because we all care very much for Paulin. Then he begins to cry. Oh, I cannot tell you, you can't imagine how that made me feel to see Paulin cry. He wanted so badly to win. I think he would have gotten dressed and gone out on the ice to help if he could have. But he couldn't and I think in that moment, seeing him weep, it came home to me stronger than ever the one thing he taught me above all else. He taught me how to win, and that's one of his great strengths.

Winning comes from motivation. If you are motivated, it will happen for you. *Si tu es motivé ça va se faire tout seul!* If you're motivated, it will happen by itself. It's very important for your body and your head. If you're having a difficult game, your body will know it's difficult and adapt to it. I think each person is capable of motivating himself. I think it's a good thing to be self-motivated. If you can motivate yourself, it's because you know yourself and that leaves even more for you, *plus pour toi*.

Some of the best players are already taken, but the scouts and GMs are still here to catch what's left. Every NHL team has representatives here to watch the top Juniors in the seventy-first Memorial Cup.

"This Memorial Cup is unique," says the coach of the St Louis Blues, Ted Hampson. "Many of the best, like Sheldon Kennedy or Andy MacVicar or Neil Carnes, have already been drafted. Many of the kids who are available have already been passed over for one reason or another."

Kennedy, the high-scoring right-winger of the Broncos, has been taken by Detroit. MacVicar, the Petes' left-winger, has been drafted by Buffalo and Carnes, the Laval Titans' centre, is the property of Montreal Canadiens. But the scouts and hockey executives are here to shop anyway.

"There's still plenty to see," says Max McNab, executive vice-president of the New Jersey Devils, observing that some of the flashiest players available this year are on the small side.

"Donald Audette is a prime example," says McNab. "The way he plays, he jumps out at you. Although he's small, some teams are becoming more willing to give the small player a chance."

McNab sees a trend towards less fighting in the NHL and believes this will eventually open the league to the small players.

"That kind of change can come out of a single meeting," he says. "The NHL may decide to outlaw fighting entirely, and then skill, not size or muscle, will be decisive."

Such a development could benefit a defenceman such as Danny Lambert, an outstanding Junior. He's only five foot seven and 175 pounds, but his play earned him a nomination as this year's top defenceman. Scout Bart Bradley of the Boston Bruins says small defencemen have it tough in the NHL.

"But [Greg] Hawgood worked out very well for us," he says. "We won't turn down a defenceman because of size."

Tracey Katelnikoff, the Blades' captain and career scoring leader, was invited to the Washington Capitals' camp last year, but returned home when his father died.

"With Tracey, it's not so much size," says the Capitals' Jack Button. "The rules are that a player can't be drafted until he's had three years of Junior experience. That's why we waited until last year [to invite Katelnikoff] and the fact it didn't work out was beyond anyone's control. He's hard-working, he's talented and he's a leader."

Button stresses that talent is not enough, that leadership is paramount: "If a player can't inspire others, then it's probably because he can't inspire himself."

Last night we beat Laval, 5–4. It was close, and Todd played pretty well, but you could tell each game he's lost his edge just a bit. He's been losing it a bit more and more and more. You can just tell that something is going to happen. I think when it comes to playing against Swift Current, well, I know it's not going to happen, but I can play against Swift Current. I played pretty well against them in that first game and I deserve the chance now. I helped get us here and I deserve it.

o 7

Memorial Cup Final, Blades vs. Broncos, May 13:
Second Period.

Tracey, sitting on the bench as the second period of the final burns into eternity, finds that by forcing his mind onto other things he can forget or at least hold off temporarily the alarm bells in his long-suffering body. He thinks of the song by the rock group Queen, "We Are the Champions." Who's going to play that song tonight? What's a champion, anyway?

There's a commotion on the ice, pushing and shoving as Drew Sawtell draws a penalty for high sticking. As DooBee skates off, giving Broncos the power play, Katelnikoff, body screaming in protest, skates on with the penalty-killers. The Blades play it very tight, carefully, checking the Broncos, breaking into their attempts to set up a box, skating them off to the side, crunching them along the boards, firing the puck away down the ice. They keep it up with great success, killing the seconds off one at a time, trying to run out the clock. Nothing fancy, let's just do it guys, let's get it done.

Then, all of a sudden, Tracey feels a break in the rhythm of shoot it down, bring it back, shoot it down, bring it back. The Blades fire it in and the Swift Current goalie, Trevor Kruger, stops the puck behind the net. He fires it around the boards to the left side to Tisdale. Tracey sees Tisdale start up the ice with it and he visualizes what's going to happen just as it happens, anticipating Tisdale's pass and getting his stick out. He feels the puck slap into it, absorbs the shock through his aching hands, feels the hot wire of pain flare up into both shoulders; but the puck is his, he's got it in control. Kruger is slow getting back from behind the net and Tracey's tempted by the open net, even though the angle is tricky. Still he holds off because the Blades are short, he doesn't want to get sucked into trying for a goal and then getting caught out of position. A split second passes as he checks again. It's too much, I don't think I can get the angle, he thinks, so he waits again, even though it means giving Kruger a chance to get back into a pretty good position.

He fires, finally, with his head down, the wires throughout his body white hot, burning from hands to shoulders, from ankle to thigh. Geez, if this were a game during the regular season I'd be in bed, he thinks, even as the shot speeds away. Nothing fancy, just a wrist-shot, and he doesn't even see it go under Kruger's glove. But the decibel level rises suddenly and he looks up to see the twine fluff out. It is 17:30 of the second, 22 seconds left in the penalty to DooBee, and Katelnikoff has scored a shorthanded goal. The score is tied, 2–2, and the crowd gives one of those roars that penetrate to the innermost recesses of a player's being. God, I'm glad I'm here, he thinks. Tracey feels the adrenaline released in a fresh rush as he raises his arms over his head, saluting the crowd and himself, celebrating his pure and crystal joy. Two minutes and 13 seconds later, at 19:43, Kory Kocur chases Brian Sakic as he races to the Broncos' end for the puck. KoKo overtakes Sakic, gets in front and fires it through Kruger's legs. The Blades lead, 3–2, as the second period ends and the noise of the crowd still rings sweetly as they go back to the dressing-room. But Tracey's pain has flared up again, this time almost beyond enduring. He gets another shot of freezing, grits his teeth and waits.

The evening before Peterborough Petes meet the Broncos in the semi-final match, Mike Ricci lies on his bed in the Ramada Renaissance. He starts thinking about winning the league final against Niagara Falls, a series in which the

favoured Thunder resort to goon tactics as they start to fall
behind. Then he thinks about the nature of toughness. The
lessons learned against Niagara Falls can be re-applied
against the Broncos. He tapes those thoughts:

> Niagara Falls were probably a more highly skilled team
> than us with all their big scorers. They played really
> dirty, with spearing. They must have taken us for a
> spear every period or even every shift almost. At least a
> slash. They ran our goalie a couple of times and I think
> that was the turning point in the series. A lot of people
> said we were intimidated. But we weren't.
>
> It just goes to show that toughness isn't always fight-
> ing. Toughness is also how you can handle it when
> you're taking a weapon in the face or in the legs and
> getting speared and stuff, getting run if you're a goalie.
> It shows toughness of character when you can take it
> when it's necessary, and not take the penalty.
>
> I don't think they played a smart game, while we
> played really tough. We kept our head in it and didn't
> retaliate. I imagine we could have matched them with
> the roughness. But we didn't do that. We just went out
> and won. That's what you have to do with guys who are
> coached to play like that.
>
> Me not being a fighter—sometimes I hear about
> that. I don't fight that often, although I think if I did
> get into a fight I could handle myself quite well. I think
> I'd rather go out there and hit [check] a guy or go out
> and score a couple of goals than fight a guy. Most guys
> in this league are just as strong as I am and it would be
> tough for me to hurt one of them. Still, sometimes you
> get that feeling inside where you want to hurt some-
> body. I know I do and a lot of guys do. You lose the
> rockers, you lose your head, and I think that's what cost
> Niagara Falls the series. Toughness is staying cool
> when other guys are losing the rockers.

Semi-final, Petes vs. Broncos, May 12. The Peterborough
Petes find themselves helping to establish a first in

Memorial Cups, though it's not something they'd ever intended. They lose, 6–2, to the Swift Current Broncos before 8,378 at SaskPlace. The loss means the Broncos will meet the Saskatoon Blades in the final, the first time it has been contested by two Western Hockey League teams.

The Swift Current goals are scored by Trevor Sim and Tim Tisdale, both with two; Blake Knox and Kimbi Daniels. Ross Wilson and Mike Ricci score for the Petes. Dick Todd, fighting to keep his voice even, has critical words for referee Dean Forbes, who calls six penalties against the Petes and two against the Broncos in the first period.

"We're not accustomed to having every little thing called," he fumes. "Every time you pass in front of the net or bump a player [it seemed to result in a penalty]."

Todd's frustration is understandable, but it comes partly out of frustration at the way things have gone for his team. Although they show flashes, at no time in this series do the Petes play up to the hard-hitting, disciplined style of game that earned them berth in the Memorial Cup in the first place.

"Yes, we put ourselves in a tough position," Todd says. "That position was highlighted by our health problems. At one time we had six people ill and that hurt us. Particularly, it hurt us to have Mike Ricci off his game and he never fully recovered."

Ricci, who admits before the game that he is still playing at only 65 percent because of the chicken-pox, manages the Petes' second goal on a two-man advantage in the final period, closing the gap to 4–2.

"Having scored doesn't make me feel the slightest bit better with the team losing," says Ricci outside the dressing-room after the game. Then he turns away, refusing for a while to speak further. He does eventually reveal his feelings, but for now he wants to talk about hockey, the game he loves, what it means to him. It's as though by reminding himself of the game's grander scope, he can diminish the pain of having been beaten. He is extremely modest. It's a measure of the depth of those feelings that beginning merely days after the Petes have been eliminated from the Memorial Cup, he records on tape some thoughts he would be unlikely to reveal in person.

When I was a young kid, we'd play so much road hockey, and you know, we'd play road hockey at lunch time, road hockey sometime before school, road hockey after school. And then, some of us would be playing in leagues and we'd go play hockey then. My parents would always sort of give me shit because I'd never do school work, or anything else, except go out and play hockey. They'd always say, "Aren't you tired of it yet?"

I never got tired, but I did take time a few summers to play soccer. My dad liked that. I played with the Scarborough Blues in 1986, we were all fifteen-year-olds, but we were good enough to play under-seventeens and we made it to the Canadian finals. The team lost 1–0 to B.C. I left before the Ontario Cup, heading off to Peterborough for my first training camp. That was the end of soccer.

Sometimes during the season I'd get tired and think I wanted a rest. Well, now that it's over, I've got a rest and I'm missing the hockey already. Hockey has been such a big part of my life so far that now I can't turn it off. It's hard to do without it. Hockey is certainly not play for me, and it's not work either. Hockey is just my life, that's all.

This year, I made a pretty big name for myself, but next year I hope to just explode and evolve as the best. I want to be the best there is and the best I can be and hopefully that is the best. I think I can do a little bit more. I think I have more in me that I can really kick out. I need to get my legs stronger, my body stronger, and that's what I'll do. I think everyone should strive to do better things every year. I think that's what a lot of people say they try and do, but a lot of people are satisfied with being average and not improving.

I want to do something to impress me. It's very hard

for me to impress myself. I expect a lot, but that's what I try to do. I haven't yet, and I don't think I ever will impress myself fully, but that's the way I live my life. For someone else, maybe not. But for me, that's the best way.

People say there's a lot of pressure on me because I'm touted to be the number one pick in the NHL Entry Draft. I'm going to take that in stride, whatever happens. I think next year is going to be the most important year of my life. I know that's a lot of pressure, but if I don't become the number one pick, I'm certainly not going to quit. I want to be in the NHL and a lot of second and third picks make the NHL. I'd rather be the first pick, but it's how you do in the NHL that's the payoff. I think the NHL's been a dream of mine since I was born. I was a pretty good soccer player, but never did I care as much about that as I did about hockey.

You know, I'm really happy. I'm going after my dream. A lot of people don't get that opportunity. It makes me proud that I set a goal and I'm going after it and I'm doing it all by myself. A lot of people have helped, but no one's giving it to me.

Down by a 3–1 score after two periods, the Petes show more life in the third, and in fact outshoot the Broncos, 40 to 32, in the game. But it doesn't show on the scoreboard. The Petes' defence is lacklustre and their scoring lines seem to forget where the on switch is located. Tisdale and Daniels put the game away with goals in the final two minutes. The only spark the Petes show for most of the second period is Wilson's goal, which also came on a two-man advantage. But the Petes don't do much to help their cause, apparently having taken a vow not to shoot the puck. The Broncos, who score their first two goals on the power-play, show they can also score without it when Sim gets his second late in the second period.

A while later Ricci's emotions become calm enough that he's ready to talk about the Memorial Cup itself.

I'm a bit achy right now, I think the long season's beginning to wear out on me. I think it was a pretty disappointing Memorial Cup for me, personally, because we didn't win. This puts a damper on the whole year, but I'm trying not to let it affect me at all, shutting it out. It's not my fault I got the chicken-pox.

We still have plenty of reasons to be proud. I can remember around Christmas when we were in a big slump, all the guys saying, we need this, we need that to make the Memorial Cup. Our team stayed the same and still, with everyone saying we needed this, we needed that, we made it to the Memorial Cup. If it hadn't been for the illnesses, to me and the other guys, we could have done a lot better, probably won. I think we had the best team there. We were all pretty disappointed when we lost, but when you think that we doubted ourselves, a lot of guys thought we didn't have the team to do it and we went out and did it. . . . Well, that's a great feeling.

John Tanner records his own reaction to the loss:

We lost to Swift Current, 6–2, and it's hard to swallow. I almost want to cry, but I don't feel as bad as I would if I'd been playing. I feel cheated that in the end I couldn't even get a chance to perform. It was like all faith was taken away from me. It really bugs the heck out of me. There's a relief that it's over. But, oh God, it's going to be so hard watching Saskatoon and Swift Current play for the title in the final. You sit and say to yourself, "Why couldn't we be here? Why couldn't we at least get to the final game, because once you get there, anything can happen?"

Like I said before, Todd's been losing it a bit more and more and more and he proved it against Swift Current. He would have stopped a few beach balls if they'd been out there, but he just didn't seem to have control of himself or of his game. He wasn't challenging and his confidence wasn't there. I played much better against Swift Current than he did.

It was so crushing to the players in the dressing-room. The guys were crying and although I can understand how upset they are, they're the ones who let themselves be distracted. That's what cost us, was this total distraction. They got sidetracked by the T-shirts and sweatshirts, all the handouts, the crowds, the hype and the excitement. They forgot what they came for. I admit it was exciting, but I don't feel I was much of a part of it.

○ 8

Memorial Cup Final, Blades vs. Broncos, May 13:
Third Period.

Tracey Katelnikoff skates out for the third period, the Blades leading, 3–2. He knows this is a crucial time for both teams. Each team has enjoyed the momentum. First, the Broncos building a 2–0 lead, then the Blades, leading by one. At this point, the Blades are in danger of losing their edge. They've scored three straight goals to gain the lead and now they must fight off the unconscious urge to relax, however slightly. The Broncos, because they first led the game and now trail by a goal, are psychologically prepared to try harder. It becomes like a physical game of chess. Who can psych out the other, who will psych out themselves. The tiniest advantage, the merest misstep, can be crucial.

At 5:51 of the third, it seems the Blades are the first to flinch. Kimbi Daniels catches the Blades, if not exactly sleeping, at least unaware. He gets the puck from somewhere, moves slightly inside the blue line, walks it in a bit more, then fires it, an easy wrist-shot that doesn't even look dangerous. Duck soup. But the shot moseys in somehow, somehow beats Greener to the short side, leaves him shaking his head with frustration and rage. He'd be willing to out and shoot himself if that would help, but once it's done, it's done.

The score is tied, 3–3, and that's the way it stays. The hockey the two teams are playing is fast and exciting. It is perfect hockey. It makes the adrenaline pump and the heart thump like a machine gun. And the more they keep it up, the more the suspense builds. Watching the game, you do not want to take your eyes off the ice for an instant. You fear to blink, lest you miss something crucial, something never to be recalled.

Tracey, as he immerses himself in this sublime rhythm, finally reaches a state where the pain is either gone or it simply doesn't matter, he's not sure which. It is hard to understand it, but he reaches a state where the pain almost doesn't hurt. How can pain not hurt? He doesn't know.

The game heads for sudden-death overtime. Marcel Comeau says just one thing to his team as they sit in the dressing-room waiting for the overtime bell. It is the kind of thing only a skilled coach seems able to think of, neither too much nor too little, exactly capturing the mood, the kind of line the players will never forget.

"Here's the chance for one of you guys to be a hero," he says, his face deadpan. "And the other twenty-two can pat him on the back."

The Petes stay on in Saskatoon to watch the final, but John Tanner has by now cut himself off almost completely from his teammates. When he tapes his thoughts, he refers to his teammates as "they" or "them":

> To be very honest, I feel so not a part of it. I've never felt so outside. It seems like the team doesn't even remember I was there. Maybe I'll mature to the point where I can accept that. Personally, I just want to go home.

Later in the day, Mike Ricci expresses his satisfaction with life in general and with his team in particular. If anything, he draws closer to his teammates in defeat. He also talks about the mental attitude necessary to bridge the hills and valleys along the road to his goal: He says:

> One of the biggest things you should have is that you not get too high when you win, or too low when you

lose. If you stay at a steady level you'll be all right. Everything's so good here, on this team and in the town. It's a great town, Peterborough, and I wish we could have won the Cup for them.

A thing about Junior hockey is that you're away from your parents a lot. I've lived in Peterborough for two years now, about twenty months in Peterborough and four months at home in Toronto. It gets so it's tough going back. I'm so used to being away that sometimes your parents get hurt. They think you don't want to be around them anymore, you don't love them anymore. It's just that I am so used to being alone. I see my parents a lot, at games and when I can. But they're really sensitive people and they take it really badly sometimes.

But often, when I do things in hockey, I do it because they deserve it. In a way, I do it for them. They have done so much stuff for me that they deserve something. Taking me through hockey all these years . . . anything I wanted to do they let me do. When I had to leave home at fifteen they were hesitant, but they let me go then because they knew that's what I wanted. They've been great to me and I hope one day to repay them. Hopefully, they can read this in the book. . . . They probably think I don't love them . . . and stuff like that . . . but oh . . . I do . . . I just hope they know I do.

Patrice Brisebois watches the game, but his tears have been wept and already the contest between the Blades and the Broncos has become just another hockey game. The thought of the Titans' loss still rankles, but Patrice enjoys his days of unaccustomed leisure and his time with Michèle. These are days to gather his forces, and to savour his dreams. He talks of it in his diary:

My dream is to be a hockey player in the NHL. *C'est mon but, c'est mon rêve.* That's my goal, that's my dream. My life would be complete. My other goal is to have a Porsche. If I got those two things, I think I'd be the happiest guy in the world.

Oh yes, well there's one other thing. I want to marry the girl of my dreams, Michèle. We get along so well together. We want two, three, four children. Two at least. Boys, girls, it doesn't matter.

But the NHL. If you're a player in the NHL, that's something. *T'es une grosse vedette.* You're a big star. Everyone watches you on TV. Kids look up to you. You get lots of money. I'm going to do all I can to get there. I've always wanted to be a hockey player, I've always done everything I could, every step of the way.

C'est le plus beau sport au monde qui jamais était inventé. It's the most beautiful sport that was ever invented.

The disappointments of the season evaporate for John Tanner the moment he begins to think about fishing. Some of his most treasured moments have been spent with his father in the family boat on Lake Ontario. As he tapes his thoughts, the sound of his voice becomes lighter and another John Tanner shows through. It's as if he's suddenly been renewed:

I just can't wait to get in the lake. It's something I've been waiting for all year. Now that I'm done my hockey, why shouldn't I go fishing? I deserve it. I've got all the equipment, I've got all the technical knowledge. The alewife and the smelt, they'll just be finishing spawning. There should be some good fishing, probably located in fifty- to one-hundred-foot waters, put some small spoons down there, some plugs, maybe I can get some nice salmon. I figure, I'm not a charter-boat captain, but I can go out there and I'll never get skunked. You just have to know the fish's basic habits and its habitat. There's a lot of things you have to know about the fish and there's nothing more exciting to me.

The ultimate challenge is not stopping the puck, it's catching the big salmon. Last year I had a huge one on and lost it. This year if I get it on, no way I'm gonna lose it. The thing is, unlike hockey, there's no pressure. To go fishing, half the reason's just to relax. Dad says if I studied my homework the way I study the fishing magazines, I'd be in Princeton right now. I don't think Dad has the same interest in fishing that I do. I think he just likes to spend time with me and that's good.

But I like having the knowledge. There are so many techniques for salmon, and to me knowing about them is part of the joy. Dad and I'll go fishing off Bronte, catch a few rainbow. Last time, caught two Chinook, twenty pounds and an eighteen-pound. Caught 'em about thirty feet down over about 110 to about 90, all on these new lures I got. We used a silver green over certain depths, long leads, like way back. I got a good tan out of it, too. Geez, it's so much fun, so many fish to be caught in that lake. I wouldn't want to eat 'em, but it sure is fun to catch 'em.

I got my new *Ontario Fisherman* [magazine] the other day. My mom sent me a nice Care package with a note. Bunch of Reese's Pieces, and gum, and strawberries. You know, Mom thinks of everything all the time. And a nice note, with five dollars. This time she didn't write, "For Emergencies," the way she usually does. Soon as I look at the *Ontario Fisherman* I think, geez, why am I playing hockey? Why couldn't I just be fishing? On the other hand, I guess I can't make $200,000 a year fishing, can I?

I'm looking forward to going up north with Dad for a week. Actually, I'm dying to go up north. It's been a long year. That's probably the best time of my whole year. I wait for it all year, just to go fishing for a week. And the tranquillity up north. You got your loons in the morning, the fishing all day. And there's no one to bother you. . . . Just me and my dad. And there's pike and walleye out there. And that's about all that's out there. . . .

I've never, even when I was sent down to Junior D and C as a kid, I never thought my career was over. I never thought I was gonna end up another hockey bum, a guy who sits in the bars while he's nineteen and up, and talks to his friends while he's drunk about what he could have been and how he could be, like I know a lot of people do. I always felt confident I would make it and so far I've done very well.

But sometimes I just wonder what's going to happen if I don't make it? Sometimes I wonder, Gee, am I going to have nothing? I'm scared about that. Sometimes you wonder. I've always wanted one thing and I just wonder at how I'll handle it when maybe I don't get the one thing, or the one thing is over. What do I do? You know. If I don't make it, it's going to be pretty hard to just walk into a charter fishing business. That's not exactly a career goal, but it's something I'd love to do, someday.

Someday I'd just love to retire. Have a cottage up on a remote lake. Whatever it costs, I'd just love to do that. I love waking up in the morning, seeing the mist across the water, the sun isn't quite up, it's just over the horizon. The loon calls across the water, across the flat water. You walk outside and the mosquitoes bite you all over. Ah, it just gives you a great feeling. That's what I want someday and, hopefully, I'll get it.

Rob Lelacheur sits in the dressing-room after the third period, in the silence that descends after Comeau's remark. The players laugh, but to Rob it seems that Daniels' goal that tied the game has taken the life out of the Blades. He thinks back over the round robin and before that to the league play-offs, trying to figure why this should be so. He analyzes key games in his mind, looking for cause and effect.

We came out strong the first game, beat Laval, he tells himself. That was pretty satisfying because Laval was a fast-skating, finesse team. We are a good team, but we don't have quite the talent they had. So we banged them around and we beat them. Peterborough game, we should have won but we lost, 3–2. Spent the second half of the game in their end, it's just they have a very good goaltender.

The Swift game, winning it 5–4 meant we finished first in the round robin. We were a little leery because they beat us four straight in the play-offs. At this point, a lot of people started saying we shouldn't have been there. But they knew a year ahead of time we were going to be there [as hosts of the tournament]. Just as soon as we won a game or two, they started to get upset and start whining. When we beat Swift, that was probably the happiest point of the year because that put us in the final. We were in the Cup. They weren't.

I only played about six shifts. But I knew there was a lot more experience on the back end and Marse decided to go with those guys. It'll be me next year, hopefully.

Rob accepts that as far as he is concerned, as far as playing is concerned, his season is over. He accepts that, yet he's still a member of the team and he can't stop worrying about the silence that now envelops the dressing-room. Marse isn't going to let him out on the ice to maybe score a goal or administer a crucial check. But there's something wrong here in the dressing-room. And maybe he can figure out what it is and do something, here and now, to put it right. So he worries.

When we were down, 2–0, early in the game, we didn't let that get us down, he thinks, replaying the sequences carefully, like a video in his mind. No, we didn't really get down. We came back and we put the burners on in the second period. There we were, just like that, up 3–2 and were we pumped. Going into that third period we were pumped and you know why? The whole year we'd only lost one game where we were leading going into the third period. And when they scored that goal in the third, that goal by Daniels, it just seemed it took the life right out of us. So here we are between the third and the overtime and it seems like we're dead in the dressing-room. It seems to me like the guys almost think we've lost already.

"C'mon guys, we got nothing to be gloomy about. We're acting like we already lost. C'mon, we've come too far to think like that. We can win this thing, guys. We can win this thing."

He hears the words, knows he's saying them, but he can't quite believe it. A rookie being the cheerleader? Rob smiles at that, because it's a long time since he's felt like one or even thought much about it. They are just players together in this room now, warriors, gladiators, all in it together. His buddies look at the smile on his face and although they don't know why he's smiling they respond to it. They pick up on it and almost immediately the tempo rises, the adrenaline rush begins to build:

"Kick ass, guys!"

"You got it, buddy."

"Yo! Team!"

"Hungry dawgs, guys."

"Dead meat!"

"Number one, guys."

"Let's do it."

"Hey, team."

"Yo, team!"

"All the way!"

"Y-a-a-a-y, team!"

They all pick up on it, chanting, chipping in, adding their part to the ritual, to the magical incantation, for that's what it is.

○ **9**

Memorial Cup Final, Blades vs. Broncos, May 13:
Overtime.

The hungry dawgs are pumped, the Special K line ready, the breakfast of champions. Let's make 'em choke on it, thinks Tracey Katelnikoff, but he says nothing. T.K. on the left, Killer at centre, KoKo on the right. They eye each other, tight as drums. Gumby and Sutts are back, face-off at the Broncos' blue line. The Blades have been keeping the play almost entirely in the Broncos' end, trying to fence them all in behind the blue line, boring in time after time, checking the smaller, faster Broncos, harrying them, worrying them, sniping away.

Kaminski wins the face-off, slips the puck to Kocur and Tracey moves in with him. KoKo has the puck going down the right side, stepping it in, winding up, firing. The puck comes sizzling down, hits the glove of the Broncos' goalie, Trevor Kruger, then seems to trickle by the post. For the slightest part of a heartbeat the Blades think it's over, they've won the Cup, the Cinderella team has outfoxed the wicked stepmother, heaven is theirs. Kruger will later admit that in the same instant he thought the puck was in, too. But there's no reaction from the goal judge, none from the on-ice officials, and if it ever happened it's gone now, disappeared in an eye blink, swallowed in a memory, and the play goes on. The Blades have outshot the Broncos, 5–0, as the Special Ks skate to the bench and the lines change one last time.

A little down the bench from where Tracey is sitting, Rob Lelacheur looks across at the Swift Current bench, trying to catch the eye of his friend, Chris Larkin. One of us will earn a Memorial Cup ring before this day is over, he thinks. He gives his friend a smile, then a conspiratorial wink. There are a whole lot of things in that glance. One friend reaching to touch another.

Look what we're doing here, buddy? Will you look at what we're *doing*? One of us is gonna beat the other and I don't know who it will be, but will you look at what we're *doing*?

Although Rob wants fiercely to win the Memorial and shares with each player on both teams the anxiety that he won't, he still feels a great joy. Whatever happens at the end of the game, whatever happens in the rest of his life, those are other things. Whether he ever gets another thing right in his life, he's got this thing right, now.

None of Rob's senses gives him any premonition of what the outcome of this game will be, even though the game is ticking into its final seconds. But at this instant, Rob feels a lightness filtering through the tension. He has no time consciously to think about it, but the truth is he knows that what's unfolding on the ice is only a minuscule part of all that's happening. An entire universe unfolds around him with him at the centre. Among the 9,078 fans watching the drama on the ice, there are 9,078 universes unfolding, with 9,078 people at their centres. And all those people, just in this one building, all in their parallel universes, but all focused on a single event. All focused on what the players are doing, on Tracey, on Rob. On heroes. On champions. Rob looks at Chris and he's not sure that Chris even sees him. He does not smile back. His Broncos have more to lose than the Blades. The Broncos finished the season 25 points ahead of everyone else. They played twelve play-off games and won twelve. Yet here they are in the final seconds and they might lose. They might—geez, can you even think it—they might *lose*.

The Blades? Well, they finished second in the regular season, got wiped by the Broncos in the play-offs. They're only *here* because they're hosts for the tournament. Yet here they are in the final seconds and they might win. Geez, can you even think it? They might *win*.

And a linesman smashes the puck down on the ice for the last face-off of the Memorial Cup.

Tracey sits on the bench as the puck drops and it is now one of those times. Think of the body as an organism and if the body is an organism, then you can make it react. An organism. Put it under a microscope and turn on the light, see it quiver. Poke it with the glass rod and see it move. Make it do what you want it to do. Command it. Don't just ask it, tell it.

That stuff has worked up to a point so far, but now there's no more left. Tracey hurts. No mind games can disguise the fact. No more cajoling the body to produce the endomorphs to damp down the pain. It is hard to convince his brain to send out a command. It's as if it has finally become appalled at the chaos and disruption its every command causes as the body strives to obey. And so Tracey sits, holding tightly to something deep within, something he fears will break if he lets it go. He feels a wave of nausea, fights it back with a groan. He doesn't know whether he groans aloud. He hopes not.

What he does not see is what is happening on the ice. He sees the first signs, the play developing as the Broncos scramble around Greenlay in the Blades' net. He sees Greener shift and weave, moving, looking, trying to see everything and do everything at once. The clock shows it's coming up to 3:15 and all of a sudden Greener's lost his stick. Kevin Yellowaga, Dean Holoien, Collin Bauer, Ken Sutton, Shawn Snesar, all see it at the same time. They close around him, protecting their goalie. The Broncos move in, frantic to capitalize on their advantage, now of all times, now or never, their first shot on goal. They move closer, moving, shifting, no one back, gambling it all.

The Broncos' big defenceman, Bob Wilkie, gets the puck at the point as the Blades fire it out. T.K., on the bench, sees the Blades' defender is nowhere in sight. Where is the defenceman? Why doesn't somebody nail that mother? But nobody does. Wilkie kind of half trips over Greener's stick, shoving it off to the side a bit, and although it's accidental it clears one more obstacle out of the path to the net.

Wilkie is way out of position himself, so all the Blades have to do is take the puck away from him or have Wilkie make a bad pass or simply lose the puck, and the Blades will have nobody between them and Kruger waiting in the Broncos' net. And although Wilkie's stick-handling ability is not his strong point, this time it's like he's got the puck tied there to his stick. He can do no wrong as he doodlebugs around at least two Blades, a 220-pound doodlebug, then slides the puck off to the tiny defenceman, Darren Kruger, in the corner.

Darren Kruger, brother and identical twin of the Broncos' goalie, Trevor. Brother of Scott, one of four Broncos who died in the bus accident one cold and rainy night.

The puck approaches at 85 mph—1,496 inches per second—and Mike Greenlay sees it come. He thinks, in the merest of flashes, of every way he could stop that puck, no matter how impossible. He flashes a burst of willpower at the stick lying useless beyond his reach, but it still lies there. Maybe if he stamps three times with his skate the ice will crack open and swallow the net, let the puck miss entirely. But he has no time for stamping his feet or cracks in the ice or blasts of willpower. He is down on his knees, trying to pick up the puck again, see where it is. But he can't see it and then it's there. It hits Tisdale's stick, then Greener feels it smack the inside of his leg. There's no more time in the here and now. This piece of eternity is done with, gone forever in the two one-thousandths of a second it takes three inches of puck to pass three inches of goal line at 85 mph. It's 3:25 in the overtime and all their lives are forever changed.

Tracey sees this and Rob sees it, and his buddy, Chris Larkin. They all see it, the Blades with horror and disbelief, the Broncos with joy. Although there's no disbelief, the belief is suspended a split second longer. All feel it, this sense of unreality, this unwillingness to accept what they see. To Tracey and the Blades there's still a chance there's been a mistake. The referee, Darren Loraas, will wave it off and they'll be saved. They know this won't happen, but it's possible, anything's possible, but, oh my God, in their heart of hearts they know and they want to die. The Broncos give them that split instant of doubt and then it's pandemonium. The Broncos get their one and only shot on net, their here and now, and it turns them into Memorial Cup champions.

Rob Lelacheur feels the tears blinding his eyes, burning his face. He will say later that he feels a part of him has been taken away, and so it has. It is gone forever and that's why he mourns. That's why we all mourn, when we miss something and know we can never get it back. He finds Chris, or Chris finds him, and they stand together in the middle of the celebration and the mourning. They hold each other in their arms, speaking their words of comfort, words of joy and sorrow, one a measure of the other. The measure of champions.

Tracey Katelnikoff stands alone, leaning over the boards, his arms resting on the top. He puts his head down, shakes it in disbelief. Tracey has come the furthest in his quest, so his is the fiercest mourning for what might have been but now can never be. He has played his last Junior game. His future in the game he loves is uncertain. And yet, because he's the grandest hero, the greatest traveller, the fiercest mourner, his is also the greatest joy. It must be, for sorrow is the obverse of joy, joy the other side of sorrow. He stands there, utterly alone and yet one with himself. You dream as long as you want, and only you can end the dream, he thinks. He thinks of this, leaning on the boards near the blue-line dot. He does not smile at this, derives no happiness from the thought. But he will.

This one is for four Broncos who couldn't be here, a gift from the hearts of twenty-three who could be. It is moments after Swift Current's 4–3 overtime victory and the Broncos' coach, Graham James, pays tribute to Trent Kresse, Scott Kruger, Chris Mantyka and Brent Ruff.

"I think now we can let them rest in peace," he says, tears in his eyes.

"It's a special feeling, getting that goal, but I'm no super hero," says Tisdale of his game-winner. It is the first time since 1980 that a Memorial Cup final has been decided in overtime. That year the Cornwall Royals beat the Peterborough Petes, 3–2.

"The win means just about everything to me," says the Broncos' Danny Lambert, the tournament MVP. The five foot seven, 175-pound defenceman had three assists in the final to finish with nine assists in the tournament.

"Wherever tomorrow leads, well, that's tomorrow," adds Lambert. "But this is the greatest thing. It is like all the wishes you ever had coming true, that's what. Then when it comes, it's just hard to believe."

This is a private time for the Saskatoon Blades, a moment to share their grief with each other. The dressing-room is quiet, with the air of death about it. Some players hug each other and sob, some sit alone. Sutts spies T.K., goes to him and puts an arm on his shoulder.

"You played a great game, Trace," he says, and he is having trouble keeping his voice level. "You're an example to us all, T.K. I'm proud to play with you. I'll never forget it."

Katelnikoff manages a smile.

"Sutts, we tried," he whispers. "I still can't believe we came that close and missed it. I know it, but I still can't believe. The big thing is we tried."

Marcel Comeau comes to Rob Lelacheur.

"I wish I could have done more," says Lelacheur, his voice choking. "Maybe it might have made a little difference."

Comeau hugs him, Lolly's head on his shoulder.

"You did just fine," says Comeau. "Don't think you didn't. We all did fine."

Then he turns to the players.

"Listen up guys," he says, for the last of what must have been a thousand or, Lord knows, 10,000 times this season. "Listen up. This is the team that wasn't supposed to be here. Wasn't suppose to have a chance. And you showed them. You showed them, guys, and I'm proud. You can be proud too."

Then they cheer, for themselves and their coach.

Rob Lelacheur tapes his thoughts after the final game.

> I've never felt so empty in my life before. Especially since my best friend [Chris Larkin] plays on Swift Current. Watching him out there, celebrating, while we stood on the bench and mourned our loss. Still, Swift deserved the Cup, not that we didn't. But they had a dream season. No team's going to repeat that for a long, long time. They played well and we just fell a hair short. Right now, I feel sorry for the older guys who'll never get a chance again. People like me, like Scott Scissons and Dave Struch, we've got three more years. We at least have some chance of getting into the Cup again, whereas those guys don't.
>
> Oh, God. It ticks me off that one of us had to lose. It makes me so mad. Everything that could have been ours: the rings, the money, the trophy. The acknowledgement. Well, it'll be a long summer. People saying you did well. You played a good series. You came close. Hearing that over and over again.
>
> Well, life goes on, I guess. . . . We'll be back again during my career in Junior hockey, don't worry. We'll be in again, that's all I have to say.

So there are Sutts and Sutts, the Sutcliffe variety and the Sutton, Soupy, Gumby and Doobee, hanging around the big blue security door, waiting for parents to show up, waiting for girlfriends, waiting for time to pass. But mostly waiting for each other. Scizzo comes and Lolly, Snesy and Smartie— sounds like the seven dwarfs, better make that nine. Smurf is there and Wags and Greener and Kooney. And Loyner, geez, don't forget Loyner. Row and Jet and Strudal, KoKo and Killer and Bates. Whitey. Bomber. And they greet each other as if they've been apart for years instead of four or five minutes. They're going off to Confetti's or Esmeralda's or Cheesetoast or David's or The Pat. They can't, never in a million years, agree on which watering hole they'll honour on this night of nights. The way they are feeling just now, maybe they'll go to them all.

T.K., the Russian, looks at them, beaming, full of something, he doesn't know what. But he knows one thing, if his aching muscles and bones would let him, he'd hug them all.

So much does he love them.

O In the End . . .

O Epilogue . . .

Donald

It is June 17, 1989, a little more than a month after the Memorial Cup in Saskatoon. But the scene today is the Met Centre in Minneapolis where the annual NHL Entry Draft of mainly Junior players is under way. The hopeful big-leaguers have been rated from the time they were Midgets and often much earlier than that by the minor-league scouts who form a network across Canada and anywhere else in the world where hockey is played. Eventually such reports attract the attention of a scout for one of the big-league teams or scouts from Central Scouting, the NHL's own talent-spotters. Donald has been annoyed and frustrated throughout his Junior career by the fact that he has never been rated by Central Scouting.

"I am sick of hearing how small I am," he complains over and over, referring to what always seems to underlie his not being rated. But today his hopes are high. He has heard that the Buffalo Sabres, who have expressed interest, could draft him in the sixth round. But Boston, Montreal, Quebec, L.A. and Edmonton have also been in touch.

For those unfamiliar with how the draft works: Each of the NHL's twenty-one teams picks a player in rotation, the order of choice being dictated by the order of finish during the regular season. The last-place finisher picks first, the first-place team picks last. In one round twenty-one players are chosen.

But the sixth round passes and Donald does not hear his name. Same thing in the seventh round, then the eighth. It is disappointing and his nervousness grows. It often happens that despite a certain amount of pre-draft courtship, the suitors have second thoughts and melt away.

"The Buffalo Sabres pick . . . Donald Audette of the Laval Titans." At first he can't believe his ears or doesn't dare, but then a smile spreads over his face. He has been chosen in the ninth round, 183rd overall.

"*Voilà!*" he says as he goes to accept his jersey and hat. Later, he writes in his diary about how he feels now that he has passed one of the last milestones towards his dream.

> I have finally been drafted by the Sabres. *Maudit, que je suis content! Enfin un grand rêve qui vient de se realiser.* Damn, I'm happy that a great dream has been realized. I've always aimed higher than what I could achieve, and now here I am. The next step is actually to play in the NHL. I think every hockey player must feel that is the greatest dream. At any rate, it's mine—to at least play part of my career in the NHL. I think if I succeed, there'll be a lot of people proud of me and what it took me to get there.

He makes an impressive showing at training camp, but it is decided to send him to the Sabres' farm team, the Rochester Americans of the American Hockey league, for a year of seasoning. He has an outstanding season, finishing ninth overall in scoring, with 36 goals and 45 assists.

"I must show what I can do," he says, a refrain he's been repeating since his Midget days. You'll never make Junior. You'll never excel in Junior. They'll never draft you, you're too small. "Now I have to show them I can play in the NHL."

But Donald Audette smiles when he says it now. He smiles about showing them because he's already shown himself.

La vie ne tient qu 'a un fil, writes Donald. Life is suspended by a thread.

Soon after the draft, he is in a car accident when another drives makes an improper turn. Although there is $7,000 damage to his car, he is not seriously injured.

Tous mes membres saufs, he says. I got out intact.

However, he is bruised and shaken and it is such a near thing that he reflects on his incredible luck.

"It makes me appreciate life and what we have in this life," he says.

Donald is especially sensitive because of his teammate Neil Carnes. The nineteen-year-old centre was one of the Titans' top players at the Memorial Cup, Montreal's third pick of 1988, and star for Team U.S.A. at the World Juniors in Anchorage. Carnes dies on July 30 in a motorcycle accident at Plymouth, Michigan, not far from his home. As Donald writes: "Now I know it can all be taken from us at any minute."

Donald makes his NHL debut with the Sabres at The Forum in Montreal, during the fourth game of the opening round in the 1990 Adams Division play-offs. Although the Canadiens went on to win the series, they lose this game, 4–2.

"The greatest part of it was to play my first NHL game in my home town," says Donald, whose command of English is now nearly complete after a year in the AHL. "I couldn't get tickets for the rest of the family, but my dad was in the stands."

Patrice

Questions, questions, questions, and all of them in English, frets Patrice Brisebois. *Il posaient cinq cent mille questions, tout en anglais*. They asked 500,000 questions, all in English. I did my best to answer them. I understand English pretty well, but I don't speak it often.

Patrice's head reels after meetings with the New York Rangers, the Buffalo Sabres and the Hartford Whalers. The Sabres say that if the Canadiens don't draft him, they will. The Whalers have already sent him a jersey and hat. They've indicated to Patrice's agent, Don Meehan, that they are extremely interested in him. One of the Whalers' scouts tells Patrice how much he likes his play:

> I was really happy. I went to bed and had a really good sleep. I wasn't nervous and I wake up the next morning in great shape. I am confident, based on what they've said, that the Whalers are choosing me in the first round. Instead, out of the blue they pick Robert Holik, a Czech, can you believe it. It's not a good team that promises you something and then does nothing.

Although he is rated fifteenth by Central Scouting and should have gone in the first round, the snub by the Whalers hurts. "Frankly, I don't like what the Whalers did," he says. There is pride at stake, too. After the Whalers' turn, the Canadiens choose Lindsay Vallis. The fact that the two are friends helps a little, but again he's been passed over. Then he thinks Buffalo will take him, but they opt for Kevin Haller.

"*Mon Dieu*," he thinks, as next the New York Rangers, then Boston and Pittsburgh pass him by.

"Pittsburgh takes a guy [Jamie Heward] who has a hurt elbow, trouble with his knees—and that's their first choice," grumps Patrice, unable to hide his disappointment at being rated fifteenth but still passed over in the first round. But he does not waste energy fretting about the past. When the Canadiens draft him in the second round, thirtieth overall, he is gleeful.

"I was so happy," he says. "*C'est une grande famille!*" It's a big family. "I knew Claude Ruel really well because my agent is one of his close friends. We would all go out to dinner and Mr Ruel would say, *Corrige ça, corrige ça*. Correct this, correct that. When I saw Pat Burns [the Canadiens' coach], I was really happy. From the age of five, every Saturday night I watched the Canadiens on television. I knew everything about the club.

"And now I've been drafted by the Montreal Canadiens," thinks Patrice. "*J'ai de la misère à l'imaginer*. I can hardly believe it." When Michèle hears the news, she shares his joy. Oh, now we don't have to move to the States or somewhere else in Canada, she tells Patrice—*On reste dans la belle ville c'est Montréal.* We stay in our beautiful city of Montreal.

"All I want now is to sign my first professional contract," Patrice tells his diary, and later in the year, after the Canadiens' training camp, that's what he does. He spends the 1989-90 season back with the Titans. He writes:

> In one or two years, I hope to be at Sherbrooke [the Canadiens' AHL affiliate]. My goal is to play in the NHL, and that's what I'll work for. I know that to be drafted and to become a member of the team are two different things. I still have many sacrifices to make if I want to be a member of the team. I've taken one step by being drafted, but making the team is the final step. Work hard, make sacrifices, keep striving to be *une vedette.* That's what I have to do.

Mike

Mike Ricci is still only seventeen at the time of the 1989 Entry Draft and won't be eligible until the draft of June 1990, in Vancouver. That doesn't mean his presence isn't felt. Scouts and general managers aren't losing sleep over it, but if they could figure out a way to load the 1990 draft in favour of their team signing him, they'd not turn it down. The 1989 draft isn't over before the media, who'd trade their souls for any label that will fit into a snappy headline, are referring to 1990 as the Ricci draft.

As the 1989-90 season unfolds, it's clear that Ricci is improving with age. He is co-captain of Team Canada, which goes to Helsinki for the 1990 World Junior Championship. This time Team Canada makes up for the loss at Anchorage, winning the gold medal. Although he must sit out two games because of a shoulder injury, he still has four assists and is the twelfth leading playmaker of the series. He finishes the season playing 60 of the regular schedule's 66 games. He is third in the league, with 52 goals and 64 assists, for 116 points. Ahead of him are Keith Primeau of the Niagara Falls Flyers, with 127 points, and Paul DiPietro of the Sudbury Wolves, with 119. Midway through the season he has a slump and although it is short-lived, it does attract the critics, who are suddenly not so certain that 1990 will be the Ricci draft. Maybe it'll be the Primeau draft, or the DiPietro, the Owen Nolan or the D'arcy Cahill. Mike Ricci keeps himself largely aloof from the discussion.

"I go out and play, that's what I do," he says. He doesn't say he's uncaring about who is ranked number one when the draft actually arrives. "I'd like to be number one as a matter of pride," he says. "Anyone would. And sometimes the band-wagon-jumpers bother me. One day I'm the greatest player and the next day it's somebody else. But I can't let that bother me. That is really nothing to do with me."

What is to do with Mike Ricci is The Game. Whenever he uses the words you can tell he capitalizes them in his mind. The Game is his reason for being. In his diary he says:

> You know, it's something special, hockey. Off the ice is one thing, but on the ice is another. Once I step on the ice there are no more insecurities. I just go out there and play. I don't care how people look at me or think of me. The Game is somewhere to go to throw all your insecurities away. I don't think I'm a particularly inse-cure guy, but there's always the odd thing you get inse-cure about. Once you step on that rink, though, it's like a new world. Like it's my world. And I just want to go out there and do the best I can.

He is named the OHL's most gentlemanly player for 1989-90 and the most valuable player in the country. He is ranked number one, the top player in Canada, in the final Central Scouting rankings for 1990. Nolan, of the Cornwall Royals, is ranked second, Petr Nedved of the Seattle Thunderbirds is third, Primeau is fourth and Scott Scissons of the Saskatoon Blades is fifth. But when it comes to the actual draft, Quebec picks Nolan, making him the actual first-round pick, number one overall. Nedved is second, going to Vancouver. Detroit choosing third takes Primeau. Mike Ricci is fourth, going to Philadelphia. And suddenly the potential superstar trans-forms before your eyes to what he really is, after all, a kid of eighteen. A smile splits his face and there are tears in his eyes.

"That's my dream," he says, looking at the Flyers' jersey. "That's my dream."

John

It's three in the morning in Minneapolis, Minnesota. Dad's sleeping and he's not snoring. Can't believe it. I'm on the other side of the room, just in case he does start up snoring. This is the pinnacle of my life. Went to a press conference today of the top three goalies and the top twelve players. I got a new blue suit, got a tie. Dad bought that. For once, I looked just 110 percent awesome.

Thought at first I'd go in the first round, but now I don't. I think Washington Capitals are going to take a goalie in the first round. I talked with Jack Button, the director of scouting for Washington, and I didn't get a very good feeling. He beat around the bush with me a whole hour and a half. We talked when I met him in Toronto two weeks ago. I didn't get a very good impression, but I know they're gonna draft a goalie in the first round, but I also know it isn't gonna be John Tanner. I can just feel it.

I don't know why. I work hard. I think I'm as good as any goalie out there and hopefully some team's going to pick that up. Maybe Quebec, who knows? I went to their fitness test and did great, 55 repeat, breasting. I feel really good, I like them, but I don't really care; I just want to go somewhere. When I look back, I realize I've worked all my life for this and tomorrow, in a few short hours, it's going to be over. It's not going to be *over*; what I realize now, it's just a foot in the door. At this point, it feels like it's going to be the pinnacle, but really it's just the beginning.

The next day John finds he's right in his assessment of Washington Capitals' intentions. They draft Olaf Kolzig,

Central Scouting's number-one-rated goalie, from the Tri-City Americans of the WHL. But then, the big moment:

> It happened today, June 17th, 1989. John Tanner became a member of the Quebec Nordiques' organization. Third round, 54 overall. It was, well, quite an experience. And just like I sort of expected, it was a big letdown, in a way. Everything culminated in one call and I'm down there and they take pictures and the Quebec press interviews you with your sweater on. And all of a sudden, it's over again. All of a sudden, you realize you've got to work twice as hard, now, to get further. That doesn't bother me, it's just sort of a letdown. It's not really what I expected.
>
> I'm disappointed a bit. I'm disappointed I didn't go a little higher. It seemed like I was going to fall right out of the third round. Like, I don't know how I would have even gone home without being drafted. I'd feel like a total idiot. I don't even know how I'd show my face anywhere. It'd probably be the toughest thing I'd ever have to face. But, thank God, I didn't have to. I was most disappointed with the fact that Mike Parsons from Guelph was drafted ahead of me. My arch rival goes to my favourite team, the Bruins, in the second round, 38 overall. I'm a better goalie than him, yet he gets picked by the team I wanted to be picked by. You know, I'm really happy to go to Quebec, though. From what I can see, they're a caring organization, a team that wants to really turn it around.

Late in the 1989-90 season, the Petes trade Tanner to the London Knights, where, to his immense satisfaction, he gets the lion's share of the goaltending duties. He finishes the season with a 2.90 goals-against average, the best in the OHL for the second year in a row. Earlier, he had enjoyed a fine training camp with the Nordiques. He made his debut as an NHL goalie at the end of the season, March 31, 1990, versus Hartford at Le Colisée. Hartford wins, 3–2. He finishes the season with Quebec's International Hockey League affiliate, the Halifax Citadel, now coached by Paulin Bordeleau.

"My people tell me John played a good game," says Gilles Léger, the Nordiques' director of farm systems.

"I thought I played a good game, too," says John, referring to his NHL debut. "I never played before so many people. Fifteen thousand and fifteen—don't forget the fifteen! I even stonewalled Pat Verbeek. Michel Bergeron saying, 'Let's go, Johnny!' Geez, that's Michel Bergeron! Talking to me! I look up out of my crouch and as far up as I can see there's people. And it seems like I can hear them all yelling my name, 'cause I'm the new goalie, kind of the new Ron Hextall.

"God, it's exciting . . ."

Rob

Rob Lelacheur has a so-so season in his second year with the Blades, but that's largely because he twists his ankle shortly after Christmas and misses twenty-five games. It is one of those injuries that everyone expects will heal in days, but it hangs on forever. Even when he is able to play again the ankle bothers him and hampers his play. He has one goal and 18 assists in the regular season, but his value as a player is not reflected in his scoring ability. His value derives from his tough style of play, his hard work, his ability to grind the opposition down. He's a stay-at-home defenceman in the Brad Marsh style, and like Marsh he is a key player on the team.

An example of the kind of thing Rob does so well comes in the first game of the 1990 play-off series with the Medicine Hat Tigers. The Tigers are out to intimidate the Blades and are doing pretty well at it, too. They're leading 3–0 at the end of the first period. But that ends when Rob takes on Tigers' defenceman Brent Thompson, the second-round selection of L.A. Kings, in the 1989 Entry Draft. Lelacheur cuts Thompson's lip, bloodies his nose and triggers a macho chain reaction, which, in the arcane chemistry of hockey, actually prevents further chippiness. It goes, let's knock off the fighting before another of our top guys gets hurt. That act of Rob Lelacheur's was a key to the Blades' winning the series, three straight.

In his dairy he writes:

> I don't know what my potential is yet. But I'm going to find out. That's one of the things that makes me angry when I see it in others. I see people who have potential, but don't do anything about it. They're just so lazy, they don't do anything. Quitters. Whiners. They'd rather make excuses than face up to reality. We were put here to do the best we can. And that's what we should do. No excuses.

Tracey

"I guess that's it for me and hockey," says Tracey Katelnikoff in the dark days following the Blades' loss to Swift Current. He is speaking to the assistant general manager, Denis Beyak, the statement more an expression of his fears than anything else.

"I'll be talking to Jack Button [the Washington Capitals' director of scouting], because I think they should give you another try," says Beyak, and later he's as good as his word.

But Button doesn't call and Tracey drifts through the summer, enjoying his first prolonged break from hockey since he can't remember when. Earlier in the summer Tracey chats with his friend Duncan MacPherson. MacPherson was a New York Islander first-draft choice in 1984, but has decided to become a player-coach in Scotland for the Dundee Tigers. He promises to call Tracey when he arrives in Dundee, to discuss Tracey joining the Tigers. However, the call never comes as MacPherson mysteriously disappears in Europe, en route to Scotland. The suspicion is that he met with a climbing accident.

Tracey enrolls in second-year psychology and economics at the University of Calgary and plays hockey for the Dinosaurs. Later, he has an operation on his back to correct a hockey-related injury, and that kills his hockey year. He enrolls at the University of Saskatchewan while he's recovering and there finishes his year.

In April 1990, Tracey undergoes a second operation, this time to repair the damage when his right shoulder was dislocated before the Memorial Cup.

"The shoulder hurts a lot, even after all this time," he says. he plans to return to the University of Calgary, work for a degree in commerce and play for the Dinos.

"A lot of things might happen, but I'm not through with hockey yet. I'll know when it's time."

Tracey smiles at this, a champion. He knows that any dream can end but there is no end to dreaming.

Printed in Canada